I0753020

MANUAL

OF

DETERMINATIVE MINERALOGY

WITH AN INTRODUCTION

ON

BLOW-PIPE ANALYSIS.

BY

GEORGE J. BRUSH,

PROFESSOR OF MINERALOGY IN THE SHEFFIELD SCIENTIFIC SCHOOL

SECOND EDITION, WITH CORRECTIONS.

NEW YORK:
JOHN WILEY & SON,
15 ASTOR PLACE.
1875.

JOHN F. TROW & SON,
PRINTERS AND ELECTROTYPERS,
205-213 *East 12th St.*,
NEW YORK.

PREFACE.

The material in this compilation was, for the greater part, prepared almost twenty years since, by Prof. S. W. Johnson and myself as a text-book for the students in our laboratory. Circumstances prevented its publication at that time, but it has served as the basis of a course of lectures and practical exercises annually given in the Sheffield Laboratory.

The plan of instruction has been to have the student work through a course of Qualitative Blowpipe Analysis as introductory to Determinative Mineralogy. For the latter subject we have employed von Kobell's *Tafeln Zur Bestimmung der Mineralien*, many of the students taking the work in the original, while others made use of either Erni's or Elderhorst's translations. These "Tables" were translated by Prof. Johnson and myself while we were students of Prof. von Kobell in 1853–4, at Munich, and it was after our suggestion, in 1860, to Prof. Elderhorst, that he introduced von Kobell's "Tables" into the second edition of his "Manual," although he did not avail himself of our translation, which was then offered to him for that purpose.

The "Tables" as now presented are based on the tenth German edition of von Kobell's book. Additions of new species have been made, and in many cases fuller details are given in regard to old species, and the whole material has been thrown into an entirely new shape, which it is believed will greatly facilitate the work of the student. The preparation of the Tables in this form, the idea of which was suggested to me by Prof. W. T. Roepper, has been performed, under my supervision, by my assistant Mr. George W. Hawes, who has also aided me greatly in revising the rest of the work, and in the reading of the proof-sheets.

The main authorities used in the original preparation and later revision of the chapters on Blowpipe Analysis were the works of Berzelius and Plattner. The third and fourth editions of Plattner, the latter edited by Prof. Richter, have been chiefly consulted. The complete work of Plattner, with still later additions by Prof. Richter, has been made accessible to English reading students through an excellent translation by Prof. H. B. Cornwall, and this cannot be too highly commended to those who desire to become fully acquainted with this important subject.

In Determinative Mineralogy, besides the works of von Kobell, free use has been made of the treatises of NAUMANN and DANA, especially of the pyrognostic characters contributed by myself to the latter work. This constitutes, in accordance with the original plan of Professor Dana and myself, the Determinative Part of his System of Mineralogy. It is proposed at some future time to add to the volume methods for the determination of minerals by their physical characters.

In conclusion, I take great pleasure in acknowledging my indebtedness to my colleague, Prof. S. W. JOHNSON, who has not only generously given me his share in the original work, but has constantly aided me by his advice in the revision here presented.

SHEFFIELD LABORATORY OF YALE COLLEGE,
NEW HAVEN, December 15, 1874.

TABLE OF CONTENTS.

CHAPTER I.

CHAPTER II.

CHAPTER III.

CHAPTER IV.

BLOWPIPE ANALYSIS.

Chapter I.

APPARATUS AND REAGENTS.

THE MOUTH BLOWPIPE.

1. THIS little instrument, for centuries employed only by artisans in soldering, and other operations requiring an intense heat, has more recently become an invaluable means of scientific research.*

It is now of the greatest service to the chemist and mineralogist, not only for the recognition of minerals, and the detection of their ingredients, but even for the quantitative separation of several metals from their ores.†

The blowpipe serves chiefly for ascertaining the general nature of a body, by revealing some one or more of its ingredients; more rarely it helps to detect all the constituents of a very complex compound, although in but few cases is it possible by its use alone to decide that besides the substances found in a body, no others are present.

The blowpipe enables us in a moment, with no other fuel than that furnished by a common lamp or candle, to produce a most intense heat. In the blowpipe flame not only are most refractory bodies (platinum) melted or volatilized, but the most opposite chemical effects (oxidation and reduction) may be produced. Almost all mineral substances may be made to manifest some characteristic phenomena under its influence, either alone or in presence of certain other substances (reagents), and their nature may be thus surely and easily detected.

2. **The Common Blowpipe** (Fig. 3) is a conical curved tube of brass, terminating in an orifice as large as a small needle. This simple instrument, when well constructed, answers most ordinary purposes. If used a long time without interruption, the moisture of the breath gathers in drops in the narrow part of the tube, and is finally projected into the flame.

3. In the **Chemical Blowpipe** a chamber is fixed near the extremity of the instrument which collects the condensed moisture. The most usual form of this

* For a brief history of the use of the blowpipe, see Berzelius' work, translated by J. D. Whitney, Boston, 1845. A more complete history is found in Kopp's *Geschichte der Chemie*, II. 44. Braunschweig, 1844.

† For Plattner's methods of assaying gold, silver, copper, lead, bismuth, tin, cobalt, nickel, and iron ores, with the help of the blowpipe, see his work cited in the preface.

instrument is shown in Fig. 1 (half size), in which A represents the condenser. To admit of emptying this reservoir, it is connected with the tubes by the ground joints *b* and *c*. The instrument is also furnished with a movable jet, a section of which, in correct dimensions, is shown at D. This admits of ready cleaning without injury in case of stoppage. Berzelius recommends it to be made from solid platinum, as it then may be easily freed from the soot which is apt to collect upon it, by igniting it in the flame of a spirit lamp, whereby the impurities are burned away. Platinum jets made of foil are too thin at the point, and are thus liable to be easily damaged.

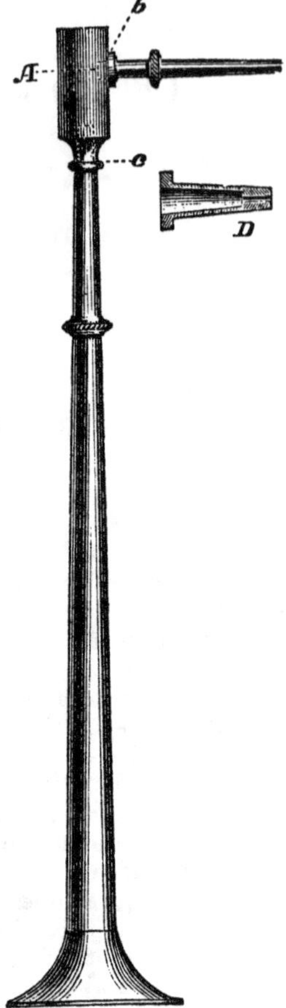

Fig. 1.

Brass jets are very durable and inexpensive, and may be cleaned, not indeed by heating, but by means of a sharpened splinter of soft wood, which should be introduced for that purpose at the larger end of the jet.

The internal form of the jet is not unimportant. The best shape is that of the section seen in the figure; it is such that the flame produced in using it is always well defined and conical, even when the blast is strongest. The jets of the blow-pipe found at the instrument-makers' usually need enlarging at the orifice. This is conveniently done with the help of a slender three-edged drill, which may be readily made by grinding down the sides of a large needle.

4. The instrument as shown in Fig. 1, without the trumpet mouthpiece, is of the original form proposed by Gahn, and employed by Berzelius. The beginner is liable to be fatigued in using it, as it requires considerable effort to keep the lips closed about the cylindrical tube for a long time. Plattner recommends the mouthpiece shown in the figure. It is made of horn or ivory, thirty-five millimetres in its outer diameter, and particular care must be taken that it has the proper curvature, so that in placing it against the lips it may not give an unnecessary or unequal pressure.

A very good mouthpiece may be made from a piece of glass tube, two inches long, and of just such diameter as fits the blowpipe tube. It is strongly and uniformly heated for half its length in the flame of a lamp, and when quite soft is flattened between two smooth metallic surfaces, to give it the form shown in Fig. 2. The other end is cemented into the blowpipe by means of a little sealing wax. This kind of mouthpiece is free from the disagreeable taste of the brass, and when inserted between the lips it displaces them but slightly from their customary position, and causes them very little fatigue.

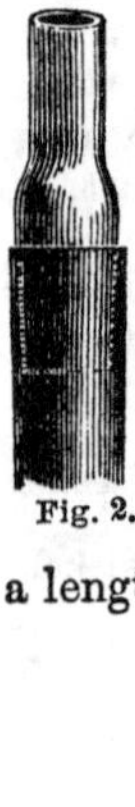

Fig. 2.

5. The blowpipe is usually made of brass, or preferably of German silver. The length of the instrument should be measured by the visual distance of the operator; from seven to nine inches is the ordinary length.

6. In Figs. 3 and 4 is shown how a common blowpipe may be materially improved with but little trouble. A blowpipe being selected that gives a good flame, it is cut in two so that the wider part of the tube has a length equal to the visual distance of the operator. The narrow tube is then reversed, and tightly fitted into the wider end of the long tube by means of a perforated cork, thus forming a reservoir for moisture, as seen at *a* in the figure.

7. Bunsen's gas blowpipe, in which illuminating gas issues from a tubular burner which surrounds the jet of the blowpipe, is sometimes convenient for laboratory use.

BLOWING.

8. In blowpipe operations it is often necessary to maintain an uninterrupted stream of air for several successive minutes. To be able to do this easily, requires some practice. It is best learned by fully distending the cheeks and breathing slowly through the nose for a time. When one is accustomed to keeping the

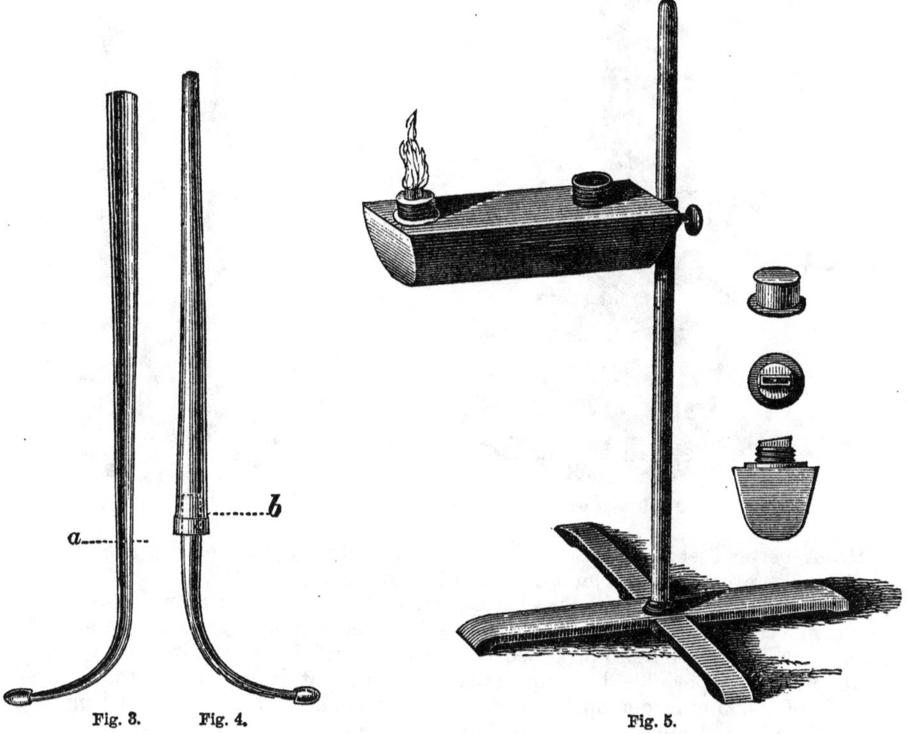

Fig. 3. Fig. 4. Fig. 5.

cheeks inflated, the mouthpiece of the blowpipe may be inserted between the lips, and the same thing repeated without attempting to blow or do more than keep the mouth full. Since the air now escapes through the blowpipe, the cheeks gradually fall together and must be again distended, yet without interrupting the outward current. This is accomplished by shutting off the communication between the mouth and the lungs by the palate, and inhaling through the nose. From the lungs thus filled the mouth is from time to time supplied, yet without any effort on the part of the muscles of the breast. A few hours' practice generally suffices to acquire the art of blowing. Beginners should keep in mind that the stream of air requires scarcely more force to produce it than results from the natural tendency of the inflated cheeks to collapse.

The lips should not be closed too firmly about the mouthpiece, else they are speedily fatigued. To the experienced operator continuous blowing is hardly an effort.*

THE FUEL.

9. When more convenient material is not at hand, stearine candles of good quality will answer for most purposes. Paraffine candles give a higher heat, but they soften in warm weather, and melt, and run down inconveniently. The common tallow candle may often suffice in an emergency, but requires constant snuffing.

Fig. 6. (⅓ size.)

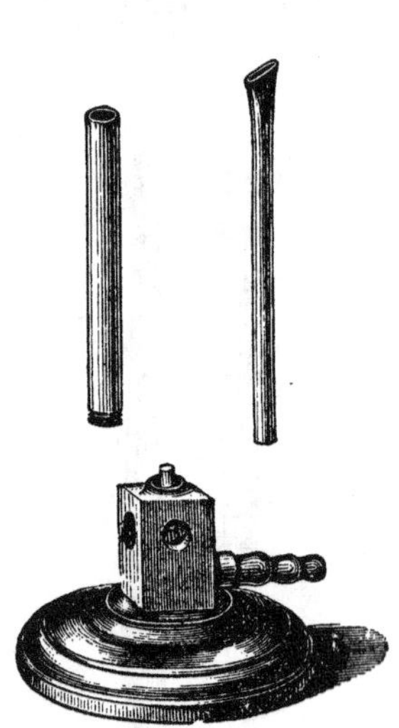

Fig. 7. (¼ size.)

10. A better fuel is olive or rape-seed oil burned in a lamp having a single circular wick rather more than a quarter of an inch in diameter, if the wick tube and lamp be so arranged that the charcoal and other supports used in blowpipe experiments can be brought close under the deflected flame. Fig. 5 represents the form of the blowpipe lamp proposed by Berzelius, and improved by Plattner. It is adapted for a portable blowpipe apparatus, since it is free from leakage, and capable of packing into a small space. The cistern A is of tinned sheet iron, and the wick tube and filling orifice are closed by screw caps.

11. The most convenient combustible is illuminating gas. A burner of the form given in Fig. 6 is used. It is about four inches high; the tube is flattened at the top and made a trifle lower on the left side, so that the blowpipe flame may be turned downward when necessary. A cock in the tube at the foot is useful. Such a lamp has the advantage of dispensing with all trimming and other inconveniences attendant on the use of an oil lamp. The ordinary Bunsen gas-burner (Fig. 7) is often provided with an extra tube to slip over the small gas jet in the in-

* Luca has described a blowpipe intended to maintain a steady stream of air with intermittent blowing, but this and other contrivances are unnecessary when the student has sufficient enterprise and patience to learn to blow the ordinary instruments, and no others wil be likely to make much progress in blowpipe analysis.

terior of the burner, in such a manner as to shut off the access of the air; the gas is then burned from the upper end, which is shaped as in the figure. The only objection to this lamp is, it is a little too high, although it may answer for all ordinary purposes.

A simpler blowpipe gas lamp may be easily made by selecting an iron or brass tube, eight inches in length, and three-eighths of an inch in bore, bending it at a right angle at the middle, and passing it through a block, properly cut, or placing it in a mould, which is then filled with melted lead. The top of the tube is then flattened, and the proper inclination given to the orifice by filing. Fig. 8 shows a lamp thus constructed.

THE BLOWPIPE FLAME.

12. When an ordinary lamp or candle is lighted, the combustion takes place only upon the outer limits of the flame, but if a stream of air is blown into the flame the combustion is transferred to the interior, is thus rendered more complete, and the flame is condensed. It is to these causes that the very intense heat of the blowpipe flame is due.

Fig. 8. (⅓ size.)

When the beginner is able to maintain a steady blast for some minutes together, he may attempt the production and management of the blowpipe flame. The operator being easily seated at the table, his arm resting upon its edge, the blowpipe is lightly grasped near the water chamber, between the thumb and first and second fingers of the right hand, and its jet brought to the edge of the flame, just above the wick or tube. The blowing should be regulated so as to produce a steady flame, which will be regular and conical if the jet be well shaped.

In Fig. 9 a common candle flame is represented, in which a light-blue segment, bounded by the line *a c*, and disappearing as the flame ascends, is seen at the base. The dark core of the flame *f* is surrounded by the illuminating portion *a b c*, and the thin, scarcely visible envelope *a e c* forms the outer coat of the flame.

13. Reducing Flame. While the candle is burning the stearine is slowly melted, sucked up by the wick, and vaporized. These vapors unite with the oxygen of the air and burn, upon the outer limits of the flame forming the hot coat *a e c* of carbonic acid and vapor of water. As the oxygen reaches no farther into the flame than the line *a b c*, the vapors inside this line are intensely heated out of the contact of the air, and any metallic oxide introduced into this yellow segment will, when hot, tend to part with its oxygen to the carbon and hydrocarbons of the flame. This is called the *Reducing Flame* (R. F.). To produce it with the blowpipe, the whole of the flame is deflected by a gentle blast, so regulated that it maintains its yellow color, and is luminous as before. The blowpipe is placed outside the flame, as shown in Fig. 10. The flame must not deposit soot upon the substance under trial, and only the extremity of the luminous part should be applied so as to envelop the assay.

14. Oxidizing Flame (Fig. 11). When the jet is carried somewhat into the flame, and the blast is a little stronger, the carbon is more completely consumed; the inner blue cone, corresponding to the part *a c* of the candle flame, becomes sharply defined, and is surrounded by a nearly colorless envelope, corresponding to the mantle *a e c*, at the extremity of which metals may be intensely

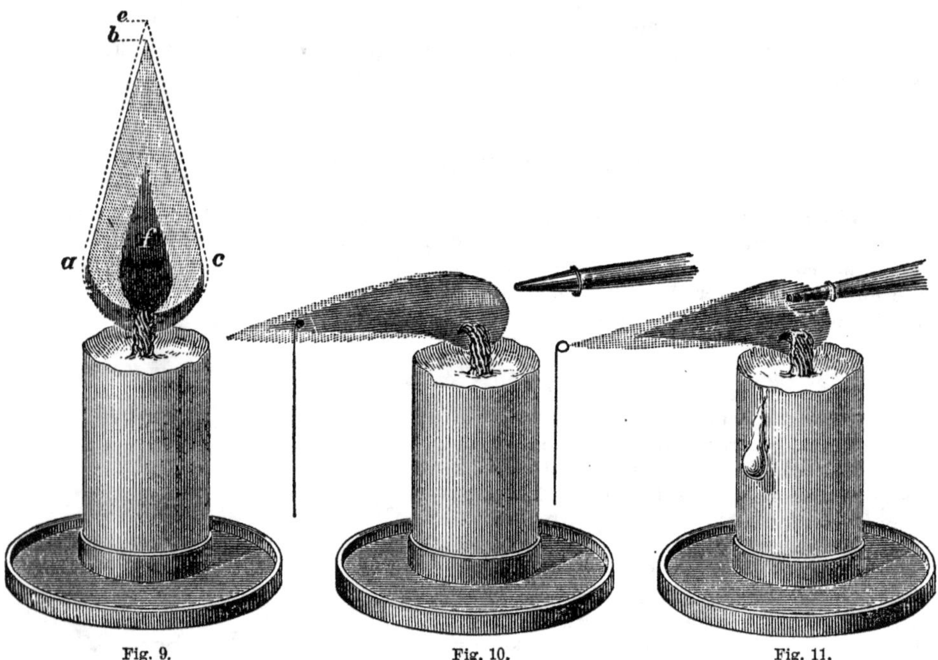

Fig. 9. Fig. 10. Fig. 11.

heated in contact with air, and will thus be rapidly oxidized. This is called the *Oxidizing Flame* (O. F.). The assay should be held as far beyond the blue point of the flame as is consistent with the temperature requisite for the most rapid oxidation, and the flame should be so managed that no luminous streaks are seen in it. A flat wick serves best for its production. The heat is most intense at the point of the blue cone, and this is accordingly used for testing the fusibility of minerals and other substances, without reference to chemical action.

SUPPORTS.

In blowpipe examinations the assay is supported by certain substances which are either infusible, or have the power of sustaining a high heat without changing their form.

15. Charcoal is used in many operations as a support for the assay. For most purposes any piece of well-burned charcoal that does not snap or become fissured in the flame will suffice. The softer kinds of wood yield the most suitable material. That made from bass-wood (linden) is the best; pine and willow charcoal are also excellent. For use it is conveniently sawn into parallelopipedons, with faces one or two inches in width, and three to six inches in length. The assay is best placed on the flat, smooth surface, at right angles to the rings of growth. It can be repeatedly used, the clean surface being renewed by scraping with a knife or file.

16. Cavities for the reception of the substance to be heated on charcoal may be made with the point of a knife. For some purposes, cavities may be made more nicely by means of a tube of stout tin plate, the edges of which are sharpened. The tube is made conical, has a length of three inches, its diameter at one end is three-eighths, at the other five-eighths, of an inch. The end of this is applied to the surface of the coal at a considerable inclination, and the tube is revolved with a scooping motion. The excavation should be made near the edge of the charcoal, should be cup-shaped, rather shallow, quite smooth, and regular.

17. Platinum Wire is used for supporting beads of fused borax or other flux in the flame. The kind designated as No. 27 (or jeweller's hole 12½), is the best. It is cut into pieces three inches long, and a loop made in the end. When not in use the hooked ends should be plunged into a little bottle containing dilute sulphuric acid, which dissolves away the matters that have been fused on them. Before use they should be rinsed with water and thoroughly cleaned.

18. Platinum Spoon. For a few operations a small platinum spoon of the form shown in Fig. 12, may be usefully employed. A cork or wooden handle should be adapted to it. A rectangular slip of platinum foil, which is used also for other purposes, may be made to answer for the spoon by bending up its corners and holding it in the platinum forceps.

Fig. 12. (½ size.)

19. Platinum Forceps. For igniting fragments of minerals, forceps tipped with platinum are indispensable. Fig. 13 represents the usual form. They are made of steel or German silver. The points are opened by pressure. The free ends may be used as an ordinary forceps for picking up small fragments of minerals, etc.; or if of steel, for detaching pieces of specimens. Fig. 14 shows a

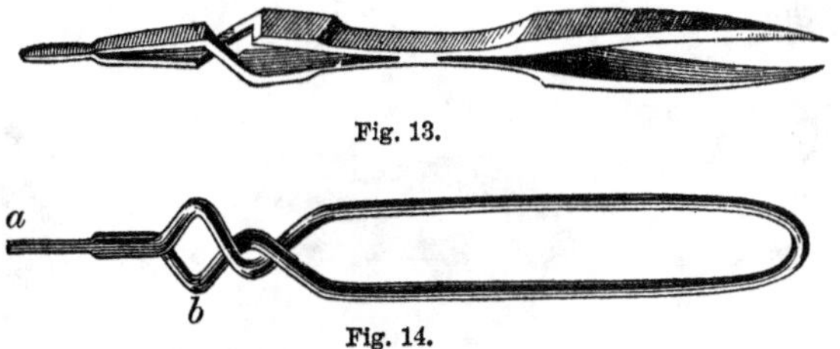

Fig. 13.

Fig. 14.

simpler form of this instrument, which any jeweller can easily construct. A piece of highly elastic brass wire, No. 12, is the best material for the tongs. The platinum tips *a* are readily hammered out from a piece of stout wire or cut from a plate, and are riveted or, better, soldered to the brass wire with silver solder. The bend at *b* is intended to prevent the points from touching the table. The forceps must be slender in order not to conduct away too much heat from the assay.

20. Glass Tubes. Tubes of hard glass, free from lead, $\frac{1}{12}$ to $\frac{1}{4}$ inch in diameter, and four to six inches long, are indispensable. They serve for the ignition of bodies in a current of air, the rapidity of which may be regulated by varying the inclination of the tube. The substance under trial is placed in the tube about

Fig. 15.

an inch from the end, the tube is then held nearly horizontally, either in the flame of the lamp or of the blowpipe. The falling out of the body may be hindered by bending the tube slightly one inch from one end. The body is then placed at the bend as shown in Fig. 15, and the proper inclination given to the tube; but for most uses straight tubes are quite as good. For each new operation a clean tube must be employed. The tube usually cracks when used a second time, and should therefore be cut off at the place where a body has been ignited. Tubes are most easily cleaned by wiping them out with a slip of soft paper rolled around some slender cylinder having a *rough* surface to hold the paper. A small rat-tail file is excellent for this use.

21. Closed Tubes and Glass Bulb Tubes (*matrasses;* Fig. 16) serve for heating bodies out of contact, or with but limited access of air. They are easily made, especially the form B, which answers nearly every purpose, from the pieces which have become too short to be used as open tubes, or by heating a tube six inches long in the middle and drawing it into two parts.

ACCESSORY APPARATUS.

22. An Agate Mortar with pestle (Fig. 17) is used for reducing minerals to a fine powder. It should be from two to three inches in diameter, and should be used only for grinding, never for pounding, hard bodies.

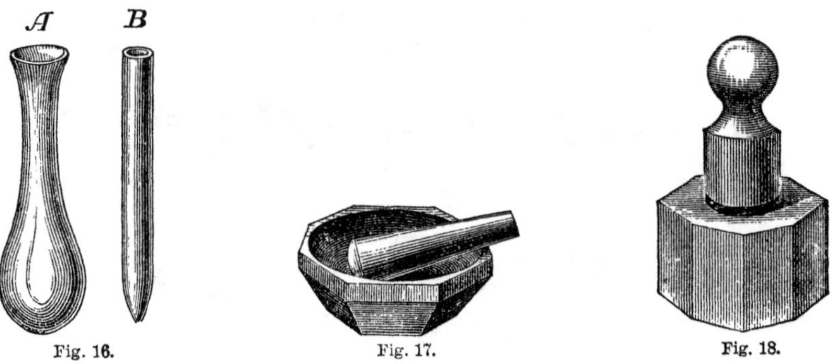

Fig. 16. Fig. 17. Fig. 18.

23. A Diamond Mortar (Fig. 18) made of cast steel and well tempered, is used for breaking up and reducing to a tolerably fine powder hard and refractory bodies. The fragments to be broken are placed in the bottom of the cavity; the closely fitting pestle is also placed in the hole, and is sharply struck with a small hammer. Minerals are thus prepared for finer pulverization in the agate mortar; but the same thing may be accomplished by wrapping the assay in several folds of paper, placing it upon an anvil and striking it.

24. Hammer. A small steel hammer such as is used by jewellers.

25. Anvil. A small parallelopipedon of hardened steel, or any convenient flat surface of steel.

26. Pliers. Cutting pliers (Fig. 19) are useful for detaching fragments from mineral specimens.

27. File. A small three-cornered file is used for cutting glass tubes. A notch is cut in one side of the tube, which is then half pulled, half broken in two.

28. Magnet. A common steel magnet, or a magnetized knife blade, serves to recognize magnetic bodies; a magnetic needle is sometimes useful for delicate determinations.

29. Lens. A magnifying glass composed of two convex lenses.

30. Watch-glasses from one to two and a half inches in diameter serve for various purposes.

31. Test-Tubes of hard glass with a suitable stand.

32. Funnels of glass one and a half to two inches in diameter.

33. Porcelain Dishes. Those with handles, called casseroles (Fig. 20), are most convenient. They are used for boiling liquids and for evaporations.

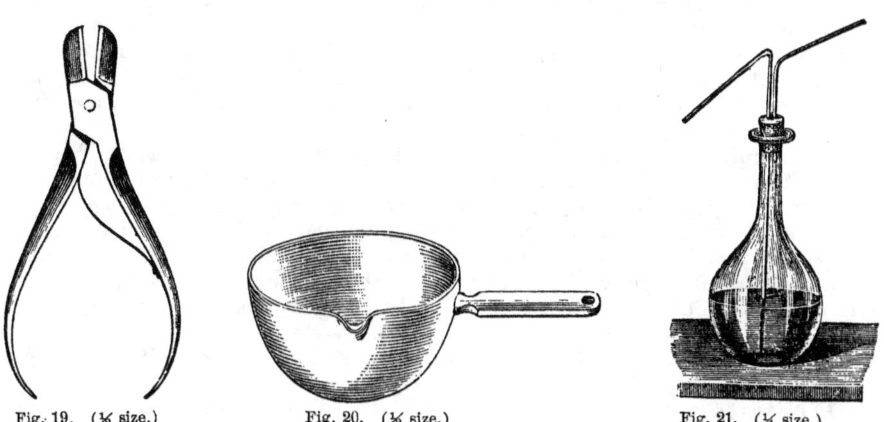

Fig. 19. (½ size.) Fig. 20. (½ size.) Fig. 21. (¼ size.)

34. A Wash-Bottle (Fig. 21), made from a small flask, or any bottle having a mouth wide enough to receive the cork through which the tubes are passed.

35. Glass Rods, three to six inches long, rounded at each end, are used for stirrers.

36. Filters. Suitable paper is cut into circular pieces, the radius of which should be a half inch less than the side of the funnel in which it is to be placed. It is twice folded upon itself, thus forming a quadrant; this is opened so as to form a conical cup, having three thicknesses of paper on one of its sides, and one on the other. It is snugly inserted into a funnel, and moistened from the wash-bottle just previous to use.

The list of appliances for blowpipe analysis may be indefinitely increased, but the simplicity of a blowpipe outfit, in rendering it non-expensive and portable, is very desirable. A little ingenuity will supply the place of much apparatus.

BLOWPIPE REAGENTS.

The substances employed to produce chemical changes in bodies for their recognition are termed reagents. The quantities needed are so small that it is usually advisable to purchase most of them; but as it is often difficult to procure reagents of proper quality, simple directions for preparing some of them, and for testing their purity, are here given.

37. Carbonate of Soda; or *Soda*, in blowpipe language. Either neutral carbonate or bicarbonate may be used. To prepare it, take four or five ounces of commercial bicarbonate of soda, free from mechanical impurities, place it in a porcelain mortar, add a little distilled water, and pulverize finely. Bring it upon a large filter in a glass funnel, and allow the water to drain off. Successive additions of water, in quantities of about one ounce, are made, until a few drops of the drainings, caught in a clean test-tube, and acidified with nitric acid, give no precipitate, nor even the faintest turbidity with a drop of clear solution of chloride of barium. The washing often requires several days, and is sometimes not complete before half of the salt has been washed away. It is thus freed from sulphuric acid, which contaminates the commercial salt. Soda that is purchased as pure should be tested for sulphur and sulphuric acid, as described in **145**, before trusting its purity. The salt as thus prepared is spread out upon paper and allowed to dry. Part of it may be bottled while moist, and used in that state; but a part must be dried at a high heat, in order to expel all water. It is then pulverized and put away for use.

38. Biborate of Soda. Borax. The commercial salt is usually pure enough. Clean crystals are selected, and coarsely pulverized. For some tests, fused borax is required. To obtain this, some of the commercial salt is melted in a platinum dish, and when cool placed in a tightly stoppered bottle.

39. Phosphate of Soda and Ammonia. Salt of Phosphorus. Microcosmic Salt. The very small quantity of this substance (1 oz.) needed for a great number of trials is best purchased. It may be prepared by dissolving in two parts of boiling water six parts of crystallized phosphate of soda, and one part (all the parts *by weight*) of white and clean sal-ammoniac, and immediately filtering while still boiling hot. The crystals that separate on cooling are freed from the chloride of sodium that adheres to them by recrystallization. *Testing.*—It must fuse on platinum wire to a colorless, perfectly transparent globule; and when oxide of copper is added, and it is again heated, it must not tinge the flame with a blue or green color.

40. Nitrate of Cobalt. Cobalt Solution. The crystals of nitrate are dissolved in ten parts of water, and filtered if necessary. For use the cobalt solution is most conveniently kept in bulbs similar to those represented in half size, in Fig. 22. The bulb A is easily made from a bit of glass tube. In order to fill such a bulb it is gently heated, and the tip placed beneath the surface of a solution of nitrate of cobalt in a shallow dish. When a drop of the solution has entered it is again heated, the drop is converted into steam, the tip is again immersed, and the solution will almost instantly rush into the bulb. It should not be more than two-thirds filled. To apply the solution, the bulb is grasped gently in the palm of the hand, and inverted, when the expansion of the air shortly forces out a drop or more, as is required.

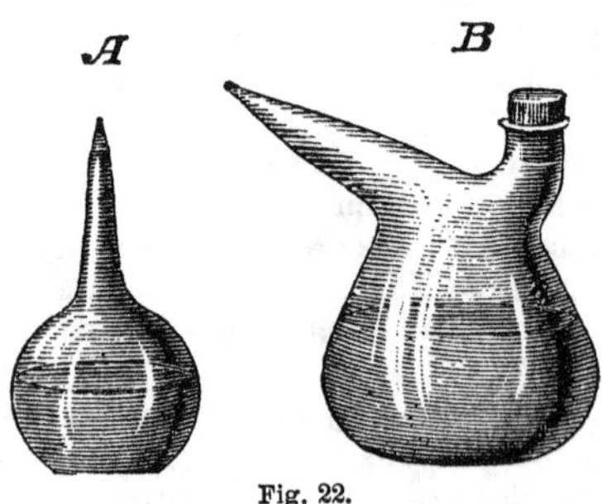

Fig. 22.

41. Nitrate of Potash. Clean crystals of the commercial salt are powdered.

42. Bisulphate of Potash. Equal weights of clean nitrate of potash and oil of vitriol are heated together in a porcelain dish, gently at first, afterwards more strongly, till the nitric acid and excess of sulphuric acid are driven off and a clear liquid remains which solidifies to an opaque mass on cooling. The salt thus obtained is pulverized, and preserved in a glass-stoppered bottle. It can also be prepared by heating pure sulphate of potash with an excess of sulphuric acid, until the excess is driven away and the mass solidifies on cooling.

43. Cyanide of Potassium. In nearly every case this reagent can be dispensed with, by one who has perfect command of the blowpipe, its only use being to facilitate difficult reductions. It can be procured of any photographer or druggist.

44. Iodide of Potassium. The clean crystals purchased of any druggist.

45. Sulphur. Flowers of sulphur.

46. Tin. Strips of pure tin-foil a half an inch wide and one inch long.

47. Zinc. Strips of common sheet zinc.

48. Lead. Pure lead, for detecting gold and silver by cupellation, is prepared by dissolving acetate of lead (sugar of lead) in hot water, filtering, and inserting strips of clean zinc into the solution. After five to six hours the precipitated lead should be scraped from the zinc in order to expose a fresh surface. When the lead is all separated, it is washed thoroughly with water, then dried by pressing between folds of blotting paper, and finally by exposure to a gentle warmth.

49. Iron. Clean wire of the thickness of a medium-sized sewing-needle. Iron in a fine state of subdivision is used for reductions in the wet way.

50. Magnesium. Bits of foil or wire are useful in detecting phosphoric acid.

51. Silver. A smooth silver coin, which must be freshly cleaned at the time of using. See detection of sulphur, **145.**

52. Bone-Ash. A little cup of bone ashes, called a *cupel*, is used for the detection of silver and gold. Bones burned to whiteness are finely pulverized and reserved for these purposes.

53. Oxide of Copper. A copper cent is dissolved in nitric acid, the solution is evaporated to dryness, and the dry mass gradually heated to redness in a porcelain dish.

54. Fluoride of Calcium. Pure *fluor-spar* is crushed and heated in a test tube until decrepitation ceases; it is then finely pulverized.

55. Oxalate of Nickel. The pure salt is best purchased, and when fused with borax before the blowpipe, must give a brown and not a blue glass.

56. Test Papers. *A. Blue Litmus Papers.*—Digest one part of the litmus of commerce with six parts of water, and filter the solution; divide the intensely blue filtrate into two equal parts; saturate the free alkali in the one part by repeatedly stirring with a glass rod dipped in very dilute sulphuric acid, until the color of the fluid just appears red; add now the other part of the blue filtrate, pour the whole fluid into a dish, and draw strips of fine unsized paper through it: suspend these strips over threads, and leave them to dry. When dry, the paper should have a fine blue color, and may be cut in narrow strips and kept in a tight box. The moistened paper should be promptly reddened by the smallest trace of acids, and is used for their detection. When the litmus paper is reddened by a very feeble acid, it may be used for the detection of alkalies.

B. Turmeric Paper.—Digest one part of bruised turmeric root with six parts of *weak* spirits of wine, filter the tincture obtained, and steep slips of fine paper in the filtrate. The dried slips must exhibit a fine yellow tint. It is turned brown by alkalies, and serves also in the recognition of boric acid, molybdic acid, and zirconia.

C. Brazil-wood Paper.—Brazil-wood is boiled with water, the liquid filtered, and paper saturated with it and dried. It is used for detecting fluorine, which gives it a yellow color; it also serves to recognize alkalies, which color it violet.

WET REAGENTS.

57. **Water.** Whenever water is used in analytical operations it should be either *distilled water*, or *clean rain water*.

58. **Hydrochloric Acid. Muriatic Acid.** The strong commercial acid will answer for most purposes, but it is also advisable to have some of the pure fuming acid which on evaporation leaves no residue and when diluted with water gives no milkiness on the addition of chloride of barium.

59. **Sulphuric Acid** concentrated, (ordinary oil of vitriol).

60. **Nitric Acid,** pure. It must leave no residue upon evaporation, nor give any turbidity with nitrate of silver.

61. **Phosphoric Acid.** The officinal concentrated solution.

62. **Ammonia.** It must be colorless, should leave no residue when evaporated on a watch-glass, nor should it cause the slightest turbidity in lime-water.

63. **Carbonate of Ammonia.** One part of the commercial salt is dissolved in four parts of water, to which one part of solution of caustic ammonia has been added.

64. **Chloride of Ammonium.** Select sublimed white sal-ammoniac of commerce. If it contains iron or other impurities it is dissolved in hot water, and set aside to recrystallize. The dried crystals are dissolved for use in eight parts of water.

65. **Phosphate of Soda.** Purify the salt of commerce by recrystallization, and dissolve one part of the pure salt in ten parts of water.

66. **Oxalate of Ammonia.** Dissolve commercial oxalic acid, which has been purified by recrystallization, in two parts of hot water; add caustic ammonia, or carbonate of ammonia, until the fluid begins to manifest a slight alkaline reaction; filter, and set aside to cool. The crystals that separate are allowed to drain, and the mother liquors are further evaporated to crystallization. Purify by recrystallization. Dissolve one part of the pure salt in twenty-four parts of water.

67. **Potassa.** Dissolve some sticks of caustic potassa in water, allow to stand, and separate the clear solution from the sediment by decantation.

68. **Chloride of Barium.** This salt may be purchased of any druggist. For use it is dissolved in ten parts of water.

69. **Nitrate of Silver.** May be procured in crystals from any druggist or photographer.

70. **Bichloride of Platinum.** Treat platinum filings (purified by boiling with nitric acid) with concentrated hydrochloric acid and some nitric acid, and apply a very gentle heat, adding occasionally fresh portions of nitric acid, until the platinum is completely dissolved. Evaporate the solution to dryness on a water bath, with addition of hydrochloric acid, and dissolve the residue in ten parts of water for use. It is used for detecting potassa in the presence of soda and lithia.

71. **Molybdate of Ammonia.** Pulverize the sulphide of molybdenum as finely as possible, and roast it in a shallow sheet-iron or earthen dish, at a low red heat, until it turns yellow, and becomes converted into molybdic acid. It is then digested with ammonia, which extracts the molybdic acid; the solution is filtered, evaporated to dryness, and the molybdate of ammonia which is left is dissolved in water acidulated with nitric acid and kept for use.

All the reagents of a well-appointed laboratory may be of occasional service in the qualitative analysis of minerals, but reagents other than the above will be but rarely needed by the student in blowpipe analysis.

Chapter 2.

SYSTEMATIC COURSE OF QUALITATIVE BLOWPIPE ANALYSIS.

72. THE student being provided with the necessary materials, and having acquired some skill in producing the oxidizing and reducing flames, is prepared to consider the various effects that may be produced with the blow-pipe. These reactions are classified, according to the apparatus and reagents that are used, under the eight following heads, as recommended by Plattner:

A.—Heating in the closed tube.
B.—Heating in the open tube.
C.—Heating on charcoal.
D.—Heating in the platinum forceps to test fusibility, and to observe the coloration of the flame.
E.—Treatment with cobalt solution.
F.—Fusion with borax.
G.—Fusion with salt of phosphorus.
H.—Treatment with carbonate of soda.

Under each of the above divisions is given, first, the method of experimenting, and, second, in tabular arrangement, the phenomena or reactions produced, which are characteristic of the substances usually subjected to blowpipe examination. The beginner should not attempt at first to work with bodies of unknown composition, but should provide himself with some substances which are well calculated to illustrate the reactions indicated.

The blowpipe lamp is placed upon a sheet of stout clean paper, so that the assay accidentally falling may not be lost. Whenever a new substance is taken for experiment, all fragments of the old should be shaken off.

The assay must not be too large; in most cases the bulk of a mustard seed is enough, in the practised hand. Beginners may use a larger quantity, but as the student progresses he should aim to reduce the size of his assays to the least amount consistent with a perfect experiment, since he will be often called upon to determine minerals upon minute fragments.

The closest observation will often be necessary for the detection of the reaction, and the success of the student is greatly dependent upon the accuracy of discrimination, quick comprehension, and careful manipulation which is acquired in these preliminary examinations.

A.—HEATING IN THE CLOSED TUBE.

73. The body, in fragments the size of a grain of wheat, or an equivalent bulk of it, if it be in form of a powder, is placed in the bottom of a tube closed at one end; the tube is held nearly horizontal, and heated over the spirit or gas lamp, very gently at first, and finally, if needful to intense ignition, with the aid of the blowpipe, and the successive phenomena are carefully watched as they appear.

Powdered substances must be so introduced into the tube as not to soil its sides; this is accomplished by placing the powder on a narrow slip of writing paper previously folded lengthwise in the form of a trough. The tube is held horizontal, and the paper trough is inserted to its bottom; the whole is now brought into a vertical position, and the paper is carefully withdrawn.

The phenomena can nearly all be produced in the simple closed tube (Fig. 16, *b*), and for most purposes this form is better than the bulb tube, since the object of these experiments is to heat the body out of contact with the air, and to produce changes among its constituents without the interposition of any reagents.

The following phenomena may be observed: *

1. Decrepitation—Fluorite, Barite, and many other minerals.
2. Glowing—Gadolinite, etc.
3. Phosphorescence—Fluorite, Willemite, etc.
4. Change of color. The most important are here tabulated.

ORIGINAL COLOR.	COLOR WHILE IGNITED.	COLOR AFTER COOLING.	SUBSTANCE.
White to yellow.	Brown.	Yellow.	Binoxide of tin.
White.	Yellow.	White.	Oxide of zinc and many of its salts.
White.	Yellow.	Yellow.	Hydrated oxide, carbonate, and other salts of lead.
Blue or green.	Black.	Black.	Hydrated oxide, carbonate, and other salts of copper.
White.	Dark yellow.	Light yellow.	Hydrated oxide, carbonate, and many salts of bismuth.
White.	Brown.	Brown.	Hydrated oxide, carbonate, and many salts of cadmium.
Yellow or red.	Deeper color.	Original color if gently heated; green if strongly heated.	Most chromates.
Red.	Black.	Red.	Sesquioxide of iron.

5. Fusion—Stibnite, Nitre, and other bodies.
6. Give off oxygen—Binoxide of Manganese, Oxide of Mercury, etc. Tested by placing a bit of charcoal in the tube, upon the assay. Heat the charcoal first, then the assay, and the charcoal will glow.
7. Become carbonized, and give a burnt odor—Amber and many organic compounds. If acid reaction, non-nitrogenous; if alkaline, nitrogenous body.
8. Give off water—All hydrates.
9. Give acid vapors—Hydrates with volatile acids. Tested by placing a blue litmus paper in the end of the tube. If the glass is etched, Fluorine.
10. Give alkaline vapors—Ammonia Salts. Tested with a piece of turmeric paper.
11. Give sublimates which condense on the cold part of the tube.

* For experiments illustrating the effects to be produced in the closed tube, the following substances are given: Fluorite, Gadolinite, Oxide of Zinc, Stibnite, Oxide of Mercury, Amber, Serpentine, Nitrate of Ammonia, Pyrite, Realgar, Arsenopyrite, Selenium, Amalgam, Cinnabar, Spathic Iron.

a. A yellow sublimate.	SULPHUR.	Either originally *free*, or from decomposition of a *sulphide.*
b. A sublimate, dark brown-red, almost black when hot, and red or reddish yellow when cold.	SULPHIDE OF ARSENIC.	*Realgar* and *Orpiment*, and other *Sulph-arsenides.*
c. In strong heat, a sublimate deposits near the assay, which is black when hot, and brown-red when cold.	OXYSULPHIDE OF ANTIMONY.	*Sulphide of Antimony* and its *compounds, with other metallic sulphides.*
d. A dark red, almost black, sublimate, and odor of decaying horse-radish at open end of tube.	SELENIUM.	Various *Selenides.*
e. Condenses in small drops, with metallic lustre.	TELLURIUM.	Various Tellurides.
f. A black, brilliant sublimate, and garlic odor.	ARSENIC.	*Native Arsenic* and many *Arsenides.*
g. A gray sublimate, consisting (use lens) of metallic globules, which may be united by rubbing with a feather.	MERCURY.	*Amalgams.*
h. A black, lustreless sublimate, red when rubbed.	SULPHIDE OF MERCURY.	*Cinnabar, Vermilion,* minerals containing both Mercury and Sulphur.
i. The body *fuses*, and yields a sublimate, which is white when cold.	1. *Perchloride of Mercury.* 2. *Chloride of Lead;* fuses to a yellow liquid, partially sublimes, and becomes opaque and white on cooling. 3. *Antimonous Acid;* fuses to yellow drops, and if air be excluded, deposits in brilliant needles.	
j. The body *does not fuse*, but gives a sublimate, which is white when cold.	1. *Salts of Ammonia.* 2. *Arsenous Acid;* easily sublimes and condenses in octahedral crystals (lens). 3. *Protochloride of Mercury;* sublimate is yellow when hot.	

12. The residue is magnetic—Spathic Iron, Pyrites, etc.

There are some other reactions more rarely observed, particularly in the study of minerals. Osmic acid forms a sublimate of white drops, which possess a disagreeable odor. Cyanogen, when liberated, is recognized by its peculiar odor. Iodine volatilizes in beautiful violet fumes. From some of its alloys Cadmium volatilizes and condenses as a black metallic sublimate. Sulphurous acid is given off by sulphides in an amount proportionate to the oxygen which surrounds the assay, but the place for its observation is in the open tube.

B.—HEATING IN THE OPEN TUBE.

74. This is essentially a roasting or oxidizing process. The substance is placed in a glass tube open at both ends, at a distance of about one inch from the end, at which point a bend is sometimes made (see Fig. 15); but for most operations a straight tube is preferable. The heat should be gentle at first and only gradually raised, otherwise some bodies may volatilize without oxidizing, and give the same sublimate as when heated in a closed tube. By changing the inclination of the tube, the current of air through it may be increased or diminished, and the oxidation made to proceed more or less rapidly. Not too much of the substance must be taken, and if satisfactory reactions be not obtained from a fragment, it should be pulverized. Bodies which decrepitate and lose volatile ingredients by heating in a closed tube, must be finely pulverized at the outset, and introduced into the tube by means of a paper trough.

A slip of moistened litmus paper should always be placed in the upper end of the tube when experimenting on an unknown substance, and when vapors begin to arise, attention should be given to their odor, and to the sublimates which condense on the inner surface of the tube. Many of the phenomena encountered in this trial are identical with those obtained in the closed tube. Only such as are peculiar or characteristic are here noticed.*

1. *Odors.—a.* Sulphur and sulphides in the open tube form sulphurous acid, giving the odor of burning sulphur, and reddening moistened blue litmus paper. When a reaction is not developed by heating a fragment, the powder must be employed.

b. Odor of decaying horse-radish.—*Selenium.* Mostly sublimes.

c. Odor of garlic.—*Arsenic.* Mostly sublimes.

2. *Sublimates.*—Carefully compare last section in case they are not noticed below. The sublimate itself should be heated to ascertain if it be volatile or fusible.

a. White, crystalline (octahedral), volatile sublimate; formed easily at moderate heat.	ARSENOUS ACID.	*Metallic Arsenic* and many *Arsenides.*
b. White, thin sublimate, crystalline nearest the assay; fusible to droplets; yellowish when hot, nearly colorless when cold. When the R. F. is directed upon it within the tube, it becomes blue, or even copper-red from reduction.	MOLYBDIC ACID.	*Molybdic Acid* and *Sulphide of Molybdenum.*
c. Dense white smoke, and at first a mostly volatile white sublimate, depositing on the upper side of the tube; afterward in most cases a white, non-volatile and infusible sublimate gathering on the under side of the tube.	ANTIMONOUS and ANTIMONIC ACIDS.	Most compounds of *Antimony.*
d. White smoke, and non-volatile fusible sublimate depositing on the under side of tube.	SULPHATE OF LEAD.	*Sulphide of Lead.*

* Substances serving to illustrate the reactions of the open tube: Pyrite, Blende, Selenium, Arsenopyrite, Molybdenite, Stibnite, Galenite, Bismuth, Tellurium, Cinnabar.

e. Fusible sublimate, dark brown when hot, lemon yellow when cold.	OXIDE OF BISMUTH.	Most compounds of *Bismuth.*
f. A gray sublimate, fusible to colorless drops that solidify on cooling.	TELLUROUS ACID.	*Native Tellurium* and many *Tellurides.*
g. A steel-gray sublimate, the upper edge of which appears red, and sometimes fringed with small white very volatile crystals of selenous acid.	SELENIUM.	*Selenium* and many *Selenides.*
h. A bright metallic sublimate, that can be gathered into a drop by sweeping it together with a splinter of wood or a feather.	MERCURY.	*Cinnabar*, and compounds containing sulphide of mercury.

3. *Residues.*—Compare table of changes in color, **73.** 4.

C.—HEATING ON CHARCOAL.

75. A small quantity of the substance is placed in a shallow cavity on charcoal, which is so situated that the flame of the blowpipe can be directed downward upon it, and its behavior in both flames observed.

A fragment may be used, or if the substance is in the form of powder, or on account of decrepitation must be reduced to powder, it may be mixed with water to a paste and placed on the coal, and heated at first gradually, afterward, when dry, to full ignition.

Much trouble is sometimes experienced in keeping the assay in its place sufficiently long to observe its behavior fully, especially when it is infusible or difficultly volatile. In such cases borax may often be employed to advantage in the following manner: The assay is held in the forceps, heated to redness, and then touched to a little grain of borax. The borax melts, and attaches itself to the body, which is now laid in the cavity so that the borax is in contact with the charcoal, and is carefully heated with the blowpipe; it usually adheres without further trouble.

In the following tables are given the characteristic phenomena that belong to this section.

1. *Odors* should be observed immediately after a short exposure to heat. Traces of *sulphur*, *selenium*, and *arsenic* are more surely detected by their odor on charcoal, than in an open tube.

a. *Odor of burning sulphur.*—*Sulphur* and sulphides. Best observed in O. F.

b. *Odor of decaying horse-radish.*—*Selenium* and selenides. Treat in O. F.

c. *Odor of garlic.*—*Arsenic* and its compounds. Traces are most surely recognized after momentary exposure of the assay to the R. F.

2. *Deflagration.*—Nitrates, chlorates, iodates, bromates.

3. *The body fuses and is absorbed by the charcoal.*—The fixed alkalies and many of their salts; also hydrates of baryta and strontia, and after very long heating their carbonates and sulphates.

4. *A white infusible residue remains, it may be after previous fusion,* which:

a. Glows brightly in O. F., indicating lime, strontia, magnesia, zirconia, zinc, and tin.

b. After ignition turns moist turmeric paper brown. Baryta, strontia, lime, magnesia.

c. Communicates a characteristic color to the flame. See page 20.

	Near Assay.		Distant from Assay, or in thin Layers.	In O. F.	In R. F.	Remarks.
a. Selenium.	Steel gray; faint metallic lustre.		Dark gray, with tinge of violet; dull.	Volatile.	Volatile with blue flame.	Selenium fuses very easily; volatilizes with brown smoke, giving the odor of decaying horse-radish.
b. Tellurium.	White.		Red or deep yellow.	Volatile.	Volatile with green flame, or, if selenium be present, with blue-green flame.	Tellurium fuses very easily.
c. Arsenic.	White.		Grayish.	Volatile.	Volatile, with faint blue flame.	Metallic arsenic volatilizes without fusing. Sublimate is deposited quite far from assay, is very volatile, and in R. F. gives garlic odor.
d. Antimony.	White.		Bluish.	Volatile.	Volatile, with faint greenish flame.	Metallic antimony fuses very easily; after being strongly heated upon charcoal, remains red-hot for a considerable time, and before solidifying becomes surrounded with crystals of antimonous acid. The sublimate is less volatile than that of arsenous acid.
e. Thallium.	White.		Near the assay brown.	Volatile.	Volatile, with intense green flame.	Thallium fuses and oxidizes very easily.
f. Silver.	Reddish brown; *when a little lead and antimony are present,* carmine red.		....	....	....	Silver fuses.
	Hot.	*Cold.*				
g. Bismuth.	Dark orange yellow.	Lemon yellow.	Bluish white.	Volatile.	Volatile.	Bismuth fuses very easily. When *sulphide* and *chloride of bismuth* are submitted to the blowpipe on charcoal they fuse, and outside of the sublimate of oxide is deposited a *white coating of sulphate or chloride of bismuth,* which is volatile in the R. F. without coloring it.
h. Lead.	Dark lemon yellow.	Sulphur yellow.	Bluish white.	Volatile.	Volatile, with azure-blue flame.	Lead fuses easily. When *sulphide* and *chloride of lead* are heated B. B. on charcoal, they fuse, and deposit a *white sublimate of sulphate or chloride of lead* outside of the coating of oxide. The white sublimate is volatile in R. F., tinging the flame blue.
i. Indium.	Dark yellow.	Yellowish white.	....	....	Volatile, with a violet flame.	....
j. Cadmium.	....	Red brown.	Orange yellow.	Volatile.	Volatile.	Cadmium fuses easily, is volatile in R. F., and burns in O. F. with dark-yellow flame and brown smoke. The charcoal exterior to the sublimate sometimes becomes iridescent. *Chloride of cadmium* fuses B. B., and yields outside of the sublimate of oxide a white coating of chloride that is volatile in R. F.
k. Zinc.	Yellow.	White.	....	Non-volatile, but glows brilliantly. After moistening with nitrate of cobalt and strong ignition becomes *yellowish green.*	Slowly volatile.	Zinc fuses easily, is volatile in R. F., and burns in O. F. with a luminous greenish-white flame. *Chloride of zinc* fuses, is partially decomposed, and partially condenses unchanged in form of a white sublimate outside of the coating of oxide. It is volatile in R. F.
l. Tin.	Faint yellow.	White.	....	Non-volatile; glows; with nitrate of cobalt and ignition becomes *bluish green.*	Non-volatile; is reduced to metallic tin.	Tin fuses easily, and in O. F. becomes covered with oxide, which may be blown away mechanically. In R. F. the fused metal remains brilliant and the charcoal is coated. *Chloride of tin* behaves like chloride of zinc.
m. Molybdenum.	Yellow; sometimes crystalline.	White.	Bluish.	Volatile, leaving a copper-red stain of oxide of molybdenum, which is not further affected.	Gives a beautiful azure blue when touched for a moment with the R. F.; continued heat gives the same as in O. F.	This sublimate is best obtained with pulverized material. When sulphide of molybdenum is heated B. B. a copper-red ring surrounds the assay interior to the white sublimate. Molybdenum is infusible.

5. *Sublimates or Coatings.*—The volatile metals and some of their compounds give B. B. on charcoal, more or less characteristic deposits or sublimates. These coat the charcoal at a greater or less distance from the assay, and it must be observed what color they possess both when hot and cold, as well as whether they disappear in the O. F. and R. F., and thereby color the flame.

These sublimates, which are mostly deposited on the unheated charcoal, are not to be confounded with the ash (usually white), which remains as a thin coating where the coal itself has been exposed to the blowpipe flame.

Compounds of some of the metals must be heated in the R. F. They are then reduced to the metallic state, volatilized, and issuing from the flame are instantly reoxidized and deposited as a coating.

The characters given in the tables belong to the unmixed bodies. Their detection is often difficult when they occur together, and not always certain, even to the experienced operator.

a—m (inclusive). See table on page 18.

n. The *sulphides* (*sulphates* which in R. F. on charcoal become sulphides), *chlorides*, *iodides*, *bromides* of *potassium*, *sodium*, *rubidium*, and *cæsium* give B. B. white sublimates, the similar compounds of *lithium* grayish white, less copious sublimates, the salts themselves fusing and being absorbed by the charcoal. These sublimates volatilize in R. F., thereby tinging the flame with the color characteristic to these alkali metals: viz., potassium, rubidium, cæsium, violet; sodium, yellow; lithium, purple.

o. The *chlorides* of *ammonium* and *antimony*, and *subchloride of mercury*, volatilize without fusing, and yield white sublimates, which disappear in R. F. without coloring the flame.

p. *Chloride of copper* fuses and tinges the flame intense azure blue. By long heating it partly volatilizes in white fumes, that smell of chlorine, and coat the charcoal with three differently colored sublimates, of which the interior is dark gray, the middle is dark yellow to brown, and the outer is bluish white. In R. F. the sublimate volatilizes, tinging the flame blue.

D.—HEATING IN THE PLATINUM-POINTED FORCEPS.

Coloration of the Flame.

76. Several bodies may be recognized by the colors they communicate to the blowpipe flame.

When the substance admits, a thin fragment may be held in the *clean* platinum forceps, and its point brought into the edge of the blue flame just within its apex.

When the body fuses so readily that it cannot be supported in the forceps, or if it attacks platinum, it must be laid in a very shallow cavity made on a narrow piece of charcoal, and held in such a manner that the flame may be thrown across it.

If the assay is infusible and decrepitates, or cannot be had in fragments, its powder is moistened to a paste with pure water (not with saliva) and spread upon the coal; it is first dried by a gentle heat and afterwards strongly ignited. Usually a coherent cake is thus obtained, which, with care, may be lifted in the forceps and its edge subjected to the flame. If a small fragment of a decrepitating mineral is taken in the forceps, and the forceps inserted into the flame in such a manner as to strongly heat their points before the mineral is heated, it may then be slowly drawn into the flame, uniformly heated, and thus often be saved.

The trial often succeeds best when the loop of a platinum wire is moistened with distilled water, touched to the powder of the assay, and then carefully heated; or if the body is easily fusible the wire may be ignited and brought rapidly in contact with it. Enough will adhere to observe if any coloration be given. Even if the substance attacks or alloys with the platinum, this method is to be recommended; it is then only needful to cut off the injured part of the wire.

The utmost care must be taken that no foreign matters interfere with the observation. The forceps, charcoal, or wire must be chemically clean, and must not alter the color of the flame when heated alone therein. If the assay is to be pulverized, the mortar and pestle must be thoroughly washed beforehand. The wire may be cleaned by dipping it in hydrochloric acid, or heating it therewith in a test tube, until apparently clean, and then rinsing it with distilled water. Merely by drawing a wire through the fingers, or wetting it with saliva, it receives a coating of soda enough to give a distinct though momentary yellow color to the blowpipe flame.

The flame itself should be what has been described as the oxidizing flame; it must at least be totally free from yellow streaks, and is best obtained from a slender wick like that of a candle. A brass wick-tube often tinges the flame green, especially if the fuel be oil.

The assay is held just within the point of the blue flame; the coloration is observed in the exterior part of the flame, and is best seen in a darkened room, or at least in a situation shielded from the direct light of day.

If the body gives no coloration or only a slight one when heated alone, it should be moistened with *sulphuric acid* and again heated, by which means phosphoric and boric acids become evident; or with hydrochloric acid, which in most cases heightens the coloration given by baryta, strontia, and copper.

1. Yellow.

Reddish yellow. Soda in all its compounds, even when present in very small quantity. Admixtures of potash, etc., even in considerable quantities, do not interfere with this reaction.

2. Violet.

Bluish violet. Potash and most of its salts, phosphates, borates, and infusible silicates excepted. In presence of very little soda the reaction of both is discernible; with more soda (1 per cent.) the yellow flame predominates. The presence of lithia also masks this reaction. Silicates containing potash only, give the flame a violet color, when, besides being free from soda and lithia, they are somewhat fusible. Indium, cæsium and rubidium also give violet flames.

3. Red.

a. Purple red. Lithia and most of its compounds. The reaction is not masked by potash, but easily by soda.

b. Red. Strontia and many of its compounds. The coloration is increased by moistening the already ignited assay with hydrochloric acid; is masked by much baryta.

c. Yellowish red. Lime and many compounds; flame not to be confounded with that produced by strontia; is masked by much baryta.

4. Green.

a. Yellowish green. Baryta and most of its salts, silicates excepted; not masked by lime.

b. Yellowish green. Molybdic Acid; also oxide and sulphide of molybdenum.

c. Emerald green. Copper and most of its salts.

d. Green. Tellurous Acid.

e. Green. Thallium and its salts.

f. Bluish green. Phosphoric Acid. Many phosphates give the coloration alone; others only after their powder is moistened with sulphuric acid to a paste, and then ignited on platinum wire. The coloration is often but momentary.

g. Yellowish (siskin) green. Boric Acid. Minerals and salts are best mixed as powder with sulphuric acid, and heated on platinum wire; coloration often momentary.

h. Dark green, feeble. Ammonia Salts.

i. Whitish green, intense. Metallic Zinc.

5. Blue.

a. Light blue. Metallic Arsenic, and arsenides of bases which do not themselves tinge the flame. Also arsenates, and arsenous acid.

b. Greenish blue. Metallic Antimony, and the sublimate of antimonous acid, on charcoal.

c. Azure blue. Lead. The metal fused in R. F., the sublimate of oxide, also salts of lead when fused on wire, in case their acid constituent does not tinge the flame strongly.

d. Azure blue. Selenium.

e. Azure blue. Chloride of Copper. Metallic copper, and most copper compounds after wetting with hydrochloric acid, color the flame for a short time purplish blue, afterwards green.

f. Greenish blue. Bromide of Copper. After a little time, green.

Fusibility.

77. The fusibility of minerals is also tested in the platinum forceps. (See scale of fusibility in Chapter IV.) As a general rule, no substances with metallic lustre should be heated in the platinum forceps, since they are apt to be injured by forming an alloy with the fused metals; but the cautious manipulator may heat any substance in the forceps without danger, by taking especial care that the fused substance does not come in contact with the forceps.

78. Many of the combinations of the alkaline earths become alkaline on heating. Such substances, if not too fusible, may be treated in the forceps, and the fragment under examination after cooling placed on a strip of moistened turmeric paper, which acquires a brownish-red color at the point of contact with the assay.

E.—TREATMENT WITH COBALT SOLUTION.

79. This operation is only applicable to bodies which are nearly or quite infusible, and which, after ignition, have a white or at least a grayish color, and is always conducted in O. F. If the substance can be heated in the form of splinters or fragments, and is somewhat porous, it may be held in the platinum forceps; the projecting extremity is moistened with the cobalt solution, then heated gradually until dry, and finally ignited as strongly as possible in O. F. without causing fusion.

Hard, compact minerals must be finely pulverized before treatment. The powder is placed in the palm of the hand and moistened with the solution of cobalt. A portion of the paste is then taken upon the loop of a platinum wire and strongly ignited in the O. F.

Certain sublimates, for example, oxides of zinc and tin, formed by heating compounds of these metals on charcoal, are treated directly with cobalt solution.

By this treatment several bodies, especially alumina, magnesia, and oxide of zinc, assume characteristic colors. The tints of blue, red, and black that appear before strong ignition are merely due to the drying or decomposition of the nitrate of cobalt, and are not to be regarded.

The color of the assay thus treated must be examined by daylight.

Minerals, and salts which fuse to a colorless glass, yield with cobalt solution the smalt-blue color which is characteristic of cobalt. A blue *infusible* mass only, indicates *alumina.*

The cobalt solution should be rather dilute, and if needful, successive portions added until decisive results are obtained.

This reagent serves to detect alumina, magnesia, etc., infallibly when they are in the pure state, and also in many of their combinations; but in various minerals the result is masked by other ingredients.

80. The colors thus obtained are given in the following table:

1. *Brown or brick red*—Baryta, under fusion and while hot.
2. *Flesh red*—Magnesia, tantalic acid, after cooling.
3. *Violet*—Zirconia (dirty violet); phosphate and arsenate of magnesia (fuse).
4. *Blue*—Alumina, silica (faint).
5. *Green*—Oxide of zinc (yellowish green), oxide of tin (bluish green), titanic acid (yellowish green), columbic acid (dirty green), antimonic acid (dirty dark green).
6. *Gray*—Strontia, lime, glucina (bluish gray).

It sometimes happens that the ash of the charcoal itself acquires a new color by ignition with this reagent. We have occasionally observed a greenish-yellow color thus produced. The operator has to assure himself that the ash of the coal he uses gives no deceptive reaction with nitrate of cobalt.

Use of Fluxes—Roasting.

81. Borax as well as salt of phosphorus exerts a very powerful solvent action when fused with metallic oxides, forming, in many cases, highly colored glasses, which are exceedingly characteristic. These salts are therefore very important reagents in blowpipe analysis; but it must always be remembered that the colors noted in the following tables are those given by the *oxides*, and where the preliminary examination has shown the substance to contain sulphur or arsenic in combination it is indispensable before going further to remove these elements, and convert the metals into oxides by *roasting.*

82. Roasting. The operation of roasting is performed as follows: The finely pulverized substance is placed in a quite shallow cavity on charcoal, pressed with a pestle or knife-blade into a *thin* layer, and heated for some time, only to dull redness, with the extreme point of the flame. When the odor of sulphurous acid ceases to be perceptible the assay is brought into the R. F., whereby the sulphates and arsenates that may have been formed in the O. F. are reduced, and arsenic is more or less driven off. When no more arsenical odors are evolved the treatment in O. F. is repeated, and these operations are alternately continued until the assay is odorless in both flames. The heat should be quite moderate, so that the body does not fuse; if it fuses, it must be removed to the agate mortar and freshly pulverized. When the roasting has been well conducted the residue is pulverulent, and of uniform appearance throughout. When much arsenic is present it is best to heat the body previously in the open glass tube.

Bodies containing selenium, tellurium, and antimony, if free from sulphur and arsenic, usually require no roasting, as the former substances, unlike the latter, do not interfere with the reactions about to be described.

F.—FUSION WITH BORAX.

83. Treatment with Borax in O. F. The fusion with borax is usually effected on the platinum wire. The clean loop is heated to redness and dipped in borax powder, and the adhering particles are heated until fused to a clear and colorless glass, or bead; this bead, while still hot, is brought in contact with a very little of the assay, and heated therewith in the O. F.

It is to be observed whether the body dissolves readily or slowly, quietly or with effervescence; and when solution has been effected, the bead is to be held before the eye, against the light, and its color, when hot and cold, is to be noted, as well as whether its transparency is disturbed while cooling. Beads should not be looked at against the light of the gas or candle, since by such lights the colors are much modified.

The phenomena of color vary in intensity, and to a certain degree in kind, according to the quantity of substance dissolved in the bead. The manifestation of opacity on cooling depends also upon the quantity of material contained in the flux, and indeed only occurs when a certain amount has been added. It is therefore necessary to begin by dissolving a little of the assay, and after noting the result, more may be cautiously added at several intervals, until the operator is satisfied.

If, by using too much of the assay, a bead has been obtained, so deeply colored that it is difficult to decide what the color is, it may be flattened in the forceps, or drawn out by a platinum wire while still hot; or most of the hot bead may be thrown off with a sudden jerk, and the remaining portion diluted with more borax.

If the operator be in doubt as to the nature of the color he has obtained, he should view it through a lens, or compare it with some known color, obtained by fusing the appropriate pure metallic oxide in another borax bead. Care must be taken finally to guard against deception arising from reflections from colored surfaces near the operator.

84. Flaming. The alkaline earths, and some other bodies, dissolve in borax, forming beads which, at a certain stage of saturation, are clear, and remain so when cold, but which, if heated slowly and gently in the R. F., especially with an intermittent flame, become opaque and enamel-like.

The application of the *intermittent flame* is called *flaming*. In most cases the bodies, which at a certain degree of saturation are made opaque by flaming, become so without flaming when the saturation is carried a little farther.

85. Treatment with Borax in R. F. After observing the behavior of a body in the O. F., it is subjected to the R. F., which must, however, be so managed that no soot deposits on the bead. After blowing a little time the bead is allowed to cool, and its color, both when hot and cold, is observed. It may sometimes be needful to add more of the assay, and repeat the heating. In case no effect be produced, or if metallic globules appear, which may often alloy with the platinum (whereby the loop is spoiled), the bead is jerked off into a clean dish, placed in a shallow cavity on charcoal, and further submitted to the R. F. for one or two minutes. In this way reductions are easily accomplished that scarcely succeed on the wire. While the bead is still glowing it is grasped in the clean pincers, flattened, and slightly lifted from the charcoal. It is thus suddenly cooled, whereby oxidation, that might occur were the bead left to cool slowly, is prevented, and at the same time it is brought into a good position for examining its color.

In special cases reduction is still further aided by help of metallic tin. A bit of tin-foil is laid in contact with the bead, and the two are fused together for a few moments in the R. F. The tin oxidizes at the expense of the higher oxide present, reducing the same to a lower oxide, while the oxide of tin formed, dissolves in the borax, without interfering with the color produced by the reduced assay.

86. With Borax in O. F. are yielded—

1. Colorless Beads by

Temperature.		
Hot and Cold.	Silica, alumina, oxide of tin, baryta, strontia, lime, magnesia, glucina, yttria, zirconia, thoria, oxides of lanthanum and silver, tantalic, columbic, and tellurous acids:	when strongly saturated become opaque white by flaming.
	Titanic, tungstic, molybdic, and antimonic acids, oxides of indium, zinc, cadmium, lead, and bismuth:	when slightly saturated.

2. Yellow Beads by

Hot.	Titanic, tungstic, and molybdic acids, oxides of zinc and cadmium:	when strongly saturated; colorless when cold, but opaque by flaming.
	Oxides of lead and bismuth, antimonous acid:	when strongly saturated; colorless when cold.
	Oxides of cerium, uranium, and iron:	when feebly saturated; paler on cooling.
	Oxide of chromium: when feebly saturated; yellowish green when cold.	
	Vanadic acid: greenish when cold.	

3. Red to Brown Beads by

Hot.	Oxide of cerium: yellow on cooling; opaque by flaming.
	" didymium; rose colored; the same when cold.
	" iron: yellow when cold.
	" uranium: yellow on cooling; opaque yellow by flaming.
	" chromium: yellowish green when cold.
	" iron containing manganese: yellowish red on cooling.
Cold.	Oxide of nickel (red brown to brown): violet when hot.
	" manganese: (violet red) violet when hot.
	" nickel containing cobalt: (with little cobalt, violet brown) violet when hot.

4. Violet (Amethystine) Beads by

Hot.
- Oxide of nickel: red brown to brown on cooling.
- " manganese: violet red on cooling.
- " nickel containing cobalt: passes into brown on cooling; if much cobalt be present, it remains violet.
- " cobalt containing manganese: on cooling, like the nickel mixture.

5. Blue Beads by

Hot.—Oxide of cobalt: unchanged on cooling.
Cold.—Oxide of copper (when highly saturated greenish blue): *green* when hot.

6. Green Beads by

Hot.
- Oxide of copper: blue after cooling, or greenish blue when highly saturated.
- Oxide of iron containing cobalt:; " " " copper:; " copper " iron:; " " " nickel: — According to the degree of saturation and the relative proportions of the oxides to each other, the green color changes on cooling into *pale green*, *blue*, or *yellow*.

Cold.
- Oxide of chromium (yellowish green): *yellow* to *red* when hot.
- Vanadic acid (greenish): *yellow* when hot.

87. With Borax in R. F. are given—

1. Colorless Beads by

Hot and Cold.
- Silica, alumina, oxide of tin, baryta, strontia, lime, magnesia, glucina, yttria, zirconia, thoria, oxide of lanthanum, oxide of cerium, tantalic acid: — when strongly saturated; become opaque by flaming.
- Oxide of didymium, oxide of manganese, the latter often takes a faint rose color on cooling:
- Columbic acid: when used in small quantity.
- Oxides of silver, zinc, cadmium, lead, bismuth, and nickel; antimonous and tellurous acids: — after long heating; gray if heated but a short time.

Hot.
- Oxide of copper: becomes opaque red on cooling, if highly saturated.

2. Yellow to Brown Beads by

Hot.
- Titanic acid (yellow to brown): when strongly saturated; become enamel blue by flaming.
- Tungstic acid (yellow to dark yellow): brownish when cold.
- Molybdic acid (brown to black and opaque).
- Vanadic acid (brownish): chrome green when cold.

3. Blue Bead by

Hot. Oxide of cobalt: unchanged on cooling.

4. Green Beads by

Hot and Cold.	Oxide of iron (yellowish or bottle green): especially when cold.
	" uranium (yellowish green): when highly saturated; becomes black by flaming.
	" chromium (pale to dark emerald green): according to degree of saturation.
Cold.	Vanadic acid (chrome green): brownish, when hot.

5. Gray or Turbid Beads, the Turbidity often appearing during the Heating by

Cold.	Oxides of silver, zinc, cadmium, lead, bismuth, and nickel, antimonous and tellurous acids:	when heated a short time; by longer blowing become colorless.
	Columbic acid: when highly saturated.	

6. Red Beads by

Cold.	Oxide of copper (opaque) if highly saturated, or with tin on charcoal.
	Sesquioxide of didymium (rose color).

G.—FUSION WITH SALT OF PHOSPHORUS.

88. The general rules given for fusion with borax apply here.

The salt of phosphorus when first heated fuses in its crystal water, and is so fluid that it easily falls from the platinum loop. If, however, a small quantity be first fused upon the wire until it ceases boiling, then the additional quantity needed will adhere without difficulty. The bead is best placed *over* the blowpipe flame, as the ascending vapors that are driven from the salt buoy up the bead and keep it from falling.

In general the behavior of the various bodies is quite similar to that with borax; there are, however, characteristic differences, as the table shows.

Salt of phosphorus is especially useful in the detection of *silica*. Most silicates, when added to a bead of it and heated, are decomposed. The bases dissolve in the flux without interfering with its transparency (unless the substance is in too large quantity), while the silica, being almost insoluble, floats as a translucent yet distinct cloud in the bead. It is best observed when the bead is hot. If the alkaline earths be present, the bead becomes opaque on cooling, but this does not interfere with the test. It must be borne in mind, however, that silica is soluble, though but slightly, in salt of phosphorus, and small quantities may, therefore, be easily overlooked. Also that some silicates, especially those of alumina and zirconia, are with difficulty decomposed by it.

When phosphate of soda and ammonia is subjected to the action of heat, the ammonia escapes with the water of crystallization, and the readily fusible metaphosphate of soda is left behind. This is a powerful solvent, and its action is quite analogous to that of biborate of soda.

89. With Salt of Phosphorus in O. F. are given—

1. Colorless Beads by

Hot and Cold.

- Silica (very slightly soluble).
- Alumina, oxide of tin (difficultly soluble).
- Baryta, strontia, lime, magnesia, glucina, yttria, zirconia, thoria, oxide of lanthanum, tellurous acid: when strongly saturated; become opaque white by flaming.
- Tantalic, columbic, titanic, tungstic, and antimonous acids, oxides of zinc, cadmium, lead, and bismuth: when not too highly saturated; otherwise yellowish to yellow and colorless only after cooling.

2. Yellow Beads by

Hot.

- Tantalic, columbic, titanic, tungstic, and antimonic acids, oxides of lead, zinc, cadmium, and bismuth: when slightly saturated, but colorless when cold.
- Oxide of silver (yellowish): when cold, opalescent.
- Oxides of iron and cerium: when slightly saturated; become colorless on cooling (strongly saturated are red when hot, and yellow when cold).
- Oxide of uranium: yellowish green when cold.
- Vanadic acid (dark yellow): paler on cooling.

Cold.

- Oxide of nickel: reddish when hot.

3. Red Beads by

Hot.

- Oxides of iron and cerium: when highly saturated; becomes yellow after cooling.
- Oxide of didymium: rose color when saturated.
- " nickel (reddish): yellow when cold.
- " chromium (reddish): emerald green when cold.

4. Violet (Amethystine) Bead by

Hot.

- Oxide of manganese (brown violet): pale red violet when cold.

5. Blue Beads by

Hot.

- Oxide of cobalt: color unchanged on cooling.

Cold.

- " copper (when strongly saturated greenish blue): green when hot.

6. Green Beads by

Hot.

- Oxide of copper: blue when cold (when strongly saturated, greenish blue).
- Molybdic acid (yellowish green): paler on cooling
- Oxide of iron containing cobalt.; " " " copper.; " copper " iron.; " " " nickel.: According to the degree of saturation, and the relative proportions of the oxides to each other, the green color changes on cooling into pale green, blue, or yellow.

Cold.

- Oxide of uranium (yellowish green): yellow when hot.
- " chromium (emerald green): reddish when hot.

90. With Salt of Phosphorus in R. F. are given—

1. Colorless Beads by

Hot and Cold.	Silica (very slightly soluble).	
	Alumina and oxide of zinc (difficultly soluble).	
	Baryta, strontia, lime, magnesia, glucina, yttria, zirconia, thoria, oxide of lanthanum:	when strongly saturated become opaque white by flaming.
	Oxides of cerium, didymium, and manganese.	
	Oxides of silver, zinc, cadmium, indium, lead, bismuth, tantalic, antimonous, and tellurous acids:	after long heating (otherwise gray).
	Oxide of nickel (especially on charcoal).	

2. Yellow to Red Beads by

Hot.	Oxide of iron (yellow to red): when cooling at first greenish, then reddish.
	Titanic acid (yellow): violet on cooling.
	Columbic acid (violet brown): particularly on charcoal.
	Vanadic acid (brownish): chrome green after cooling.
	Titanic acid containing iron. } (Yellow): when cold, brown (blood)
	Tungstic " " " } red
	Columbic " " " (brown red): dark yellow when cold.

3. Violet (Amethystine) Beads by

Cold.	Columbic acid (when highly saturated): faint dirty-blue when hot.
	Titanic acid (even by moderate saturation): yellow when hot.

4. Blue Beads by

Cold.	Oxide of cobalt: same when hot.
	Tungstic acid: brownish when hot.
	Columbic acid (when very strongly saturated): dirty blue when hot.

5. Green Beads by

Cold.	Oxide of uranium: yellowish green when hot.
	Molybdic acid: dirty green when hot.
	Vanadic acid: brownish when hot.
	Oxide of chromium: reddish when hot.

6. Gray or Turbid Beads, the Turbidity often appearing during the Heating by

Cold.	Oxides of silver, zinc, cadmium, indium, lead, bismuth, and nickel, antimonous and tellurous acids:	Reaction best obtained on charcoal. After long blowing become colorless.

7. Red Beads by

Cold.	Oxide of copper (opaque) when strongly saturated, or by aid of tin on charcoal.
	Sesquioxide of Didymium (rose colored).

H.—TREATMENT WITH SODA.

91. No attempt is here made to tabulate the phenomena that may arise in the treatment of bodies B. B. with carbonate of soda. These phenomena have either been described in the foregoing tables (sublimation), or are somewhat uncertain in their production, especially by the beginner (formation of glass with silicates), or, finally, are of a general nature (reduction of metallic oxides). We therefore translate substantially what Plattner has written under this head. According to the nature of the assay, it may either *fuse together with* or *dissolve in* soda, as when containing earths or fixed acid; or a *metallic reduction* may occur if the assay consist of reducible metallic oxides.

92. Fusibility with Soda (O. F.). A large number of bodies have the property to unite with soda at a high temperature, and to give partly fusible, partly infusible, compounds.

The fusible bodies are, however, few in number: principally silica, titanic acid, tungstic acid, and molybdic acid. When the fusion takes place on charcoal, silica and titanic acid both unite with the soda under effervescence to clear beads. The silicate of soda remains transparent after cooling if no excess of soda be present, but the titanate of soda becomes crystalline and opaque.

Molybdic and tungstic acids also combine with soda with effervescence, but the compounds are absorbed by the charcoal. Besides these acids, the salts of baryta and strontia are fusible with soda, but the mass is absorbed by the coal. Most salts of lime fuse indeed with soda, but when the acids they contain are stronger than carbonic acid, they are decomposed; the resulting salt of soda penetrates the coal, while the lime remains as a white mass on the surface.

In trying the fusibility of a body with soda, one proceeds in the following manner: If the body be in form of powder, it is mixed in the palm of the hand with soda, by means of a moistened knife-blade, to a coherent mass; if the assay be a splinter or fragment, and does not decrepitate, the moistened soda is spread upon it; if it decrepitates it must be pulverized. In both cases the assay is placed in a shallow cavity on charcoal, gently heated until thoroughly dry, and thereupon intensely ignited in the O. F. If a fragment has been used, the soda is commonly absorbed by the coal as it first fuses; but if the assay be soluble in it, it appears again and attacks the body with effervescence, and presently fuses with it to a globule. *If too little soda be used in the treatment of a body soluble in this reagent, a portion of the assay remains undissolved, and surrounded by a clear glass; if too much soda has been employed, the glass will become opaque on cooling.* It is therefore advisable to add the soda in successive small quantities, and observe the changes thus produced. *Many bodies, especially silicates, which are themselves difficultly fusible, although their bases are infusible, dissolve in a little soda to a clear glass, but with more soda they form a slaggy or infusible mass.*

If the assay be insoluble in soda, but decomposable by it, the operator will see that it gradually swells up and changes its appearance, though it does not fuse to a globule. If this be the case with an assay used in the state of powder, it may not be certain that it is actually insoluble, because too little soda may have been used; the mass must therefore be heated with a new portion of soda, or even with a second or third addition. When this appearance of decomposition occurs with a fragment of mineral, the same body must also be heated with soda in the state of powder. If the assay is both insoluble and undecomposable, the soda is absorbed by the charcoal and the body is left on the surface unchanged, whether applied as a fragment or in powder.

93. Formation of a Hepar (R. F.). The higher sulphides of the alkalies have long been known by the name of *Hepar sulphuris* (liver of sulphur), since they possess a *liver-brown* color. When soda is fused on charcoal in the R. F. with any compound of sulphur (sulphide or sulphate), sulphide of sodium is produced, and if much sulphur was present in the assay the fused mass will show the characteristic color of hepar. Whether or not the mass possess this color, whether it remain on the surface of the coal or be absorbed by it, it is only necessary to place it on a freshly scraped surface of silver (or to cut out the coal into which it has sunk, and put it on the silver), and then add a drop of water, in order after a few moments to recognize the slightest trace of SULPHUR by the production of a yellow or even black stain of sulphide of silver. Illuminating gas commonly contains sulphur-compounds, and when this test for sulphur is employed with gas for fuel, the soda should always be fused first on coal and tested before adding the assay. If sulphur should prove to be present the test must be made with a candle or oil-flame.

94. Reduction of Metallic Oxides (R. F.). The fusion of certain oxides with soda on charcoal in R. F. furnishes a most ready and delicate means of detecting their presence in minerals and salts.

Some metallic oxides are reduced to the metallic state by heating alone in R. F. when pure, but with difficulty or not at all when mixed or combined with other bodies; by addition of soda, however, the reduction is easy. There are other oxides that alone are unaltered, but by fusion with soda are reduced to the metallic state.

If the oxide of lead, for example, is fused with soda, there is no difficulty in recognizing the metallic lead, which will be found in globules on the surface of the charcoal. Oxide of iron yields, however, metallic iron which cannot be fused, and the fusible metals often escape the eye when present in small quantity. The operator must therefore employ the method of Gahn, as follows. The finely pulverized substance is mixed with soda and a drop of water to a paste, which is laid in a cavity on charcoal, and strongly heated in the R. F. The soda commonly sinks into the charcoal; more is added at intervals, until the assay has nearly or completely disappeared in the pores of the coal. A drop or two of water is now put upon the place, and all those parts of the coal near the cavity which have absorbed the assay are cut out into the agate mortar, and pulverized with addition of water to a fine powder. The water is now carefully decanted, or the mortar is held beneath the surface of water contained in a clean bowl, and gently moved to and fro, so that the coal dust is washed away from any metallic particles that may be in the mortar. By careful washing even the smallest quantity of copper, tin, or lead may be seen remaining in the mortar in the shape of flattened globules. If the metal be infusible or brittle, it will be found as a heavy, lustrous powder.

The nature of the metal can be determined by its physical properties; or the particles may be dissolved in borax or salt of phosphorus, and tested as already described. Often the sublimate that is deposited about the assay will give a clue to the kind of metal under examination.

Iron, cobalt, and nickel are obtained as metallic powder which is lifted by the magnet (best tried under water). Copper is recognized by its red color; Tin and Lead flatten under the pestle; Bismuth and Antimony are brittle, and present themselves as powder. Besides these metals, Molybdenum, Tungsten, Tellurium, Indium, Zinc, and Cadmium, and the noble metals, are also reduced by treatment with soda. Antimony, Tellurium, Bismuth, Indium, Lead, Zinc, and Cadmium volatilize partly or completely, and yield characteristic sublimates. Zinc and Cadmium usually volatilize entirely. Arsenic and Mercury are also reduced, but must be heated with soda in a tube, in order to collect the sublimates, which are metallic arsenic and mercury.

When several metals are together, they usually form an alloy. Copper and iron are, however, obtained distinct. If the assay contained arsenate of cobalt or nickel, fusible metallic globules are obtained, which are always brittle from presence of arsenic. The reactions with borax and salt of phosphorus must be the final resort, and it may happen that only the experienced operator will be able to make out satisfactorily the nature of a metallic mixture, such as may result from a reduction with soda.

PLATTNER directs attention to the three following points, as needful to be carefully attended to in successfully conducting the operation in question:

1. The operator must keep the assay a sufficiently long time exposed to the action of a strong R. F.

2. In cutting out and pulverizing the fused mass, and in washing the same, the greatest care must be exercised that no metallic particles be lost; and,

3. The remaining metal, whether in form of scales, grains, or powder, must be examined with help of a lens, and tested by means of the magnet, and if needful by fluxes (borax and salt of phosphorus).

To acquire skill in the detection of copper and tin by reduction with soda (it is most applicable for finding small quantities of these metals especially), the beginner should practise with mixtures of a copper ore or salt with increasing quantities of feldspar or some other body free from metallic oxides. One or two per cent. of tin, and much less copper, can be detected in the quantity usually employed for blowpipe assays.

95. For convenience of reference is added here a tabular view, translated from Plattner, of the behavior of the earths and metallic oxides when treated successively, (1) alone on charcoal or in the platinum forceps; (2) with borax, and (3) with salt of phosphorus on platinum wire; (4) with soda, and (5) with cobalt solution; the special reactions of the alkalies will be given under appropriate heads in the next chapter. In the table the sign O, given under some of the heads, indicates that no reaction is observed with the substance.

TABLE

SHOWING THE BEHAVIOR OF THE

EARTHS, AND METALLIC OXIDES BEFORE THE BLOWPIPE.

Earths.	Behavior alone, on Charcoal, and in the Platinum forceps.	With Borax on Platinum Wire.	With Salt of Phosphorus on Platinum Wire.	With Soda on Charcoal.	With Solution of Cobalt in O. F.
Baryta Ḃa	As hydrate fuses, boils, and intumesces, congeals on the surface, and then is absorbed by the coal. As carbonate, fuses easily to a clear glass, which becomes enamel white on cooling. After repeated fusion it boils and spirts, becomes caustic and is absorbed by the coal. Heated in the forceps, tinges the flame yellowish green.	The carbonate is soluble with effervescence to a clear glass, which by a certain addition may be made opaque by flaming. At a greater saturation becomes opaque of itself.	As with Borax.	Fuses together with soda, and is absorbed by the charcoal.	Fuses to a pale brown or brownish red globule; on cooling loses color, and on exposure to the atmosphere falls into a light-gray powder.
Strontia Ṡr	The hydrate behaves like that of baryta. The carbonate fuses on coal only on the finest edges, and throws out cauliflower-like ramifications which emit a brilliant light, and tinge the R. F. faintly red; they also react alkaline with turmeric paper. Heated in the forceps, the flame is tinged purple red.	As Baryta.	As Baryta.	Caustic strontia is insoluble. The carbonate, mixed with an equal volume of soda, fuses to a clear glass, which becomes milk white on cooling. In stronger heat the glass boils, the earth becomes caustic, and is absorbed by the coal.	Sinters, and assumes a black or dark-gray color.
Lime Ċa.	Caustic lime neither fuses nor is altered. The carbonate becomes caustic, of whiter color, glows brightly, acquires alkaline reaction, and if a fragment be thus heated, it falls to powder upon moistening with water. Heated in the forceps, the outer flame acquires a faint-red color.	Easily soluble to a clear glass, that may be made opaque by flaming. The carbonate dissolves with effervescence. A larger addition gives a clear glass, which while cooling becomes crystalline and clouded, but never so milk-white as is the case with baryta and strontia.	Soluble in large quantity (carbonate with effervescence) to a clear glass, which when considerably saturated may be made opaque by flaming. When fully saturated, the clear glass becomes milk-white on cooling.	Insoluble; the soda is absorbed by the coal, and leaves the lime on the surface.	Is perfectly infusible, and becomes gray.

Magnesia $\dot{\text{Mg}}$	The carbonate is decomposed: glows and acquires an alkaline reaction.	As lime, but is not so strongly crystalline.	Dissolves easily (the carbonate with effervescence) to a clear glass, which by flaming becomes opaque, and when fully saturated turns milk-white on cooling.	As Lime.	After long ignition assumes a pale flesh-red color, that must be observed when the assay is cold. Phosphate and arsenate of magnesia fuse and acquire a violet-red color.
Alumina $\dddot{\text{Al}}$	Unchanged.	Slowly soluble to a clear glass, which does not become opaque, either by flaming, or after complete saturation, by cooling. When added as a fine powder in large quantity, a glass results that is not clear, but on cooling becomes crystalline on the surface, and is hardly fusible.	Slowly dissolves to a clear glass, that remains clear. With too large an addition the undissolved portion is rendered semi-transparent.	Intumesces slightly, forms an infusible compound, and the excess of soda is absorbed by the coal.	After strong ignition becomes beautifully blue, best observed when the assay is cold.
Glucina $\dot{\text{Be}}$	Unchanged.	Soluble in large quantity to a clear glass, that becomes milk-white by flaming or when saturated, by simple cooling.	As with Borax.	Insoluble.	Acquires a pale bluish-green color.
Yttria. $\dot{\text{Y}}$ and Terbia. $\dot{\text{Tr}}$	Unchanged.	As Glucina.	As Glucina.	Insoluble.	O
Erbia $\dot{\text{E}}$	The yellow oxide becomes of a lighter color in R. F., and acquires a transparent appearance.	Dissolves slowly to a clear colorless glass, which turns milk-white by flaming, or after saturation by mere cooling.	As with Borax.	Insoluble.	O
Zirconia $\ddot{\text{Zr}}$	Infusible. As prepared from sulphate, glows more intensely than any other substance.	As Glucina.	Dissolves more slowly than in Borax, and more readily yields an opaque glass.	Insoluble.	Assumes a dirty violet color.
Thoria $\ddot{\text{Th}}$	Unchanged.	Soluble to small extent, forming a clear glass, which when fully saturated becomes milk-white on cooling; but if it remains clear after cooling, cannot be made opaque by flaming.	As with Borax.	Insoluble.	O
Silica $\ddot{\text{Si}}$	Unchanged.	Slowly soluble to a clear, difficultly fusible glass, that cannot be made opaque by flaming.	To a very small degree soluble to a clear glass. The undissolved portion becomes semi-transparent.	With not too much soda, soluble with effervescence to a clear glass.	With little cobalt solution becomes faint bluish in color. With more solution is black or dark gray. The thinnest edges may, however, be fused by skilful blowing to a reddish-blue glass.

Metallic Oxides & Acids	Behavior alone, on Charcoal, etc.	With Borax on Platinum Wire.	With Salt of Phosphorus on Platinum Wire.	With Soda on Coal.	With Solution of Cobalt in O. F.
Antimonous acid $\overset{\cdots}{Sb}$	*O. F.* Volatilizes, and mostly deposits around the heated point. *R. F.* Is reduced and volatilized; partly deposits again. A greenish-blue tinge is communicated to the outer flame.	*O. F.* Largely soluble to a clear glass, which is yellowish while hot, but becomes colorless on cooling. On charcoal the dissolved acid may be almost completely expelled from the bead, so that tin manifests no reducing action as below. *R. F.* The glass which has been exposed but a short time to the O. F. on charcoal becomes grayish and turbid from separation of particles of metallic antimony. By continued blowing these volatilize, and the glass becomes clear. With tin the glass is made gray to black, according as it is less or more saturated.	*O. F.* Soluble with boiling to a clear glass, which while hot appears only faintly yellow. *R. F.* On charcoal the saturated glass is at first made turbid, but afterwards becomes clear from the volatilization of the antimony. With tin the glass becomes gray on cooling, but clear again on continued blowing. The gray turbidity is caused by tin when only very little antimonous acid is dissolved in the glass.	On charcoal in both flames very easily reducible, but the metal is immediately volatilized, and covers the coal with a white deposit of oxide of antimony.	If the sublimate formed on charcoal when ignited in O. F. is heated after moistening with solution of cobalt it is partly volatilized, but another part remains, and after cooling is seen to have acquired a dirty, dark-green color.
Arsenous Acid $\overset{\cdots}{As}$	Volatilizes below a red heat.	O	O	On charcoal is reduced, evolving vapors of arsenic, which may be recognized by their garlic odor.	O
Oxide of Bismuth $\overset{\cdots}{Bi}$	*O. F.* On platinum foil fuses easily to a dark-brown mass, which is pale yellow when cold. On charcoal in both flames it is reduced to metallic bismuth, which gradually volatilizes, depositing on the support an inner coating of yellow oxide, and an outer white one of carbonate of bismuth. In R. F. these sublimates disappear without tinging the flame.	*O. F.* Easily soluble to a clear yellow glass, which with a small quantity is colorless when cold. With a larger quantity the glass is yellowish red when hot, but while cooling becomes yellow, and is opaline when cold. *R. F.* On charcoal the glass is at first gray and turbid, then the oxide is reduced to metal with effervescence, and the bead becomes clear. The reduction occurs more promptly by addition of tin.	*O. F.* Easily soluble to a clear yellow glass, which is colorless when cold. With a large quantity of oxide, the glass can be made opaque by flaming, and with still more it becomes opaque by cooling. *R. F.* On coal, especially with help of tin, the glass so changes that when hot it appears clear and colorless, but on cooling becomes dark gray and opaque.	On charcoal is immediately reduced to metallic bismuth.	O
Oxide of Cadmium $\dot{Cd}$	*O. F.* On platinum foil unchanged. *R. F.* On charcoal disappears, and condenses on the surrounding coal as a reddish-brown to dark-yellow powder, the color of which is best seen when cold. The exterior parts of the sublimate are iridescent, like the tail of a peacock.	*O. F.* Soluble in very large quantity to a clear yellowish glass, which is almost colorless when cold. When strongly saturated the glass maybe made milk-white by flaming; very strongly saturated it becomes opaque by cooling. *R. F.* On charcoal the glass boils, the cadmium is reduced, but immediately volatilizes and coats the support with dark yellow oxide.	*O. F.* Largely soluble, forming a clear glass, which with a large quantity is yellowish when hot, but colorless when cold. A saturated glass is milk-white when cold. *R. F.* The dissolved oxide is slowly and imperfectly reduced on charcoal, yielding a slight sublimate of yellow oxide on the surrounding charcoal. Tin facilitates the reduction.	*O. F.* Insoluble. *R. F.* On charcoal is immediately reduced. The metal volatilizes and deposits reddish-brown and dark-yellow oxide on the support; exteriorly the sublimate is iridescent.	O

Sesquioxide of Cerium $\overset{\cdots}{\text{Ce}}$	In O. F. the protoxide is changed into sesquioxide, which is not altered in R. F.	*O. F.* Soluble to a dark yellow to red glass (like oxide of iron); on cooling, however, the bead is yellow. At a certain saturation the glass may be made opaque by flaming; by greater saturation it becomes opaque on cooling. *R. F.* The yellow glass is rendered colorless. A highly saturated glass becomes enamel white and crystalline.	*O. F.* As with Borax: the color, however, completely disappears on cooling. *R. F.* The glass is colorless both when hot and cold (distinguishes cerium from iron). No degree of saturation causes the glass to become opaque on cooling.	Insoluble. The soda passes into the coal; the sesquioxide is converted into protoxide, and remains on the surface, of a light-gray color.	O
Sesquioxide of Chromium $\overset{\cdots}{\text{Cr}}$	Unalterable in either flame.	*O. F.* Dissolves slowly, but with intense color. In small quantity gives a glass which is yellow when hot (chromic acid) and yellowish green when cold; in larger quantity dark red while hot, yellow while cooling, and when entirely cold fine yellowish green. *R. F.* With little chrome oxide the glass is a beautiful green, both when hot and cold; on a larger addition it becomes darker, or pure emerald green. Treatment with tin causes no change.	*O. F.* Soluble to a clear glass, which is red while hot; on cooling becomes dirty green, and finally assumes a beautiful green color. *R. F.* As in O. F.; the colors appear somewhat darker; the same with tin.	*O. F.* Soluble on platinum wire to a dark brownish-green glass, which becomes opaque yellow on cooling (chromic acid). *R. F.* The glass is opaque and green (oxide) when cold. On charcoal it cannot be reduced to metal: it remains as green oxide on the surface of the charcoal, while the soda is absorbed.	O
Columbic Acid $\overset{\therefore\therefore}{\text{Cb}}$	*O. F.* Becomes yellow on heating, but white again on cooling, without further change. *R. F.* As in O. F.	*O. F.* Easily soluble to a clear colorless glass, which when strongly saturated may be made turbid by flaming. When very strongly saturated grows turbid on cooling. *R. F.* The opaline glass from O. F. is unchanged, but with the lower oxide of columbium becomes clear again, and when the latter is added in larger quantity the glass loses its transparency and assumes a bluish-gray color. In still greater quantity the glass is bluish gray and quite opaque when cold.	*O. F.* Soluble in large quantity to a clear glass that is yellow while hot, but colorless when cold. The lower oxide gives a greenish blue glass, which becomes colorless on long blowing. *R. F.* With a large quantity the glass is brown; addition of sulphate of iron makes it blood red. The lower oxide gives a fine blue, becoming brown on charcoal, and with addition of sulphate of iron gives a blood-red color.	*O. F.* With about an equal volume of soda, fuses with effervescence. With a larger quantity of soda it is absorbed by the charcoal. *R. F.* As in *O. F.* The acid cannot be reduced to metal.	While hot appears gray, on cooling becomes dirty green. If the heat be too strong, the assay sinters; and after cooling, the portions that have been most strongly heated are of a dark gray color.
Oxide of Cobalt $\dot{\text{Co}}$	*O. F.* Unchanged. *R. F.* Shrinks together somewhat, and without fusing is reduced to metal, which is lifted by a magnet, and when rubbed in a mortar assumes metallic lustre.	*O. F.* The oxide of cobalt possesses very great coloring power. The glass is smalt blue both when hot and cold. When strongly saturated the color is so deep as to appear black. *R. F.* As in O. F.	*O. F.* As with Borax: with equal quantity of oxide the color is not quite so deep as with borax, especially after cooling. *R. F.* As in O. F.	*O. F.* On platinum wire dissolves in very slight quantity to a transparent, pale, rose-red mass, that becomes gray on cooling. *R. F.* On charcoal reduced to a gray magnetic powder, which is made lustrous by rubbing.	O

Metallic Oxides & Acids	Behavior alone, on Charcoal, etc.	With Borax on Platinum Wire.	With Salt of Phosphorus on Platinum Wire.	With Soda on Coal.	With Solution of Cobalt in O. F.
Oxide of Copper $\dot{\mathrm{Cu}}$	*O. F.* Fuses to a black globule, which on charcoal soon spreads out, and is reduced to metal on its under surface. *R. F.* Is reduced at a temperature below the fusing point of metallic copper. The reduced portions have the metallic lustre of copper, but as soon as the blowing is interrupted, the surface oxidizes, and becomes brown or black. By stronger heat the reduced metal fuses to globules.	*O. F.* A small quantity gives the glass a green color while hot, which changes to blue on cooling. A larger quantity gives a glass, which when hot is dark green to opaque, and on cooling becomes greenish blue. *R. F.* At a certain saturation the glass soon becomes colorless; on cooling, however, becomes red and opaque (suboxide). On charcoal the copper may be reduced and separated so that the glass becomes colorless after cooling. On charcoal with tin easily made brownish red from formation of suboxide of copper.	*O. F.* The colors are the same as with borax, but less intense; viz.: green to dark or opaque green when hot, and blue or greenish blue when cold, according to the degree of saturation. *R. F.* A pretty strongly saturated glass becomes dark green; and on cooling, at the moment of solidification, opaque brown red (suboxide). If the glass contains but little oxide of copper in solution, and be treated with tin on charcoal, it is colorless while hot, but becomes opaque red on cooling.	*O. F.* On platinum wire soluble to a clear green glass, which loses its color and becomes opaque on cooling. *R. F.* On charcoal is easily reduced to metallic copper, which fuses to globules in a strong heat.	O
Oxide of Didymium $\dot{\mathrm{Di}}$	*O. F.* Infusible. *R. F.* Loses its brown color and becomes gray.	*O. F.* Soluble to a rose red colored glass, which is unchanged in R. F.	As with Borax, but more difficultly insoluble.	Insoluble. The soda is absorbed by the charcoal, leaving on its surface the oxide with a gray color.	O
Oxide of Gold $\dddot{\mathrm{Au}}$	Ignited in either flame, is converted into metal which is easily fusible to globules.	*O. F.* Is reduced without dissolving, and on charcoal may be fused to globules. *R. F.* As with O. F.	As with Borax.	As with Borax; the soda, however, is absorbed by the charcoal.	O
Oxide of Indium $\dot{\mathrm{In}}$	*O. F.* Becomes dark yellow when heated, and lighter again on cooling. Infusible. *R. F.* Gradually reduced and volatilized, coating the coal and coloring the outer flame violet.	*O. F.* Dissolves to a clear glass, feebly yellow while hot, colorless when cold, and cloudy when much is added. *R. F.* Unchanged. On coal is reduced; volatilized, coats the coal, and colors the flame violet, which is perceptible notwithstanding the soda.	As with Borax; but the glass when treated with tin on charcoal becomes gray and turbid on cooling.	*O. F.* Insoluble. *R. F.* Is reduced on coal, and the metal volatilizes in part, coating the coal with oxide, and partly remains in the flux in almost silver-white grains.	O
Oxide of Iridium $\ddot{\mathrm{Ir}}$	Is reduced by ignition, but the metallic particles cannot be fused.	*O. F.* Is reduced without dissolving, but no globules can be obtained. *R. F.* As with O. F.	As with Borax.	As with Borax; the soda passes into the charcoal.	O

Sesquioxide of Iron $\overset{\cdots}{Fe}$	*O. F.* Unchanged. *R. F.* Becomes black and magnetic (proto-sesquioxide).	*O. F.* In small quantity yields a glass which is yellow when hot, and colorless when cold; with more oxide the glass is red when hot, and yellow when cold; with still more the hot glass is dark red, and when cold is dark yellow. *R. F.* The glass is bottle green (proto-sesquioxide). On charcoal with tin, is at first bottle green, then vitriol green (protoxide).	*O. F.* With a certain quantity of oxide, the hot glass is yellowish red; upon cooling becomes first yellow, then greenish, and finally colorless. With a very large quantity, the hot glass is dark red; on cooling it becomes brownish-red, then dirty green. When cold it is brownish red. The colors disappear sooner by cooling than those of the borax glass. *R. F.* With little oxide the color is not altered; with more it is red when hot, and on cooling first yellow, then greenish, and finally reddish. On charcoal with tin the glass becomes green and finally colorless on cooling.	*O. F.* Insoluble. *R. F.* On charcoal is reduced, and by pulverization and washing the metal is obtained as a gray magnetic powder.	0
Oxyd of Lanthanum $\dot{La}$	Unchanged.	*O. F.* Soluble to a clear colorless glass, which at a certain saturation can be made opaque white by flaming, and more strongly saturated becomes opaque by cooling. *R. F.* As in O. F.	As with Borax	Insoluble. The soda passes into the charcoal, and the oxide remains behind as a gray powder.	0
Oxide of Lead $\dot{Pb}$	Red lead heated on platinum-foil blackens, and by gentle ignition is converted into yellow oxide; more strongly heated this oxide fuses to a yellow glass. On charcoal in *O. F.* and *R. F.* is immediately reduced to metallic lead, which gradually volatilizes by continued heating, and covers the charcoal with a yellow deposit of oxide of lead, beyond which a thin white coating of carbonate of lead is formed. These coatings disappear when heated in *R. F.*, tinging the flame azure blue.	*O. F.* Easily soluble to a clear yellow glass, which is colorless on cooling, is rendered opaque by flaming at a certain grade of saturation, and still more highly saturated becomes opaque and enamel yellow on cooling. *R. F.* The glass containing oxide spreads itself out upon charcoal and becomes turbid; by continued blowing the oxide is reduced with effervescence to metallic lead, and the glass becomes clear.	*O. F.* As with Borax; more oxide is necessary, however, to produce a glass which is yellow while hot. *R. F.* The glass containing oxide becomes grayish and turbid on charcoal. With a large dose of oxide, the charcoal is coated with a yellow sublimate. Addition of tin makes the glass more turbid, but it is never entirely opaque.	*O. F.* On platinum wire easily soluble to a clear glass, which is yellow and opaque when cold. *R. F.* On charcoal immediately reduced to metallic lead, which coats the charcoal with yellow oxide when further heated.	0
Oxide of Manganese $\overset{\cdots}{Mn}$	*O. F.* Infusible. The higher oxides are converted by strong ignition into reddish-brown proto-sesquioxide, yielding oxygen. *R. F.* As in O. F.	*O. F.* Colors intensely. The hot glass is amethystine red, on cooling becomes violet red; with too large quantity the glass becomes opaque, and appears black, unless flattened, or drawn into threads. *R. F.* The colored glass becomes colorless (protoxide). If the glass is deeply colored, the reduction succeeds best on charcoal, especially with addition of tin.	*O. F.* The glass requires much oxide before it becomes colored. When hot it is brown violet, on cooling it becomes reddish violet. The glass cannot be rendered opaque by a large addition. When the glass contains too little manganese to color it, the amethyst tint is developed by bringing the hot bead in contact with a grain of nitre. *R. F.* The colored glass speedily becomes colorless.	*O. F.* On platinum wire slightly soluble to a clear green mass, which becomes opaque and bluish green on cooling (manganate of soda). *R. F.* Cannot be reduced on charcoal; the soda is absorbed and the manganese remains behind as oxide.	0

Metallic Oxides & Acids	Behavior alone, on Charcoal, etc.	With Borax on Platinum Wire.	With Salt of Phosphorus on Platinum Wire.	With Soda on Coal.	With Solution of Cobalt in O. F.
Oxide of Mercury. Hg	Is immediately reduced and volatilized.	O	O	Heated in closed tube (as well alone) it is reduced, and condenses in the cold parts of the tube as a grayish metallic sublimate, which may be united to globules by rubbing with a feather, or better by cutting off the part of the tube containing the sublimate, placing it in a test tube with a little dilute hydrochloric acid, and boiling the latter.	O
Molybdic Acid Mo	*O. F.* Fuses with a brown color and volatilizes, condensing on the surrounding charcoal in form of a yellow sublimate, which nearest the assay consists of small crystals. The sublimate is white (the crystals colorless) when cold. Interior to this deposit is seen best when cold a thin, non-volatile, dark copper-red coating of oxide of molybdenum. The white coating touched with the R. F. becomes of a deep azure-blue color. *R. F.* Mostly absorbed by the charcoal, and is reduced to metallic molybdenum, which may be obtained by washing as a gray powder.	*O. F.* Easily and largely soluble to a clear glass, which appears yellow while hot, but is colorless when cold. With a very large quantity the glass is dark yellow to dark red when hot, and opaline or opaque bluish gray when cold. *R. F.* The strongly saturated glass becomes brown or even opaque. In a good flame, oxide of molybdenum separates in the form of black flocks, which are very perceptible in the then yellowish glass, when the latter is flattened.	*O. F.* Easily soluble to a clear glass, which with a moderate quantity of the assay is yellow green when hot, and almost colorless when cold. On charcoal the glass becomes dark green in consequence of reduction. *R. F.* The glass from O. F. becomes dark dirty green; on cooling, however, fine green similar to chromium; on coal the same. With tin, the green color becomes somewhat darker.	*O. F.* On platinum wire fuses with effervescence to a clear glass, which becomes milk-white on cooling. *R. F.* On charcoal fusion with effervescence first occurs; the fused mass is then absorbed by the support, and most of the molybdic acid is reduced to metal, which may be separated as a steel-gray powder by washing.	O
Oxide of Nickel Ni	*O. F.* Unchanged. *R. F.* On charcoal is reduced to metal. The coherent metallic powder cannot be fused; strongly rubbed in the mortar it assumes a metallic lustre, and is highly magnetic.	*O. F.* Colors intensely. In small quantity it colors the hot glass violet, which becomes pale red brown on cooling; with larger quantities these colors are darker. *R. F.* The glass from O. F. becomes gray and turbid from separation of metallic nickel. By long blowing the metallic particles cohere and leave the glass colorless. On charcoal the reduction proceeds more rapidly, especially on addition of tin, which fuses with the nickel to a globule.	*O. F.* Dissolves to a reddish glass, which becomes yellow on cooling; with larger quantity the hot glass is brownish red, and becomes reddish yellow on cooling. *R. F.* The glass from O. F. is unaltered on platinum wire. On charcoal with tin, all the nickel is reduced after continued blowing, and the glass becomes colorless.	*O. F.* Insoluble. *R. F.* On charcoal easily reduced to small brilliant metallic particles, which are highly magnetic.	O

Oxide of Osmium. $\ddot{Os}$	*O. F.* Is converted into osmic acid, which volatilizes, yielding no sublimate, but giving vapors which have a very penetrating and pungent odor, and attack the eyes. *R. F.* Is reduced to a dark-brown infusible powder (metallic osmium), which may easily be oxidized again to osmic acid.	0	0	Is easily reduced to an infusible metallic powder, which may be obtained pure by washing.	0
Oxide of Palladium. $\dot{Pd}$	Is reduced on ignition, but the metallic particles cannot be fused together.	*O. F.* Is reduced, without dissolving in the flux. The metallic particles cannot be united to a globule even on charcoal. *R. F.* As in O. F.	As with Borax.	Insoluble. The soda is absorbed by the charcoal, leaving the Palladium behind as an infusible powder.	0
Oxides of Platinum $\ddot{Pt}$ Rhodium $\dddot{R}$ and Ruthenium $\dddot{Ru}$	As Palladium.	As Palladium.	As Palladium.	As Palladium.	0
Oxide of Silver $\dot{Ag}$	Easily reduced to metallic silver, which fuses to globules.	*O. F.* Is partly dissolved, and partly reduced to metal. The glass on cooling becomes opaline or milk-white, according to the degree of saturation. *R. F.* The glass from O. F. becomes at first gray from separation of metal, then clear and colorless, all the silver separating and fusing to a globule.	*O. F.* Both the oxide and the metal yield a yellowish glass. A highly saturated bead appears opaline on cooling; its color is yellow by transmitted daylight, and red by candle-light. *R. F.* As with Borax.	Is immediately reduced; fuses to metallic globules, while the soda is absorbed by the charcoal.	0
Tantalic Acid. $\dddot{Ta}$	Is unchanged, except in color becoming faintly yellow when hot, and white again on cooling.	*O. F.* Easily soluble to a clear glass, which at a certain saturation is yellowish when hot, becomes colorless on cooling, and may be made turbid by flaming. At a greater degree of saturation becomes enamel white on cooling. *R. F.* As in O. F.	*O. F.* Largely soluble to a clear glass, which if very highly saturated is yellowish when hot, and becomes colorless on cooling. *R. F.* The glass from O. F. is unchanged.	*O. F.* Mixed with a little more than an equal volume of soda, it fuses on charcoal with effervescence to a bead, but soon spreads out on the coal and with more soda it passes into the charcoal. *R. F.* As in O. F. No reduction to metal takes place.	After long ignition appears light gray; on cooling, however, becomes pale red, like magnesia. If it is not quite free from alkali it sinters, and becomes bluish black.

Metallic Oxides & Acids	Behavior alone, on Charcoal, etc.	With Borax on Platinum Wire.	With Salt of Phosphorus on Platinum Wire.	With Soda on Coal.	With Solution of Cobalt in O. F.
Tellurous Acid $\ddot{\text{Te}}$	*O. F.* Fuses, and is reduced with effervescence. The reduced metal volatilizes, however, immediately, and a white coating of tellurous acid deposits on the support. The edges of the sublimate have commonly a red or dark yellow color. *R. F.* As in O. F. The outer flame is tinged bluish green.	*O. F.* Soluble to a clear colorless glass, which becomes gray from separation of metallic tellurium when heated on charcoal. *R. F.* The clear glass from O. F. heated on coal becomes first gray and finally colorless, all the tellurium being reduced and volatilized and coating the coal with tellurous acid.	As with Borax.	On platinum wire soluble to a clear colorless glass, which becomes white on cooling. On charcoal it is reduced and volatilized with the formation of a coating of tellurous acid.	O
Binoxide of Tin $\ddot{\text{Sn}}$	*O. F.* The protoxide of tin takes fire and burns like tinder, and passes into binoxide. The binoxide glows strongly, and while hot appears yellowish; on cooling, however, becomes dirty yellowish white. *R. F.* By long blowing the oxide may be reduced to metallic tin, with formation of a slight sublimate of oxide, which coats the charcoal very near the assay.	*O. F.* Very slowly soluble in small quantity to a clear colorless glass, which remains clear after cooling, and is not made turbid by flaming. A bead saturated with oxide, allowed to become perfectly cold, and then heated to gentle ignition, becomes turbid, loses its round form, and manifests indistinct crystallization. *R. F.* A glass that is not saturated suffers no change. On charcoal, from a bead containing much oxide, a portion may be reduced.	*O. F.* Very slowly soluble in small quantity to a clear colorless glass, that remains clear on cooling. *R. F.* The glass from *O. F.* is not altered, either on platinum wire or on charcoal.	*O. F.* On platinum wire unites with soda with effervescence, to a swollen infusible mass. *R. F.* On charcoal is reduced to metallic tin.	Assumes a bluish-green color, which must be observed after the assay is perfectly cold.
Titanic Acid $\ddot{\text{Ti}}$	In both flames becomes yellow when heated; on cooling resumes its white color. Is not otherwise changed.	*O. F.* Easily soluble to a clear glass. The glass is yellow while hot, colorless when cold, and may be rendered turbid by flaming, if it contains a large quantity of the assay. When the glass contains a very large quantity, it becomes opaque white on cooling. *R. F.* Dissolved in small quantity the glass is yellow, with more it becomes dark yellow to brown. A saturated glass may be made enamel blue by flaming.	*O. F.* Easily soluble to a clear glass, which when containing much of the substance is yellow while hot, and colorless on cooling. *R. F.* The glass from O. F. is yellow while hot, but on cooling reddens, and assumes finally a beautiful violet color. If the assay contains iron, the glass on cooling becomes brown yellow to brown red. On charcoal with tin the glass becomes violet, if not too much iron be present.	*O. F.* On charcoal soluble with effervescence to a dark-yellow glass, which on cooling crystallizes with production of so much heat that the globule becomes again of itself white hot. When fully cold the glass is white or grayish. *R. F.* As in O. F. No reduction to metal can be accomplished.	Assumes a yellowish-green color, similar to oxide of zinc, but less fine.

Tungstic Acid. $\dddot{W}$	*O. F.* Unchanged, unless in very intense heat, when, as in *R. F.*, it becomes black, being reduced to tungstic oxide, but does not fuse.	*O. F.* Easily soluble to a clear colorless glass. Added in pretty large quantity it appears yellow while hot. With more of the substance the bead may be made enamel-like by flaming, and with a still larger quantity it becomes opaque white on cooling. *R. F.* The glass containing but little tungstic acid is unaltered in R. F., but as the quantity is increased, the bead acquires a yellow or dark-yellow color, and on cooling becomes yellowish-brown (oxide). The same reactions succeed on charcoal with less of the substance. Tin darkens the color of the glass when not too much tungsten is present.	*O. F.* Easily soluble to a clear colorless glass, which when highly saturated is yellow while hot. *R. F.* The glass from O. F. soon becomes dirty green while hot, but is blue when cold; by longer blowing it is bluish green when cold. On charcoal, especially with tin, it becomes dark green. If the assay contain iron, the hot glass on platinum wire is yellow, and on cooling becomes brown to blood red, like ferriferous titanic acid. This glass becomes blue when treated on charcoal with tin, except when the content of iron is too large.	*O.F.* On platinum wire dissolves to a clear dark-yellow glass, which on cooling becomes crystalline, and opaque white or yellowish. *R. F.* With a little soda on charcoal may be reduced to metallic tungsten; with more soda the assay is absorbed into the charcoal, and yellow or brown tungstate of soda having a metallic lustre is obtained.	0
Sesquioxide of Uranium $\dddot{\mathrm{U}}$	*O. F.* Infusible, but is converted into dark yellowish-green oxide. *R. F.* Becomes black passing into protoxide.	*O. F.* Behavior like that of oxide of iron, but the colors are less deep. When very strongly saturated, the glass may be made enamel yellow by flaming. *R. F.* Gives the same colors as oxide of iron. The green glass at a certain saturation may be rendered black by flaming, but becomes neither enamel-like nor crystalline. With tin on charcoal the glass becomes dark-green (protoxide).	*O. F.* Soluble to a clear yellow glass, that becomes yellowish-green on cooling. *R. F.* The glass from O. F. becomes dirty green; on cooling, however, is fine green (protosesquioxide). With tin on charcoal the green color becomes darker (protoxide).	*O. F.* Insoluble. With little soda shows signs of fusion; with more soda the mass becomes yellowish-brown; with still more of the reagent, the assay penetrates the charcoal. *R. F.* As in O. F. No reduction occurs.	0
Vanadic Acid. $\ddot{\dddot{V}}$	Fusible. The portions in contact with the charcoal are reduced, and pass into the support; the remainder assumes the color and lustre of graphite, being converted into a lower oxide of vanadium.	*O. F.* Soluble to a clear glass, which is colorless with a small quantity, with more appears yellow, and on cooling becomes greenish yellow. *R. F.* The glass from O. F. is brownish while hot, and on cooling becomes fine chrome green (oxide).	*O. F.* Soluble to a clear glass, which when the quantity is not too small, has a dark-yellow color while hot, and on cooling becomes pale yellow. *R. F.* As with Borax.	Fuses with soda, and is absorbed by the charcoal.	0

Metallic Oxides & Acids	Behavior alone, on Charcoal, and in the Platinum Tongs.	With Borax on Platinum Wire.	With Salt of Phosphorus on Platinum Wire.	With Soda on Coal.	With Solution of Cobalt in O. F.
Oxide of Zinc. $\dot{Zn}$	*O. F.* Becomes yellow on heating, but resumes its white color when cold. It is infusible, and glows vividly on strong ignition. *R. F.* Gradually reduces and disappears; the metal volatilizing and re-oxidizing is for the greater part deposited as oxide on the charcoal, forming a coating which is yellow while hot, and white when cold.	*O. F.* Easily and largely soluble to a clear glass, which while hot is yellowish, on cooling becomes colorless. When considerably saturated may be made opaque by flaming, and when more highly saturated becomes opaque on cooling. *R. F.* The saturated glass when first heated becomes turbid and grayish (separation of a part of the oxide), by longer blowing is rendered clear again. On charcoal the oxide is gradually reduced, the metal volatilizes and deposits as oxide on the surrounding parts of the support.	As with Borax.	*O. F.* Insoluble. *R. F.* On charcoal is reduced. The metal, however, volatilizes immediately, and if the heat be strong, burns with a bright greenish-white flame, while the charcoal is coated with oxide.	Assumes a fine yellowish-green color, best observed when cold.

Chapter 3.

ALPHABETICAL LIST OF ELEMENTS AND COMPOUNDS,

WITH THE MOST CHARACTERISTIC BLOWPIPE AND OTHER REACTIONS EMPLOYED IN THE FOLLOWING TABLES FOR THE DETERMINATION OF MINERAL SPECIES.

96. Alumina. The only characteristic blowpipe reaction is the blue color it assumes when ignited with cobalt solution. It may be thus detected in most minerals of which it is a large ingredient, provided they are infusible and do not contain too large a quantity of colored metallic oxides, or of magnesia. Very hard minerals, like corundum, must be finely pulverized (**79**). From acid solutions, when neutralized with ammonia, alumina is thrown down as a flocculent white precipitate.

97. Ammonia. The slight green tinge that salts of ammonia impart to the blowpipe flame (**76**) is too faint and uncharacteristic to serve for their detection.

Ammonia is recognized by its well-known odor. The body to be tested is mixed with dry soda, the mixture placed in a closed glass tube, and gently heated, when the ammonia is evolved in the gaseous state, and may easily be recognized by its characteristic odor, as well as by the alkaline reaction it gives with reddened litmus and with turmeric paper.

It must be borne in mind that organic substances containing nitrogen yield ammonia when ignited with soda.

98. Antimony. 1. Is almost invariably recognized by its characteristic sublimates. The body should be tested first in the open tube (**74**, 2, *c*); afterward, and generally in case of metallic compounds, on charcoal (**75**, 5, *d*).

2. Where antimony is combined with bismuth and lead, it is best detected by treating the substance with fused boric acid on charcoal, in such a manner that the flux is covered with the blue flame, and the metallic globule lies at its side partly out of the flame. The oxides of lead and bismuth are absorbed by the boric acid, and the charcoal becomes coated with a sublimate, which, when the blowing has not been too strong, consists of oxide of antimony, entirely free from the oxides of lead and bismuth.

3. A small quantity of antimony, combined with copper or with other metals which retain it strongly, may volatilize so slowly that no sublimate forms on the charcoal. Under these circumstances, the alloy is heated in O. F. with a bead of salt of phosphorus, until the latter has dissolved a part of the antimony. The glass is then removed to a clean place on the charcoal and treated with tin in R. F. If the glass becomes turbid and black, antimony is indicated. Bismuth, however, gives the same reaction.

4. In examining sulphide of lead for antimony, compare **118**, 2.

5. Compounds of antimony and arsenic, heated for a short time in the open tube, yield a mixture of crystals of arsenous acid and amorphous antimonous acid. A small amount of antimony mixed with sulphide of arsenic is detected by gently heating the dry mixture in a closed tube; the sulphide of arsenic volatilizes, while the dark-colored sulphide of antimony mostly remains where the assay was placed. The tube is then cut off between the two sulphides, and the sulphide of

antimony is transferred to an open tube and tested as usual. When the quantity is extremely small the tube is crushed, and the fragments with adhering sulphide are introduced into the open tube.

99. Arsenic. 1. The testing in open tube (**74**, 2, *a*), closed tube (**73**, 11, *f*), and on charcoal (**75**, 5, *c*), usually lead to its detection.

Arsenous and arsenic acids and their salts, as well as the sulphides of arsenic, are examined by pulverizing and placing them in a glass bulb, covering them with six times their weight of a dry mixture of equal parts of cyanide of potassium and carbonate of soda. The bulb should not be more than half filled with the mixture (Fig. 23). It is first gently heated; if moisture is given off, it is removed by inserting a piece or roll of bibulous paper. It is again gently warmed, and if necessary wiped out with paper, and the operation repeated until the mixture is *perfectly dry*. Finally, the bulb is heated strongly for some minutes in the spirit-lamp or blowpipe flame; a mirror of metallic arsenic deposits in the cool part of the tube. If the tube be cut off between the mirror and the sealed end by notching with a file and breaking, and the mirror be heated in the spirit-lamp, the arsenical odor will then be perceptible.

Fig. 23. Fig. 24.

2. Arsenous acid can also be detected by introducing the assay into a closed glass tube drawn out to a small diameter (Fig. 24), and inserting a splinter of charcoal above it. The charcoal is first heated and then the assay; the arsenous acid is reduced as it passes over the hot charcoal and is deposited as in the previous case as a metallic mirror.

3. The higher arsenides, when treated in the open tube, yield a sublimate of arsenous acid, but the lower arsenides of nickel, cobalt, and iron do not part with their arsenic at a high temperature, even in the presence of reducing agents; and for its detection in these cases Plattner recommends the following method: Mix the finely divided assay with five times its weight of nitrate of potassa, and heat as intensely as possible in a platinum spoon. The metals are thus oxidized, and the arsenic becomes arsenic acid. The spoon with the fusion is now boiled with water, until it is as far as possible dissolved. The liquid containing all the arsenic as arsenate of potash is decanted or filtered from the insoluble metallic oxides, and, 1. Evaporated with addition of a few drops of sulphuric acid (enough to expel all nitric acid) to dryness in a porcelain capsule; the residue is pulverized, mixed with cyanide of potassium and carbonate of soda, and heated as just described; or, 2. It is made slightly acid by acetic acid and boiled to expel any carbonic acid, and a crystal of pure nitrate of silver added, when a reddish-brown precipitate of arsenate of silver will be formed.

4. A small amount of arsenic in the presence of much sulphur is often difficult

to detect by its odor on charcoal. In such cases it is best to mix the assay with an excess of carbonate of soda, which will retain the sulphur, and the arsenical fumes can then be easily recognized.

100. Baryta. All the salts of baryta except silicates yield the characteristic yellowish-green coloration of the flame. When observed through copper-green glass the baryta flame appears bluish green.*

In Harmotome and Brewsterite, baryta is detected by dissolving the finely pulverized mineral in pure hydrochloric acid with aid of heat, filtering the solution and adding dilute sulphuric acid; a white precipitate of sulphate of baryta is formed, which may be collected upon a filter, washed, and then examined for the coloration of the flame.

Strontia may interfere with the baryta reaction. The presence of the sulphate of baryta with the sulphate of strontia can be detected by fusing the mixture with three or four parts of chloride of calcium in a platinum spoon, and boiling the fused mass with water. If a cloudiness is produced, by adding to the clear dilute solution a few drops of chromate of potassa the presence of baryta is indicated. Strontia is only precipitated from the concentrated solution (Chapman).

101. Bismuth. 1. Bismuth is detected by the characteristic lemon or orange yellow sublimates which it and its compounds give when treated alone or with soda on charcoal in R. F. (**75**, 5, *g*). The presence of other easily oxidizable metals may make this reaction uncertain; the wet way must then be resorted to, and for this purpose the pulverized compound is digested for some time with hot nitric acid, the liquid poured off from any undissolved matters, or if necessary filtered, then evaporated almost to dryness, and the concentrated liquid poured into a test-tube half filled with water. If bismuth be present, a white precipitate of basic nitrate is formed, which may be collected on a filter, washed with pure water, and examined on charcoal. If the precipitate be small, it should be gathered into the apex of the filter; the latter is then dried, the part containing the precipitate torn off, and tested on charcoal.

2. If a compound of bismuth be treated with a mixture of equal parts of iodide of potassium and sulphur, and fused B. B. on charcoal, a beautiful red sublimate of the iodide of bismuth will be deposited.†

3. In the presence of lead and antimony bismuth can be detected in the following manner: The mixture of the three oxides is added to an equal volume of sulphur and treated in a cavity upon charcoal with R. F.; the oxides are thus converted into sulphides. The assay is then placed upon a flat coal and treated with the O. F. and R. F. until the antimonial fumes have nearly ceased. The residue is placed in a mortar and pulverized, and mixed with an equal volume of a mixture of one part of iodide of potassium and five of sulphur; it is then heated in an open glass tube, and if bismuth be present, a distinct red sublimate of iodide of bismuth will be deposited a short distance above the yellow sublimate of lead. The sublimate of iodine which is liable to be deposited higher up the tube must not be confounded with the bismuth sublimate.‡

See also **98**, 3.

102. 1. **Boric** (boracic) **acid** is recognized by the intense yellowish-green color it or its compounds with fluorine communicate to the flame. This color is given to the outer flame by most borates, provided they do not contain an ingredient which of itself tinges the flame.

* The strips of colored glass alluded to in this chapter are such as are used for colored glass windows, a cobalt-blue glass, a green glass colored either with oxide of copper or iron, and a red glass colored with red oxide of copper. Strips 3 × 6 inches are a convenient size.

† Von Kobell. Journal für Praktische Chemie (2), III. (1871), 469.

‡ Cornwall. Am. Chemist, March, 1872.

2. Borate of soda alone tinges the flame pure yellow, but if it be moistened with sulphuric acid or mixed with bisulphate of potash, boric acid is set free, and the green color is instantly produced.

3. Silicates in which the above methods fail to indicate the boric acid, are reduced to a fine powder, the assay mixed with its own bulk of pulverized fluor-spar, and three times its bulk of bisulphate of potash; the whole is moistened to a paste, a portion of which is taken on a platinum loop, and at first gently heated to dry it, then more intensely in the edge of the blue flame. At the instant of fusion the green coloration appears, but is usually only momentary, so that the observer must direct his attention closely to the assay during the ignition.

4. As in the above trials copper and phosphoric acid may be mistaken for boric acid; it is sometimes best to use Rose's test with turmeric paper. To the solution of any borate hydrochloric acid is added until the liquid gives a distinct acid reaction (till blue litmus is reddened by it); a strip of turmeric paper is half immersed in the solution for some time, and the paper dried at a gentle heat (not over 212° F.). The smallest trace of boric acid gives the immersed portion of the paper a reddish-orange color. Silicates are fused with carbonate of soda in a platinum spoon, the mass is boiled with water until it is as far as possible dissolved, the solution is then supersaturated with hydrochloric acid, and tested as above.

The orange or reddish-orange color thus produced must not be confounded with that communicated to turmeric paper: 1st. By alkaline solutions. 2d. By acid solutions of zirconia (**159**). 3d. By moderately strong hydrochloric acid.

5. If alcohol is poured over a borate with the addition of a sufficient quantity of concentrated sulphuric acid to liberate the boric acid, and the alcohol kindled, the flame, particularly on the edges, appears of a very distinct yellowish-green color, especially upon stirring, and upon heating the alcoholic mixture.

103. Bromine. 1. When bromides are added to a bead of salt of phosphorus which has previously been saturated with oxide of copper, and the blowing continued, the bead becomes surrounded with a beautiful blue flame inclining to green on the edges, and this color continues so long as any bromine remains. As these reactions may be confounded with those given by chlorine, Berzelius recommends fusing the substance under examination with dry bisulphate of potash in a glass bulb. If a metallic bromide is present, bromine and sulphurous acid are set free, and the glass bulb becomes filled with a yellow vapor of bromine, which, although mixed with sulphurous acid, may be distinctly recognized by its characteristic odor. As a confirmatory test, if moistened starch or starch paper be exposed to these vapors yellow bromide of starch will be formed.

2. If a soluble bromide be placed upon a piece of clean silver along with a fragment of sulphate of copper or sulphate of iron, the silver becomes almost immediately coated with a black stain.

104. Cadmium. This metal can only be detected as oxide, as it is volatilized at a comparatively low temperature. The substance for examination in a pulverized state is heated in the R. F. on charcoal, whereby metallic cadmium is volatilized, and immediately on coming in contact with the atmosphere is converted into oxide which gives the characteristic coating on coal (**75**, 5, *j*). Should the substance contain not more than one per cent. of cadmium, as for instance in many zinc ores, it is best to mix the powder with soda and heat carefully in the R. F., when the coal near the assay becomes coated with a sublimate of oxide of cadmium before any sublimate of zinc is formed, cadmium being much more volatile than zinc.

Caesia. This rare alkali imparts a beautiful violet to the blowpipe flame, and when mixed with potassa and rubidia can only be distinguished by the employment of the spectroscope.

105. Carbon and Carbonic Acid. 1. *Carbon* in the form of diamond or of graphite, disappears when heated for some time B. B.; the former leaves no residue, the latter generally more or less of a red ash.

Fused with nitrate of potassa, carbon detonates, forming carbonate of potassa. *Carbonates* effervesce when treated with dilute hydrochloric acid; a few require to be pulverized, and in some cases heat is necessary before the effervescence * takes place.

2. Some carbonates lose their carbonic acid by simply heating in the closed tube; in these cases it may be detected by inserting a strip of moistened litmus paper in the tube, when the blue color will be changed to red, but on drying the original blue color will be restored.

3. Organic substances, except oxalates and formates, decompose in the closed tube, yielding a burnt odor, and usually oily products. *Anthracite* gives off moisture, but no empyreumatic oil. (See *Coal*, in the tables, chapter iv.)

106. Cerium. When in combination with other earths, cerium cannot with certainty be detected B.B. In most silicates where it, with lanthanum and didymium, occurs in considerable quantity, it may be readily detected after separation of silica and precipitation by ammonia, by treating the washed ammonia precipitate with oxalic acid, which dissolves out iron with alumina, leaving the cerium earths as insoluble oxalates; this residue when washed and ignited gives a cinnamon-brown powder, which is the characteristic color of sesquioxyd of cerium.

107. Chlorine. 1. Chlorides, like bromides, may be detected by adding a small portion of them to a bead of salt of phosphorus which has previously been saturated with oxide of copper; the bead becomes instantly surrounded with a beautiful and intense purplish-blue flame, without any of the tinge of the green which is observed in examining a bromide.

2. The soluble chlorides give the same reaction as described under bromine with sulphate of iron and copper on a silver plate.

3. Nitrate of silver produces, even in highly dilute solutions of hydrochloric acid or metallic chlorides, white curdy precipitates of chloride of silver, which upon exposure to the light change first to violet and then to black.

108. Chromium. 1. Chromium is detected by the emerald-green color which its compounds impart to the borax and salt of phosphorus beads. Chromium must not be confounded with vanadium, which gives the same reactions in R. F., but differs by yielding a yellow bead with salt of phosphorus in O. F., which flux never acquires other than a green color from chromium.

2. Minerals containing but little oxide of chromium associated with other metals which color the fluxes, are best treated by fusing on platinum wire or in a platinum spoon with a mixture of equal parts of soda and nitre. The mass is heated for some time in O. F., whereby chromic acid is formed. The fusion is dissolved in water, and the solution poured off from the residue; to this solution a drop or two of acetic acid, and afterward a crystal of acetate of lead, are added, when a lemon-yellow precipitate of chromate of lead is formed. This may be collected on a filter, washed, and tested with borax and salt of phosphorus.

3. A mineral which contains a small amount of chromium, and is not decomposed by nitre, is fused with one and a half times its volume of soda and three-fourths its volume of borax to a clear bead; this is pulverized, dissolved in hydrochloric acid, and evaporated to dryness, dissolved in water; the residue of silica filtered off; the protochloride of iron changed to sesquichloride by boiling with a few drops of

* Care must be taken not to confound minerals which contain a carbonate as an impurity with pure carbonates. If the substance under examination be a pure carbonate it can be completely dissolved in nitric acid, and effervescence will continue so long as any portion remains undissolved.

nitric acid, and the chromium, alumina, iron, etc., precipitated with ammonia. The precipitate is collected, and tested as above.

109. Cobalt. 1. In most cases can be recognized by the characteristic blue bead it gives in both flames with borax. This color is variously modified by other metals.

2. Should iron be present, the glass will appear green while hot, and blue when cold. If the substance contains copper or nickel, the cobalt-blue color can hardly be perceived, and the bead must be treated on charcoal, with tin in R. F., until it becomes transparent, and effervescence has ceased. The copper and nickel will be reduced to the metallic state, and the glass will have a perfectly pure blue color.

3. Compounds of cobalt with arsenic, and arsenides of other metals, when fused upon charcoal until arsenic fumes cease to be given off, then treated with borax in R. F., give, when freed from iron, a pure smalt-blue color; if iron be present it will be oxidized before the cobalt, and the bead will have a bottle-green color. The metallic globule is then treated with a fresh quantity of borax, and this operation is repeated until the bead gives a pure cobalt reaction.

In testing metallic nickel for cobalt it is necessary to combine the nickel with arsenic, which may be done by mixing the finely divided nickel with metallic arsenic, placing it in a depression in the charcoal, and fusing in R. F. The fused globule is then tested with borax, as just described in case of an arsenide. The volatile metals in combination are recognized by their sublimates on charcoal.

110. Columbium. If a mineral which contains columbic acid be powdered and fused with bisulphate of potassa, the fused mass powdered and dissolved in water, the columbic acid, and tantalic acid if present, will be insoluble; while the bases and titanic acid, if present, will be dissolved, and can be thus separated. The residue is treated with sulphide of ammonium, to free it from tungstic acid and oxide of tin, if these be present, and after filtration and thorough washing it is treated with dilute hydrochloric acid to remove traces of iron. The residue is treated with hydrochloric and sulphuric acids, with the addition of metallic zinc. If only a tantalate be present, no coloration ensues, or but a slight one. If a columbate is similarly treated, the separated columbic acid rapidly assumes a blue color, which gradually fades, and finally becomes brown.

111. Copper. 1. The green color which most copper compounds give to the blowpipe flame, and the reactions of its oxides with the fluxes, render its presence easily detected. The production of a red bead with salt of phosphorus in R. F. is rendered more certain by the treatment of the bead on charcoal with a small amount of tin.

2. Copper may also be detected by saturating a salt of phosphorus bead with the substance containing it, and adding chloride of sodium, when the bead will color the flame beautifully blue, owing to the formation of chloride of copper.

Many minerals give this reaction by simply moistening in hydrochloric acid and exposing in the platinum forceps to the flame; silicates should be first pulverized, moistened with hydrochloric acid, and evaporated to dryness in a porcelain capsule; then made into a paste with water, and heated on platinum wire.

3. In case the copper is combined with nickel, cobalt, iron, and arsenic, the greater part of the cobalt and iron may be separated by treating with borax on charcoal. The remaining metallic globule is fused with a small quantity of pure lead, and then boric acid is added; this last dissolves the lead and the rest of the cobalt and iron, while most of the arsenic is volatilized. The cupriferous nickel globule, which still may contain a little arsenic, is treated with salt of phosphorus in O. F.; the bead obtained will be dark green while hot and clear green when cold. This last green is caused by a mixture of the yellow of oxide of nickel and the blue of oxide of copper.

4. According to Guericke,* a very delicate test for copper is to mix the substance under examination intimately with chloride of silver, and fuse on iron wire; in this manner the smallest quantity of copper may be detected by the blue color imparted to the flame.

112. Didymium. See p. 36.

113. Erbium. See Yttria.

114. Fluorine. 1. Hydrofluoric acid imparts to Brazil-wood paper a straw-yellow color. Silicates containing even a small quantity of fluorine, when heated in the closed tube, give off hydrofluo-silicic acid; this is decomposed into silicic acid, which is deposited near the assay and hydrofluoric acid, which passes off, and the latter may be detected by inserting a strip of moistened Brazil-wood paper at the open end of the tube.

2. When fluorides are heated in a glass tube with bisulphate of potash, hydrofluoric acid is given off. This etches the tube immediately above the assay, and gives the reactions with Brazil-wood paper just mentioned.

3. The best method for the detection of fluorine in all cases is to mix the assay with previously fused salt of phosphorus, and heat in the open tube in such a manner that the flame passes into the end of the tube.

In this way hydrofluoric acid is formed; it may be recognized by its peculiar pungent odor and its corrosive action on the inner surface of the glass tube, rendering it opaque and lustreless at the points where moisture has condensed. For a confirmatory test the reaction with Brazil-wood paper may be employed.

As the heat required in this experiment is so great that the glass tube often becomes soft and unmanageable, it has been recommended to use a piece of platinum foil rolled together and inserted into the end of the glass tube, as in Fig. 25.

FIG. 25.

The substance to be tested is placed with the flux upon the projecting part of the foil, and the flame directed as before.

115. Glucina gives no reactions which admit of being determined B. B. with certainty (see page 33). It is not of frequent occurrence, being only found in combination with silica and alumina.

116. Gold may usually be recognized by its physical characters. It is separated from the easily volatile metals by simple heating on charcoal in O. F. If associated with copper or silver, it must be fused with a large excess of metallic lead and subjected to cupellation (see **142**). The copper becomes absorbed and passes off with the lead, while the silver remains alloyed with the gold. If the globule is quite yellow it is proof that but little silver is present; it is then to be tested with salt of phosphorus to prove the presence of silver, which after fusion will impart an opaline appearance to the cool bead. If it be more of a silver color, the amount of gold will be small, and in order to prove its presence the globule must be digested with hot nitric acid in a test-tube or porcelain capsule; the silver is thus dissolved, and the gold remains in a fine powder or as a spongy mass. If this powder be washed and fused with borax on charcoal it will yield a globule of metallic gold. In combination with infusible metals, such as platinum, iridium, palladium, and rhodium, the alloy obtained B. B. is less fusible. For their separation the wet reagents must be employed.

117. Indium. Colors the flame beautiful violet. (See table, p. 36.)

* Pharm. Centralblatt, 1855; 195.

4

118. Iodine. 1. Iodides, added to a bead of salt of phosphorus which has previously been saturated with oxide of copper, tinge the outer flame an intense emerald-green color. (Compare bromine and chlorine, **103, 107**).

2. Iodides, like bromides, are decomposed by fusion with bisulphate of potash; free iodine is liberated, and may be distinguished by its characteristic violet color and its disagreeable odor. If an iodide be added to a mixture of carbonate of lime and caustic lime, then intimately mixed with a small quantity of chloride of mercury and heated in a closed tube, iodide of mercury will be sublimed; this is easily recognized by its first yellow and then red-yellow color. It is best to draw the tube out to a narrow neck a short distance from the assay, and for the success of the experiment it is necessary that all the substances employed be perfectly free from moisture. This test is said to be even more delicate than the starch test, which is used in the wet way.

119. 1. **Iron** is distinguished by the characteristic color its oxides impart to borax and salt of phosphorus, as well as by its compounds yielding a magnetic powder with soda on charcoal. (See treatment with soda, **94.**)

2. In the presence of easily reducible metals, such as lead, tin, bismuth, antimony, or zinc, iron may be detected by treating the assay with borax and charcoal in R. F., until everything except the iron has been reduced, when the borax glass will have a bottle-green color. If the substance contains much tin, or if the bottle-green glass is fused with tin-foil in R. F., the iron becomes entirely reduced to protoxide, and the bead has a pure vitriol-green color.

3. In case the substance contains cobalt, nickel, and copper, the two latter will be reduced by the tin, while the cobalt will color the bead blue. To detect the iron it is only necessary to heat a portion of the blue bead, with addition of fresh borax, on platinum wire in O. F.; the bead will be green while hot and blue on cooling.

4. To distinguish the presence of protoxide of iron in minerals, Chapman recommends the following method:—"A small quantity of black oxide of copper is dissolved in a bead of borax and platinum wire so as to form a glass which exhibits, on cooling, a decided blue color. To this the test-substance in the form of powder is added and the whole is exposed for a few seconds, or until the test-matter begins to dissolve, to the point of the blue flame. If the substance contain protoxide of iron it will be converted into sesquioxide at the expense of some of the oxygen of the copper compound, and opaque red streaks and spots of red oxide of copper will appear in the glass, as the latter cools. If only sesquioxide of iron is present, the glass on cooling will remain transparent, and will exhibit a bluish-green color.

120. Iridium. (See p. 36.)

121. Lanthanum. (See page 37.)

122. Lead. 1. Compounds of lead give globules of metallic lead when heated with soda on charcoal B. B. It is recognized by its physical properties, as well as the characteristic coating it gives upon the coal (**75**, 5, *h*). The coating is modified by the presence of various other volatile metals. In the presence of zinc, the characteristic color of the lead coating is recognized on cooling, since the oxide of zinc becomes white. In the presence of bismuth, the oxide of which often obscures the lead, it is detected by heating the sublimate in the R. F., when the flame will be tinged with the azure-blue color which is characteristic of lead in the absence of selenium. The presence of selenium in such cases is evident from its odor.

2. Combinations of sulphide of lead with other metallic sulphides are tested for lead by treating in the R. F. either alone, or with borax to separate iron; and the lead is recognized by its coating. In such combinations the oxide of lead is sur-

rounded by a white coat of sulphate of lead, which renders the presence of small amounts of antimony uncertain. The safest way under such circumstances is to mix the powder of the substance with soda, which retains the sulphur; this mixture, when treated in the R. F., gives the pure lead coat, and if antimony is present it is detected by its white sublimate beyond the sublimate of oxide of lead.

3. In solutions of the salts of lead, sulphuric acid gives a white precipitate of the sulphate of lead, which is nearly insoluble in water and dilute acids. It is best to add a considerable excess of dilute sulphuric acid, evaporate the solution on a water-bath, and add water to the residue, when delicate tests are to be made in the wet way.

123. Lime. Lime imparts a characteristic yellowish-red color to the flame. When observed through copper-green glass the lime flame appears siskin-green; with cobalt-blue glass it is pale greenish-gray, and is almost entirely obscured. Many lime salts react alkaline to test papers after ignition. It is distinguished from baryta and strontia in the wet way, by the fact that sulphuric acid gives no precipitate in dilute hydrochloric solutions. Sulphuric acid gives a precipitate in the concentrated solution which distinguishes it from magnesia.

124. Lithia. The red color which pure lithia salts give to the flame is more or less modified or entirely obscured when mixed with other substances. Seen through green glass the lithia flame appears orange colored, with red glass is colored deep red, but with cobalt glass of sufficient thickness the flame is invisible. Silicates containing only a little lithia scarcely color the flame red; but if the pulverized mineral be mixed with one part of fluor-spar and one and one-half of bisulphate of potash, the whole made into a paste with a little water and exposed on platinum wire to the point of the blue flame, the outer flame will be colored distinctly red. Chapman has proved that the lithia flame, unlike strontia, is not obscured by the presence of baryta. He suggests fusing lithia minerals with chloride of barium; the phosphate, triphylite, when thus treated gives a beautiful crimson color.

125. Magnesia is recognized by its reaction with nitrate of cobalt (**80**, 2).

In combination with other earths, the wet way must be employed for its detection. Sulphuric acid does not produce a precipitate in its concentrated solution.

126. Manganese. The reactions of manganese with the fluxes are so peculiar and delicate that it may be recognized even when it exists in the smallest quantity, and in the presence of almost every other substance. The soda test in O. F. on platinum wire is the most delicate. If a reaction be not obtained with soda alone, a small fragment of nitre should be added to the assay, and the mass again heated. When testing substances which do not dissolve readily in soda it is well to add a little borax to the bead, and this also makes the test much more delicate (Chapman).

127. Mercury and amalgams give a sublimate of metallic mercury when heated in a closed tube. Compounds of mercury heated in a closed tube with soda yield metallic mercury, which condenses on the tube above the assay. When a gray sublimate is obtained, without distinct metallic globules, the part of the tube coated with it is cut off and boiled in a test tube with a little dilute hydrochloric acid; by this treatment the mercury collects into shining globules. In case mercury exists in so small a quantity that the sublimed metal is not perceptible, it may be detected by inserting a piece of gold-leaf held on the end of an iron wire into the tube, just above the assay; on heating, the mercury is volatilized and unites with the gold, giving it a white color.

128. Molybdenum. The sublimate which molybdic acid gives on charcoal (**75**, 5, *m*) and its reactions with borax and salt of phosphorus serve to distinguish it in most instances.

When it is present in small quantity, particularly when associated with copper and tin, as in some furnace products, it is necessary to have recourse to the wet way. The solution of a mineral containing molybdenum in hydrochloric acid, or the hydrochloric solution of the fusion with nitre and soda of an insoluble substance, when boiled with tinfoil is colored dark blue by the separated molybdate of molybdenum (compare Tungstic Acid, **153**). Molybdic acid can also be recognized by heating the finely pulverized substance in a porcelain dish with concentrated sulphuric acid, and then adding alcohol. The fluid when cold acquires a fine azure-blue color, especially upon the sides of the dish.

129. Nickel may be recognized by the color its oxide imparts to borax and salt of phosphorus, together with its easy reduction to the metallic state in R. F.

Arsenical compounds of nickel, cobalt, iron, and copper are treated with glass of borax (see Cobalt, **109**). When the borax is no longer colored blue from cobalt, but acquires a brown color, which is violet when hot, the metallic globule is separated from the borax, and treated with salt of phosphorus in O. F. If copper as well as nickel be present in the assay, the glass thus obtained will be green both while hot and cold; treated with tin on charcoal it will become red and opaque on cooling. A small quantity of nickel occurring in cobalt compounds cannot always be detected by the foregoing method. In such cases Plattner recommends saturating one, or if necessary several borax beads with the substance on platinum wire. The beads are then fused on charcoal in R. F. with from 50 to 80 milligrammes (0.75 to 1 grain) of fine gold; the oxide of nickel, together with a small portion of the cobalt, is reduced to the metallic state and unites with the gold. The metallic globule is then freed from the flux and treated on charcoal in O. F. with salt of phosphorus. The bead itself will be colored blue, as cobalt is easier oxidized than nickel, or perhaps if a little nickel be also oxidized it will be dark violet while hot and dirty green on cooling; in both cases the globule is separated from the flux and treated with a new portion of salt of phosphorus. If the original bead with borax was not too saturated, this second bead with salt of phosphorus will be of a pure nickel color. Should copper as well as nickel be present in the gold globule, the salt of phosphorus bead will be green while hot, and retain its green color on cooling; treated with tin in R. F. as before described, the bead will become red.

130. Nitrates. When nitrates are fused in a glass tube with bisulphate of potash, dark reddish-yellow nitrous fumes are evolved. The color is best observed by looking lengthwise through the tube held against a white ground.

All nitrates detonate when heated on charcoal; those of the alkalies and alkaline earths detonate violently, and are converted into carbonates.

131. Osmium. See p. 39.

132. Oxygen. Oxygen is evolved from some compounds by simple ignition. The substance under examination is placed in a closed tube with a bit of charcoal above it, the charcoal is first brought to ignition, and then the substance is heated, when, on liberation of oxygen, the ignited splinter of coal will glow with increased brilliancy.

133. Palladium. See p. 39.

134. Phosphates. 1. The green color (**76**, 4, *f*) which phosphates give to the flame serves in many cases for their detection. This coloration is heightened by the addition of a drop of concentrated sulphuric acid, but is rendered unsatisfactory in the presence of other substances giving a green flame.

2. If a pulverized phosphate is fused in a closed tube with a bit of metallic magnesium or sodium, the phosphoric acid will be reduced, and if the fused mass on cooling is moistened with water, phosphoretted hydrogen will be given off, recognizable by its characteristic disagreeable odor.

3. When a few drops of neutral or acid solution containing phosphoric acid are poured into a test tube filled to the depth of an inch with a solution of molybdate of ammonia with nitric acid, there is formed in the cold or after a short time a pulverulent yellow precipitate of phospho-molybdate of ammonia. The reaction is hastened by very gently warming, care being taken not to heat above blood heat. A yellow coloration of the fluid must not be regarded as proof of the presence of phosphoric acid, since silicic acid produces a strong coloration, but it does not give a precipitate. Arsenic acid gives the same reaction.

135. Platinum. See p. 39.

136. Potassa may often be detected by the violet color it communicates to the flame. In presence of other bodies that tinge the flame, especially soda and lithia, this reaction is masked. The potash flame when observed through cobalt-blue glass * appears purple, and may thus be easily detected even in the presence of lithia and soda. With green glass it is colored azure blue, and with red glass deep red.

In presence of soda, potassa may be recognized by fusing borax with addition of a small quantity of boric acid on platinum wire, then adding enough oxide of nickel † to make the glass brown when cold; the substance is dissolved in the bead thus obtained; if potassa be present it will be of a beautiful blue color on cooling. With soda alone a brown bead will be obtained.

For the detection of potash in compound substances it is often necessary to have recourse to the wet way. Bichloride of platinum produces in the neutral and acid solutions of the salts of potassa a yellow crystalline heavy precipitate of the platinchloride of potassium. Very dilute solutions are not precipitated by this reagent, hence they should be evaporated before testing; or better, evaporate to dryness after addition of the reagent and then dissolve the residue in alcohol, in which the platinchloride is insoluble.

137. Rhodium. See p. 39.

138. Rubidia. This rare alkali gives B. B. a violet flame, and when mixed with cæsia and potassa can only be distinguished by spectroscopic examination.

139. Ruthenium. See p. 39.

140. Selenium. The reaction for selenium on charcoal (75, 5, *a*) is so characteristic that the slightest traces of it can thus be detected.

Selenites and selenates are reduced to selenides on charcoal in R. F. with the characteristic odor of selenium.

141. Silica. 1. When silica is heated with soda, a clear glass is obtained if the soda be not in excess. This reaction distinguishes silica from the earths; silica may, however, contain alumina and still fuse with soda to a clear glass.

In most silicates the silica may be detected by help of salt of phosphorus (see p. 26). The experiment should be performed with a small fragment, from which the bases will be dissolved, while the skeleton of silica will maintain the same form as the original assay and float about in the bead. Only when a fragment is unaffected the powder is used, but when thus tested the result is less satisfactory.

2. When a finely powdered silicate is fused with an excess of carbonate of soda, the resulting mass dissolved in dilute hydrochloric acid, and evaporated to dryness, the silica is rendered insoluble; and on moistening the residue with strong hydrochloric acid, and dissolving in hot water, the silica will remain behind, and can be separated from the bases if desired.

3. Most of the hydrous silicates, and many which are anhydrous, but which con-

* The blue glass should be of sufficient thickness to entirely obscure a lithia flame; there is no objection to using two or three thicknesses of glass if necessary.

† Oxalate or carbonate of nickel (emerald nickel) may be employed. It must be free from cobalt (not give a blue glass with borax).

tain an excess of base, are decomposed by strong hydrochloric acid; the bases then unite with the hydrochloric acid, while the silica separates either as a gelatinous hydrate, or as a non-gelatinous powder.

142. Silver. Silver is recognized by its physical characters as well as by the brown coating it gives when heated on charcoal in O. F.

When associated with volatile and easily oxidable metals, it may be separated by heating on charcoal in O. F. If the silver be associated with a large quantity of lead or bismuth, it is best to subject it to cupellation. The following process serves for the detection of silver in most argentiferous minerals: The substance is mixed with its own bulk of borax glass and an excess of pure lead (except in cases where lead or its oxide already exists, as in litharge, minium, cerusite, etc.), the mixture is placed in a cylindrical cavity in the charcoal, and fused in R. F. The flame should at first be directed entirely upon the borax glass; after the earthy substances have been dissolved and the metallic particles united into one globule, this globule is subjected for a short time to the O. F., thereby separating such volatile and easily oxidizable substances as may be present. The remaining globule containing a large excess of lead and all the silver, together with the larger portion of the nickel and copper, is then separated from the flux and subjected to cupellation.

For this purpose finely pulverized bone-ash is mixed with a small quantity of soda, and made into a stiff paste with water. This paste is placed in a circular cavity in charcoal, half an inch in diameter and one quarter inch deep, and the surface of it made concave and smooth by pressing it with an agate pestle or other suitable convex surface. This *cupel* is now carefully exposed to a gentle heat till perfectly dry.

The lead globule, freed from all adhering flux, is placed upon the cupel, and treated in O. F. Should much nickel or copper be present, an infusible coating is formed which prevents the desired oxidation; this may be counteracted by the further addition of a small quantity of pure lead. The blast is kept up until all traces of lead have become oxidized; this is indicated by the cessation of the rainbow-colors of the oxide of lead which play over the surface of the button. When the quantity of litharge that is formed in the process of cupellation is large, the globule of silver, still containing lead, may be removed to a fresh cupel and there refined. The instant when the last traces of lead disappear can then be more readily perceived; this point is indicated by the sudden brightening of the globule. The remaining metal, when free from gold, has a silver-white color. It may be tested for gold as described under that metal.

143. Soda. Soda is readily distinguished even in compound substances by the intense yellow color it imparts to the outer blowpipe flame. The soda flame is invisible when observed through cobalt-blue glass and red glass; with green glass it is orange colored. Soda is not precipitated from solution by bichloride of platinum.

144. Strontia. The crimson color imparted to the outer flame serves in most instances for the detection of strontia and its salts. In the presence of lime this reaction is less characteristic, and a small amount of soda obscures it altogether. The color is intensified by moistening with hydrochloric acid. When the strontia flame is observed through cobalt glass it appears of a pale purple to rose-red color, through green glass it is orange, and with red glass it has a deep red color.

After ignition its salts give an alkaline reaction on test paper, and it is distinguished from lime, which also gives a red flame, in that its dilute solutions are precipitated after some time by sulphuric acid.

145. Sulphur. Sulphuric Acid. Free sulphur fuses and sublimes; on charcoal burns with a blue flame, forming sulphurous acid. The higher sulphides give off sulphur when heated in a closed tube; the neutral sulphides and sub-sulphides give off sulphurous acid when heated in an open tube. The sulphurous acid may be detected by its odor or by its reddening and bleaching action on a strip of moistened blue litmus paper. Small quantities of *sulphides* and the sulphur in sulphates may be detected by fusing with two or three parts of soda on charcoal in R. F. In using this test it should be kept in mind that illuminating gas often contains sulphur; where this is the case a candle or lamp flame should be used (see **93**). The sulphur is hereby converted into sulphide of sodium, which, placed on a clean silver surface and moistened with water, causes a brownish or black stain on the silver. In the presence of selenium this reaction cannot be used.

The soda used for the detection of sulphur should always be tested by itself for sulphur, which is a common impurity, and if it give the reaction, it should be treated as described on page 30.

The solution of a sulphate in hydrochloric acid gives a precipitate of the sulphate of baryta, on addition of chloride of barium.

The following is a delicate test for sulphides in the wet way. An amount of the assay powder that can be taken upon the point of the knife is mixed with a like volume of iron powder (*ferrum alcoholisatum* of the apothecary), the mixture placed in a cylinder of glass two and a half inches long and about an inch in diameter, and hydrochloric acid is poured upon it (one volume concentrated acid and one volume water). A strip of filter paper, which has been moistened with acetate of lead and again dried, is placed beneath the cork that fits the tube, which is then closed, the paper projecting from the tube a short distance. In about one minute the color of the paper is observed, and the glass shaken if necessary. If sulphur be present the paper will be blackened by the formation of the sulphide of lead.

146. Tantalum. See *Columbium*, **110**.

147. Tellurium. 1. Tellurides heated in the open glass tube, give a white or grayish sublimate, fusible B. B. into colorless or nearly colorless drops. On charcoal they give a white coating, and color the R. F. green.

2. When a substance containing tellurium is triturated with soda and charcoal dust and fused in a closed tube, then allowed to cool, and a little hot water dropped into the tube, the water assumes a beautiful purple color from the dissolved telluride of sodium.

3. Tellurium compounds when gently heated in a matrass with much concentrated sulphuric acid, impart to it a purple color, which disappears on the addition of water, while a blackish-gray precipitate is formed.

148. Terbia. See *Yttria.*

149. Thallium. Colors the flame intensely green. (See p. 18.)

150. Thoria, gives no reactions which permit its determination with certainty.

151. Tin. In the metallic state, tin is easily distinguished by its physical characters and its reactions in O. and R. F. on charcoal (**75**, 5, *l*). Sulphides containing tin must be roasted, and the roasted mass treated with a mixture of soda and borax in R. F.; the product is metallic tin, which can be further tested on charcoal. Oxides containing tin are best treated with soda or cyanide of potassium on charcoal; if much iron is present borax should be added. When tin and some of its compounds are treated with nitric acid, oxide of tin separates as a white precipitate, which can be separated and tested as above.

152. Titanium. 1. The violet color given by titanic acid with salt of phosphorus in R. F. serves in most cases for its detection. In the presence of iron the violet color first appears when the bead is treated with tin in R. F. on charcoal.

2. If a substance containing titanium is fused with carbonate of soda, and the

resulting mass dissolved in hydrochloric acid, and then heated with tin or zinc, the titanic acid is reduced to sesquioxide of titanium, coloring the liquid violet, and finally the violet hydrated sesquioxide separates.

When the fusion of a substance with six or eight parts of bisulphate of potassa is dissolved in a very little water, the clear solution decanted from the insoluble residue and a few drops of nitric acid and five or six volumes of water added, titanic acid if present will separate on boiling as a white precipitate.

153. Tungsten. Tungstic acid gives a blue color with salt of phosphorus in R. F.; with much iron the bead becomes dark red, but treated on charcoal in R. F., with tin it gives a blue color.

When a tungstate is fused with carbonate of soda and treated with hydrochloric acid and zinc as above (see Titanic Acid), a fine blue color is obtained.

Tungstic acid is insoluble in acids; hence if a tungstate like scheelite is decomposed by acids, the tungstic acid separates as a yellow powder.

154. Uranium. The reaction with phosphorus salt serves in most instances for its detection.

155. Vanadium. In the absence of other colored metallic oxides, vanadium may be detected by borax and salt of phosphorus; it may be distinguished from chromium by the color which it gives to salt of phosphorus in the O. F.

156. Water. Water may be detected by heating the assay in a matrass or closed tube, care being taken to free the tube from all moisture before inserting the assay. If a substance contains hygroscopic water, or if it be a soluble hydrous salt, the water is almost immediately given off and condenses in the upper part of the tube in distinct drops. Insoluble substances containing water require to be heated somewhat higher. See further under examination in the closed tube, **73.**

157. Yttria. (Erbia and Terbia.) For the detection of these rare earths recourse must be had to analysis in the wet way.

158. Zinc. The reactions of this metal on charcoal, together with the green color which the oxide gives with cobalt solution, allow of its being detected when it exists in considerable quantity—and even in extremely small quantities, if it be not associated with other metals whose reactions are such as mask those given by the zinc. If a small quantity of zinc be associated with large quantities of lead, bismuth, or antimony, it is with difficulty detected. If a mixture of different metallic oxides be fused with a mixture of two parts soda and one to one and a half parts borax, zinc will be volatilized, and in the moment of coming in contact with the air, is oxidized and gives a coating on the coal. If the substance contain a large amount of lead, this is also oxidized and coats the coal, but on moistening with cobalt solution and heating in O. F., the lead coating is reduced by the charcoal, and the zinc coating becomes green on cooling. If the quantity of zinc is extremely small, it is best to moisten the coal with cobalt solution before heating the assay. In the presence of tin and antimony it is almost impossible to detect small quantities of zinc B. B.

159. Zirconia. This earth as usually obtained gives out an exceedingly brilliant light when heated B. B. A dilute hydrochloric acid solution of zirconia, or of minerals containing zirconia, imparts an orange-yellow color to turmeric paper when it is moistened with the solution.

Chapter 4.

TABLES FOR THE DETERMINATION OF MINERAL SPECIES BY MEANS OF SIMPLE CHEMICAL EXPERIMENTS IN THE WET AND DRY WAY.

TRANSLATED FROM THE TENTH EDITION OF FRANZ VON KOBELL'S "TAFELN ZUR BESTIMMUNG DER MINERALIEN." *

Introduction to the Tables.

THE object of the following Tables is to facilitate the determination of mineral species. By means of a few simple experiments before the blowpipe and in the wet way, the mineral is quickly limited to a group of a few species; among the members of this group the mineral is distinguished by other trials, and when from these various experiments the mineral species is finally decided upon, the conclusion is confirmed or corrected by reference to the physical characteristics given in the columns upon the right, and further confirmatory evidence may, if necessary, be obtained by reference to a treatise on mineralogy. An acquaintance with the use of the blowpipe, such as is gained by the study of the preceding pages, and with the manner of performing the simplest operations of solution and precipitation, is all that is necessary in making the requisite trials.

It is hoped that this little work will be of service to chemists, miners, and others, who though not making mineralogy a special study, yet have occasion to decide upon the names of minerals.

The Tables are so constructed that it is necessary to follow them through from the beginning, comparing the characteristics of each group and division with those of the specimen in hand. A trial of fusibility, a fusion with soda, heating the pulverized substance with acid, and a few precipitations, usually lead to the desired object, when the order of the Tables is strictly followed, and the experiments are made with proper care.

The method which has been adopted in the arrangement of these Tables will be comprehended at a glance. The minerals are arranged in two great groups, *metallic* and *non-metallic*, under which heads are various classes, divisions, subdivisions and sections, the more general ones being placed upon the left, until finally we reach more specific characters, followed by the names of the species, in the middle of the page, while the remaining columns are devoted to the confirmatory evidence of color, streak, cleavage, fracture, hardness, specific gravity, fusibility, and crystalline form. In a few cases these physical characteristics are the distinguishing features of the species, but generally the mineral will be recognized by its blowpipe and chemical reactions, and the student is strongly advised to make these primary, since the chemical composition of the minerals is what is desired to

* This chapter includes, essentially, all the material contained in the tenth edition of Professor Von Kobell's Tables, but an entirely different mode of arrangement is here given, with much additional matter. The tabular form in which the minerals are arranged was suggested by Professor W. T. Roepper, of Bethlehem, Pa., who kindly permitted me to consult a manuscript translation made by him from one of the earlier editions of Von Kobell, in which a similar arrangement is employed. The Tables here presented, while following the general idea of Professor Roepper as to tabulation, have been worked up independently, and contain new features which it is hoped will be of service to the student.

be known, and naming minerals from their color or other physical properties often leads to serious errors, especially with inexperienced observers, and these alone need the caution, since the experienced person well knows the impossibility of always recognizing minerals from the evidence of sight. It is thought by this arrangement of the Tables that more definite ideas of the groupings of minerals will be gained by the student, and that he will more readily comprehend which are the general and which the specific reactions of the smaller divisions. Almost all the established mineral species are included, but for the sake of convenience, their relative importance, or frequency of occurrence, or facility of determination, has been indicated arbitrarily by the size of the type in which the name of the species is printed.

An attempt has been made, as far as possible, so to arrange the groups and divisions, that such errors of observation as are likely to be made, shall not prevent one from arriving at a correct conclusion. Since some minerals occur in one variety with metallic, and in others with non-metallic lustre, and since the fusibility of a mineral often varies, or may be underrated or overrated by the experimenter, and since the constituent elements of some mineral species are not constant, such are found under both or all of the divisions to which they might be assigned.

The following general directions may serve to assist in the use of the Tables :—

Lustre. Under the head of metallic lustre only those minerals are included which are perfectly opaque. To determine this a fine splinter or thin edge should be held between the eye and the light, or fine fragments should be placed upon a white plate, when, if the slightest translucency is observed, it is included under "non-metallic." It is evident that opacity alone does not make metallic lustre, but that the mineral must also possess the lustre which suggests it to be metallic, and must not grind to an earthy powder as do some non-metallic minerals which otherwise might be called metallic. In this, as in many other determinations, good judgment in the operator will be constantly required.

Fusibility. For determining the fusibility of minerals, the following scale is employed:

Scale of Fusibility.

1. Stibnite (antimony glance).......	Fusible in the flame of a candle, in large fragments.
2. Natrolite.......................	Fusible in the flame of a candle, in small fragments.
3. Almandine Garnet (alumina-iron-garnet.........................	Infusible in the candle flame, but easily fusible B.B., even in somewhat large pieces.
4. Actinolite.......................	Fusible B.B., in rather fine splinters.
5. Orthoclase.......................	Fusible B.B., in finer splinters.
6. Bronzite.......................	B.B. becomes rounded only on the finest points and thinnest edges.

Splinters of these minerals are kept ready for use, and in determinations their fusibility is compared with that of like splinters of the assay. The evidence of fusion is the rounding of sharp edges. It should be remembered that some minerals swell up before the blowpipe but do not fuse, and other phenomena take place which without careful observation might be mistaken for fusion. Only the O. F. should be used, since some substances, which are infusible in the O. F. are easily fusible in the R. F., on account of the reduction of some of their oxides to a lower fusible state.

Hardness.—In testing hardness, the scale proposed by Mohs, and almost universally adopted, is here employed.

Scale of Hardness.

1. Talc.	3. Calcite.	5. Apatite.	7. Quartz.	9. Corundum.
2. Gypsum.	4. Fluorite.	6. Feldspar.	8. Topaz.	10. Diamond.

The scale represents the crystallized varieties of the minerals mentioned. The hardness of a mineral is found by finding what numbers will scratch, and what are scratched by the mineral to be tested. Thus, if a mineral will not scratch apatite, but will scratch fluorite, it is of a hardness between 4 and 5; or if the mineral is scratched by apatite and not by fluorite, it is of a like hardness. Sharp corners must be used in scratching, and particular care should be taken in this as in all other cases, that impurities do not come in to modify the result; thus a grain of sand in some of the impure varieties of galena, if it happen to come upon the corner which is used, would make the mineral appear quite hard, and without proper caution many such errors will be made.

Color.—Great care must be taken in forming any conclusions from the color of minerals. In minerals of metallic lustre, the color is generally constant, and often very characteristic, in some of the non-metallic species the same is true; but experience will teach how greatly the colors of non-metallic minerals vary, and varieties are constantly found differing in color from all that were previously known. Hence, especially in non-metallic minerals, the color which is given should only be regarded as an aid or suggestion in the determination.

Streak.—The streak of a mineral is tested by scratching it with a knife or file, or better, if not too hard, it may be drawn across a piece of unglazed porcelain, and the color of the mark which it leaves behind observed.

Specific Gravity.—Considerable skill can be gained by noticing the comparative weight of minerals held in the hand, and though no accurate determination can thus be made, the column giving specific gravity can be used in the field, as designating whether minerals are heavy or light. For accurate determinations, the apparatus, described in the foot-note below,* gives very quick results and in

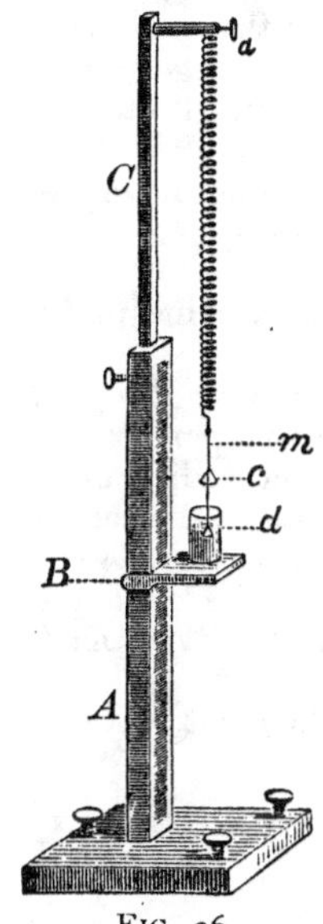

FIG. 26.

* The specific gravity of minerals is easily taken by means of an instrument devised by Prof. Jolly. See Fig. 26. This consists of a graduated strip of looking-glass set in a vertical rod (A) properly supported. A steel or brass wire in the form of a spiral is suspended from *a*, and bears upon its lower end the two pans, *c* and *d*. The spring can be placed at any desired height by elevating the smaller rod (C), as shown in the figure. The pan *d* is suspended in water in the glass, which rests upon the sliding support B. At *m* is a signal which serves as a mark for the stretching of the spiral. The reading is taken by bringing the mark and the image of the mark in the mirror scale to a level. The scale *d* being in the water, the position of the mark *m* is taken $=$ x. A fragment of the mineral, weighing from one to five grammes, is now placed in *c*, the support B moved downward till the instrument again comes to rest, the scale *d* being still in the water, and the position of the mark *m* again taken $=$ y. Then y—x $=$ weight in air. The fragment is now transferred to *d* and the position of *m* again noted $=$z. Then y—z $=$ loss of weight in water. Divide weight in air by loss of weight in water and we have the specific gravity. As the weight is not absolute, the manner in which the scale is graduated is of little importance if it be regular, and hence the apparatus is easily constructed. This spring balance is known in Germany as the *Federwage*, and is furnished by Mechaniker Berberich in Munich, for nine florins.

most cases with advantage, can be made to replace the ordinary chemical balance.

Testing for Water.—In order to detect water, a fragment of the assay is placed in the bottom of the closed glass-tube or matrass and heated strongly. Water, if present, condenses in drops on the cold part of the tube. A trace of moisture will be found by heating almost any mineral in this way; a little practice enables one to decide whether or not the mineral is actually hydrous. Decrepitating minerals may be enveloped in a piece of copper foil, and thus placed in the tube and heated.

Decomposition by Acids.—In testing whether a mineral be decomposable by hydrochloric acid, it must first be pulverized as finely as possible in a mortar, and then gently boiled with tolerably concentrated acid for ten minutes or more, unless the solution is sooner completed. The digestion is carried on in a small glass flask, a large test tube, or a casserole. In cases where the fact of the decomposition is not evident to the eye, by the formation of a jelly, disappearance of the powder or other effects, the acid must be separated by decantation or filtration from the residue, ammonia or carbonate of soda added in excess, and then a few drops of phosphate of soda. When both these reagents give no precipitate, or cause but a few flocks to appear, the mineral may be pronounced nearly or quite undecomposable. The production of a decided precipitate is evidence that it has been decomposed.

Gelatinization. When silicates are decomposed by hydrochloric acid, the silica sometimes separates in the pulverulent condition, when the mineral is said to be soluble in acid with the separation of silica without forming a jelly; sometimes the silica separates from the bases in its soluble condition, and then when the solution is boiled nearly to dryness, it will have the consistency and appearance of jelly. Such minerals are said to gelatinize with hydrochloric acid.

Many silicates not appreciably attacked by acids gelatinize after they have been previously ignited, as for example garnet, vesuvian, etc. Several splinters or little pieces of the assay are fused or strongly ignited, then pulverized and boiled in a test tube with rather dilute acid; on evaporating the solution gelatinous lumps will be seen in the remainder; or after standing some time (twelve hours) an evident fixed jelly will be found. After adding water, and stirring with a glass rod, the solution may be tested for bases if desired. Other silicates, which gelatinize with acids or are easily decomposed, will not gelatinize or are but little affected by hydrochloric acid after ignition.

Pyro-electricity. Some minerals when heated become electric, and have the power of attracting light substances. Light fibres of wool or cotton, or a deer's hair held between the fingers, may be used to test this property.

The methods for all the other commonly recurring reactions will be found under their proper heads in the preceding chapters.

In seeking the name of a mineral it is necessary always to begin with the first group and proceed in regular order to those following; for it often happens that a mineral belonging to one group has also the characters of the succeeding ones, while the minerals of the latter divisions may not show the reactions of the earlier groups. The same rule is of the greatest importance in the distinctions between subdivisions and species. Upon page 63 is given a summary of the classification—this is merely introduced to save turning the pages, and to give a more definite view of the larger subdivisions.

The method of using the table is best learned by some examples, first, without the use of the general classification.

Aluminite.

It is not metallic, turning over the pages which are headed minerals with metallic lustre, we come on page 72, to the minerals without metallic lustre, to which group our mineral belongs. Looking now in the column on the left we see **A.—B.B. easily volatile or combustible,** which our mineral is not; looking along this column there follows **B.—B.B. fusible from 1–5, etc.** Our mineral is infusible; turning over to page 89 we come to **C—infusible or fusible above 5.** Looking in the next column we see that the members of DIVISION 1 are characterized by giving a blue color when moistened with cobalt solution and ignited; the mineral upon trial is found to belong here. This group is seen to be divided into two sections; in the minerals of the one water is present, in the other it is absent. By heating the specimen in a closed glass tube it yields much water; it must, therefore, be sought in section *a*. The minerals of the first sub-section give, on fusion with soda, a sulphuret which blackens silver, and since the assay gives this reaction it belongs here. Of the minerals which belong to this sub-section, the first is insoluble in hydrochloric acid and the others are not; on trial the powder of the mineral easily dissolves and it is, therefore, aluminite. Looking now in the columns on the right the determination may be substantiated by a comparison with the physical properties there tabulated. The chemical constituents and generally the formulas of the minerals are given, and should always be noted, so as to fix in the mind the composition of the various species. The formula for aluminite is $\dddot{\bar{A}}l\,\dddot{S} + 9\dot{\bar{H}}$. In our examination we have detected all three of its ingredients: the alumina by the blue color with nitrate of cobalt; the sulphuric acid by the fusion with soda, and the water in the closed tube; but when in the determination of a species all the constituents are not determined, those who possess the requisite knowledge can, if desirable, detect the remaining substances by the ordinary methods of mineral analysis.

An example showing the use of the general classification will now be given.

Bornite (variegated copper).

Looking at the classification on page 63 the metallic lustre of the mineral places it under I. It is not a malleable metal. It is fusible and therefore belongs under **A.** B.B. it gives no odor of arsenic or selenium; gives no white coating which colors the R.F. or other reaction for tellurium, gives no fumes of antimony, but gives the reactions for sulphur, mentioned in division 5, and hence belongs to this division. We are now referred to page 67 on which this division is seen divided off in the second column. Looking now in the third column, it is not malleable, it gives no reaction for manganese, its streak is not red, it gives no globule of lead with charcoal (turn to next page), but moistened with hydrochloric acid it gives to the flame the blue color of chloride of copper, and it forms a sky-blue or green solution with nitric acid, which becomes deep violet-blue on addition of an excess of ammonia; of the minerals which give this color the first give a bismuth reaction, on trial the assay does not, but it fuses to a brittle steel-gray magnetic globule, it hence belongs among these minerals. It has not the brass-yellow color of the first three minerals but has the variegated shades of the next, and is therefore bornite.

The ordinary varieties of mineral coal are included in the tables (see page 96).

It hardly need be again remarked, that only pure and homogeneous material will give satisfactory reactions for the determination of minerals. If it is believed that the material being tested is not pure, regard must be paid to the impurity, and the reaction judged of accordingly; as, for example, many specimens of *wollastonite* (tabular spar) effervesce in acids, and after ignition impart a brownish red color to moistened turmeric paper. These qualities do not belong to the pure mineral, but come from an admixture of calcite. Too great haste should not be exercised in deciding upon the name of a mineral, since oftentimes the difficulties in the way of an accurate determination can only be overcome by long and careful labor.

On beginning the study of determinative mineralogy, it is best to examine known species, until confidence is gained in one's ability and accuracy. The following minerals are given by Von Kobell to his students; when these have all been determined, the student will be prepared to determine any mineral which can be distinguished by this method:—

Aluminite,
Alunite,
Anhydrite,
Antimony-Glance,
Apophyllite,
Argentite,
Arsenopyrite,
Atacamite,
Barite,
Borax,
Bornite,
Bournonite,
Calamine,
Calcite,
Cassiterite,
Celestite,
Cerussite,
Chalcopyrite,
Chalcocite,
Cinnabar,
Cobaltite,
Cryolite,
Cuprite,
Datolite,
Diallogite,
Dolomite,
Fluorite,
Galenite,
Glaucodote,
Gypsum,
Hematite,
Lapis-lazuli,
Lievrite,
Lepidolite,
Limonite,
Magnesite,
Magnetite,
Malachite,
Manganite,
Molybdenite,
Natrolite,
Niccolite,
Orpiment,
Pectolite,
Psilomelane,
Pyrite,
Pyrolusite,
Pyromorphite,
Pyrrhotite,
Realgar,
Scheelite,
Smaltite,
Smithsonite,
Siderite,
Sphalerite,
Strontianite,
Talc,
Witherite,
Wolfram,
Wollastonite,
Wulfenite.

(Page 63)

ANALYTICAL TABLE

SHOWING

GENERAL CLASSIFICATION

OF

MINERALS.

ABBREVIATIONS USED IN THE TEXT OF THE TABLES.

Amorph ..Amorphous.
B. B......Before the Blowpipe.
Div ......Division.
Fib.......Fibrous
F. Fus....Fusibility.
Gran......Granular.
H.........Hardness.
HCl ......Hydrochloric acid.
Infus......Infusible.
KI........ Iodide of potassium.
Mass......Massive.
n.........Near.
O. F......Oxidizing flame.
p. c.......Per cent.
R. F......Reducing flame.
S.... .. .Sulphur.
Sp. Gr....Specific gravity.
Stalac.....Stalactitic.
I..........Isometric.
II. ....Tetragonal.
III........Hexagonal.
IV........Orthorhombic.
V... .....Monoclinic.
VI........Triclinic.

GENERAL CLASSIFICATION.

I.—MINERALS WITH METALLIC LUSTRE.

(Of those minerals whose lustre may be doubtful, only such are here included as are perfectly opaque on the thinnest edges.)

The native malleable metals and mercury are easily distinguished from others (see p. 64).

The remaining minerals form the following groups.

A.—Fusible from 1-5, or easily volatile.

PAGE

1. B. B. on charcoal give the strong garlic odor of arsenic 64
2. B. B. on charcoal or heated in an open glass-tube give the strong horse-radish odor of selenium. 65
3. B. B. on charcoal give a white coating which colors the R. F. green and greenish-blue. In a small test-tube, *gently* heated with much concentrated sulphuric acid, impart to the acid a hyacinth-red color, which upon addition of water disappears, and a black gray precipitate of tellurium is thrown down 66
4. B. B. on charcoal, or in the open glass-tube, give dense antimony fumes 66
5. B. B. with soda give a sulphur reaction, or placed in the open glass-tube give sulphurous acid which reddens a strip of moistened blue litmus paper placed in the end; but do not give the reactions of the preceding divisions 67
6. Not belonging to the foregoing divisions 69

B.—Infusible or fusible above 5, and non-volatile.

1. B. B. in O. F. give to the borax bead the amethystine red of manganese 70
2. B. B. on charcoal after long heating in R. F. become magnetic 70
3. Not included in the foregoing divisions 71

II.—MINERALS WITHOUT METALLIC LUSTRE.

A.—B. B. easily volatile or combustible 72

B.—B. B. fusible from 1-5, and non-volatile, or only partially volatile.

Part I.—*B. B. with soda on charcoal give a metallic globule, or fused alone in R. F. become magnetic.*

1. B. B. with soda on charcoal give a globule of silver 72
2. B. B. with soda on charcoal give a globule of lead 73
3. Moistened with hydrochloric acid give a beautiful blue color to the blowpipe flame, and give with nitric acid a solution which, on addition of an excess of ammonia, becomes violet-blue (copper) 74
   - *a*) B. B. on charcoal evolve a strong arsenical odor 74
   - *b*) B. B. on charcoal evolve no arsenical odor 75
4. B. B. impart a beautiful sapphire-blue color to a borax bead (cobalt) 76
5. B. B. fused in the forceps or on charcoal in R. F. give a black or gray magnetic mass, but do not give the reactions of the preceding divisions 76
   - *a*) During fusion evolve a strong arsenical odor 76
   - *b*) Soluble in hydrochloric acid without leaving a perceptible residue, and without gelatinizing 76
   - *c*) Soluble in hydrochloric acid, forming a jelly, or with the separation of silica ....
   - *d*) Only slightly acted upon by hydrochloric acid ....
6. Not belonging to the foregoing divisions ....

Part II.—*B. B. with soda on charcoal give* NO *metallic globule, or fused alone in R. F. do not become magnetic.*

1. B. B. after fusion and continued heating on charcoal or in the forceps have an alkaline reaction, and change the color of moistened turmeric paper to red-brown* ....
   - *a*) Easily and completely soluble in water ....
   - *b*) Insoluble or difficultly soluble in water ....
2. Soluble in hydrochloric acid, some also in water, without a perceptible residue; the solution is not gelatinized by evaporation ....
3. Soluble in hydrochloric acid, forming a stiff jelly upon evaporation ....
   - *a*) B. B. in the closed tube give water ....
   - *b*) B. B. in the closed tube give no water or but traces ....
4. Soluble in hydrochloric acid, leaving a residue of silica without forming a perfect jelly ....
   - *a*) B. B. in the closed tube give water ....
   - *b*) B. B. in the closed tube give no water or but traces ....
5. Slightly attacked by hydrochloric acid, and B. B. give a deep amethystine color (manganese) to the borax bead ....
6. Not belonging to the foregoing divisions ....

C.—Infusible or fusible above 5.

1. First ignited B. B., then moistened with cobalt solution, and again ignited assume a beautiful blue color (alumina) ....
   - *a*) B. B. in the closed tube give water ....
   - *b*) B. B. in the closed tube give no water or but traces ....
2. Moistened with cobalt solution and ignited B. B. assume a green color (zinc) ....
3. After ignition B. B. have an alkaline reaction and change the color of moistened turmeric paper to red-brown ....
4. Nearly or perfectly soluble in hydrochloric or nitric acid without gelatinizing or leaving a considerable residue of silica ....
5. Gelatinize with hydrochloric acid, or are decomposed with the separation of silica ....
   - *a*) B. B. in the closed tube give water ....
   - *b*) B. B. in the closed tube give no water or but traces ....
6. Not belonging to the foregoing divisions ....
   - *a*) Hardness under 7 ....
   - *b*) Hardness 7 or above 7 ....

* Kenngott has shown that many silicates and other compounds before and after fusion have an alkaline reaction w[hen] they are placed upon turmeric paper in the form of *powder* and moistened with water; but they do not show this reaction w[hen] in fragments.

(Page 64)

MINERALS WITH METALLIC LUSTRE.

NATIVE METALS.

A. Fusible from 1—5, or easily volatile.

DIVISION 1 (in part).

Native Metals.

Easily recognized by their malleability.

General characters.	Specific characters.	Species.	Composition.	Color.*	Streak.	Cleavage or Fracture.	Hardness.	Sp. Gr.	Fusibility.	Crystallization.
Alone, B. B., on charcoal, a bismuth coating.	With sulphur and iodide of potassium gives a red coating (bismuth), and leaves a globule of gold.	Maldonite.	Au^2Bi.	Pinkish-white.		Cubical.	1.5—2	8.2—9.7	Easily.	I. (?)
Soluble in nitric acid; the dilute solution gives a precipitate with hydrochloric acid.	The precipitate becomes violet-gray on exposure to light.	SILVER.	Ag.	White.	White.		2.5	10.5	2.—2.5	I.
Have more or less the color of gold.	Only soluble in aqua-regia without a residue.	GOLD.	Au.	Yellow.	Yellow.		2.5	19.3	2.5—3	I.
	Decomposed by aqua-regia with separation of AgCl.	Electrum.	Au + Ag.	Pale yellow to white.			2.5	12.5—15.5	2.5—3	I.
Of a copper-red color.	Moistened with hydrochloric acid colors O. F. sky-blue.	Copper.	Cu	Copper-red.	Copper-red.		3.	8.9	3.	I.
Give a lead coating on coal.	Easily fusible; soluble in nitric acid; the solution gives a heavy precipitate with sulphuric acid.	Lead.	Pb	Lead-gray.	Lead-gray.		1.5	11.4	1.	I.
Infusible. Insoluble in hydrochloric acid; soluble in aqua-regia.	Insoluble in nitric acid.	PLATINUM.	Pt(Ir,Rh,Pd,Fe).	Steel-gray.	Light-gray.		4.—4.5	16—19	Infus.	I.
	Soluble in nitric acid.	Palladium.	Pd.	Steel-gray.	Steel-gray.		4.5—5.	11.5	Infus.	I.
Attracted by the magnet.	Infusible. Soluble in hydrochloric acid.	IRON.	Fe(Ni, etc.).	Iron-gray.		Octahedral.	4.5	7.5		I.
☞ Compare the malleable minerals, *Hessite*, Div. 3, p. 66; and *Argentite*, Div. 5, p. 67.										
Fluid.		MERCURY.	Hg.	White.				13.5		I.

A. Fusible from 1—5, or easily volatile.

DIVISION 1.

B. B. on charcoal give the garlic odor of arsenic.

General characters.	Specific characters.	Species.	Composition.	Color.*	Streak.	Cleavage or Fracture.	Hardness.	Sp. Gr.	Fusibility.	Crystallization.
B. B. volatile without fusion.	Gives in the closed tube a metallic sublimate.	ARSENIC.	As.	Tin-white.	Tin-white.	Granular.	3.5	6.	Vol.	III.
With soda on coal give a globule of lead. Soluble in nitric acid, with separation of sulphate of lead.	Very fusible; gradually volatilizes; gives no copper reaction.	Dufrenoysite.	$2PbS + AsS^3$.	Lead-gray.	Brown.	Basal.	3.	5.5	Easily.	IV.
	Decrepitates strongly.	Sartorite.	$PbS + AsS^3$.	Lead-gray.	Brown.	Basal.	3.	5.3	Easily.	IV.
		Jordanite.	Pb, As, S.	Lead-gray.	Black.	Prismatic.			Easily.	IV.
Fused B. B., and then moistened with hydrochloric acid color the flame blue (chloride of copper). A nitric solution is rendered blue by ammonia.	In the nitric solution, hydrochloric acid gives a heavy precipitate of AgCl.	POLYBASITE.	$9(Ag, Ȼu)S + (Sb, As)S^3$.	Iron-black.	Iron-black.	Uneven.	2.3	6.25	Easily.	IV.
	With S and KI, gives on coal a red sublimate (bismuth).	Rionite.	Cu, Bi, As, Sb, S.	Iron-black.	Iron-black.					
	Easily cleavable; the others are not.	ENARGITE.	$3ȻuS + AsS^5$.	Iron-black.	Grayish-black.	Prismatic.	3.	4.4		IV.
	In the nitric solution, ammonia gives a reddish-brown precipitate (iron).	Tennantite.	$4(Ȼu, Fe)S + AsS^3$.	Iron-black.	Gray.		3.5—4	4.5	1.5	I.
	Same reaction for iron.	Epigenite.	Cu, Fe, As, S.	Steel-gray.	Black.	Granular.	3.5		Easily.	IV.
	Gives no precipitate with ammonia.	Binnite.	$3ȻuS + AsS^3$.	Steel-gray.	Cherry-red.	Brittle.	4.5	4.4	Easily.	I.
	Gives no sulphur reaction.	DOMEYKITE.	Cu^6As.	Tin-white.	Blackish.	Brittle.	3.5	7.5	Easily.	Massive.
☞ Compare *Tetrahedrite*, p. 67.	Same.	Algodonite.	$Cu^{12}As$.	Steel-gray.	Bronze.	Tough.	4.	7.6	Easily.	Massive.
	Same.	WHITNEYITE.	$Cu^{18}As$.	Bronze.	Bronze.	Hackly.	3.5	8.3	Easily.	Massive.
Give to the borax bead a sapphire-blue color.	The concentrated solution is rendered turbid by addition of water (bismuth).	Alloclasite.	$2CoS^2 + CoAs + 4BiAs$.	Steel-gray.	Black.	Rhombic.	4.5	6.6	Easily.	IV.
	Gives metallic arsenic in closed tube.	SMALTITE (cobalt-speiss).	(Co,Fe,Ni)As.	Tin-white.	Gray-black.	Octahedral.	5.5	6.4—7.2	Easily.	I.
	As above.	Skutterudite.	Co^2As^3.	Gray-white.		Cubic.	6.	6.7	Easily.	I.

* The color of metallic minerals must be observed on a fresh fracture, as many of them change and become tarnished and dull on exposure to air and light.

(Page 65)

MINERALS WITH METALLIC LUSTRE.

A. Fusible from 1—5, or easily volatile.

DIVISION 1 (continued).

DIVISION 2.

		General Characters.	Specific Characters.	Species.	Composition.	Color.	Streak.	Cleavage or Fracture.	Hardness.	Sp. Gr.	Fusibility.	Crystallization.
A. Fusible from 1—5, or easily volatile.	DIVISION 1. *B. B. on charcoal give the garlic odor of arsenic.*	Give to the borax bead a sapphire-blue color.	Gives metallic arsenic in the closed tube. The dilute solution gives precipitate with chloride of barium of BaO SO_3.	Glaucodot.	$(Co,Fe)S^2 + (Co,Fe,)As$.	Gray-white.	Black.	Rhombic.	5.	6.	Easily.	IV.
			As above.	Glaucopyrite	Fe,Co,Cu,Sb,As,S.	Gray-white.	Gray-black.		4.5	7.18	Easily.	IV.
			Gives no arsenic in closed tube. Dilute solution gives a precipitate with chloride of barium of BaO SO_3.	COBALTITE (cobalt-glance).	$CoS^2 + CoAs$.	Red-white.	Gray-black.	Cubic.	5.5	6.	Easily.	I.
			☞ Compare *Bismuth*, frequently associated with cobalt ores, Div. 6, page 69.									
		When dissolved in aqua-regia form an apple-green solution; with ammonia in excess the solution becomes sapphire-blue.	Of a copper-red color.	NICCOLITE (copper-nickel).	Ni^2As.	Copper-red.	Brown-black.	Uneven.	5.—5.5	7.4	Easily.	III.
			Gives in the closed tube a sublimate of metallic arsenic.	Rammelsbergite.	$NiAs_2$.	Tin-white.	Gray-black.		5.5	7.	Easily.	IV.
			In the dilute nitric solution chloride of barium gives a heavy precipitate.	Gersdorffite (nickel-glance).	$NiS_2 + NiAs_2$.	Gray-white.	Gray-black.		5.5	5.6—6.9	Easily.	I.
			Gives a red-brown precipitate with excess of ammonia (iron).	Chathamite (var. Smaltite)	Ni,Co,Fe,As.	Gray-white.	Gray-black.	Granular.				I.
			Gives antimony fumes, and a sulphur reaction with soda on coal.	Corynite.	$NiS^2 + Ni(As,Sb)$.	Gray-white.	Black.	Uneven.	4.5—5.	6.	Easily.	I.
			As above.	Wolfachite.	$NiS^2 + Ni(As,Sb)$.	Silver-white.	Black.		5.5	6.37	Easily.	IV.
			☞ Compare *Ullmannite*, Div. 4, p. 67.									
		In the closed tube give metallic arsenic, and then fuse, and after long heating become magnetic.	Gives sulphur reaction in open tube, soluble in nitric acid, with separation of sulphur; in solution ammonia gives a reddish-brown precipitate (iron).	**Arsenopyrite** (Mispickel).	$FeS_2 + FeAs$.	Silver-white.	Gray-black.	Uneven.	5.5	6.2	2.	IV.
			Gives only a slight sulphur reaction. In closed tube, after arsenic is driven off, fuses with great difficulty.	LÖLINGITE (Leucopyrite).	Fe,As.	Silver-white.	Gray-black.		5.5	6.8—8.7	Diff.	IV.
		☞ Comp. *Bismuth*, Div. 6, p. 69; *Antimony*, Div. 4, p. 66; *Pyrargyrite*, Div. 1, p. 72; *Geocronite*, Div. 4, p. 66; all sometimes containing arsenic.										
	DIVISION 2. *B. B. on charcoal, or heated in an open glass-tube, give the strong horse-radish odor of selenium.*	With soda in a matrass give metallic mercury.	B. B. volatile without fusion; with soda upon charcoal yields metallic lead.	Lehrbachite.	Pb,Hg,Se.	Lead-gray.	Black.	Granular.	2.	7.8	Vol.	Massive.
			B. B. fuses and then volatilizes. Gives no lead.	Tiemannite	Hg,Se.	Lead-gray.	Black.	Granular.	2.5	7.2	Easily.	Massive.
			Gives a reaction for sulphur, in open tube or on charcoal.	Guadalcazarite.	$6HgSe + ZnS$.	Iron-black.	Black.	Compact.	2.	7.15	Easily.	Massive.
		Mostly volatile without fusion, coats the coal at first with a metallic gray, then white, then greenish-yellow sublimate.	B. B. with soda yields with difficulty lead globules, the nitric solution gives a precipitate with sulphuric acid.	Clausthalite.	PbSe.	Lead-gray.	Gray-black.	Cubic.	2.5	7.—8.		I.
		Give with borax a pure silver globule.	B. B. fuses easily: in O. F., quietly; in R. F., with intumescence.	Naumannite.	Ag,Pb,Se.	Iron-black.	Black.	Cubic.	2.5	8.	Easily.	I.
		B. B. on charcoal fuse to globules, which after moistening with HCl color the flame azure-blue.	Solution in nitric acid gives a heavy precipitate with hydrochloric acid (AgCl).	Eucairite.	(Ꞓu,Ag,)Se.	Lead-gray.	Shining.	Granular.			Easily.	Massive.
			Nitric solution gives a precipitate with sulphuric acid (PbO,SO_3).	Zorgite.	(Pb,Ꞓu,)Se.	Lead-gray.	Dark-gray.	Granular.	2.5	7.5	Easily.	Massive.
			The nitric solution is not precipitated by either sulphuric or hydrochloric acid.	Berzelianite.	Ꞓu,Se.	Silver-white.	Shining.		Soft.			Massive.
			Contains 18 per cent. of thallium; colors the flame strongly green.	Crookesite.	(Ꞓu,Tl,Ag,)Se.	Lead-gray.			2.5	6.9	Easily.	Massive.

(Page 66)

MINERALS WITH METALLIC LUSTRE.

A. Fusible from 1—5, or easily volatile.

DIVISION 3.

DIVISION 4 (in part).

A.—Fusible from 1—5, or easily volatile.

Division	General Characters.	Specific Characters.	Species.	Composition.	Color.	Streak.	Cleavage and Fracture.	Hardness.	Sp. Gr.	Fusibility.	Crysta-tio
DIVISION 3. *B. B. on charcoal give a white coating which colors the R. F. green, or greenish-blue. In a tube gently heated with concentrated sulphuric acid, give a hyacinth-red color, which on addition of water disappears, yielding a black-gray precipitate of tellurium.*	Wholly volatile; fuses easily; fumes strongly.	Burns with a greenish flame. Soluble in nitric acid.	Tellurium.	Te.	Tin-white.	Tin-white.	Hexagonal.	2.—2.5	6.2	1.	III.
	Wholly soluble in nitric acid.	The solution gives a heavy precip. with sulphuric acid. Soft but not malleable.	Altaite.	Pb, Te.	Tin-white.	Tin-white.	Cubic.	3.—3.5	8.1	1.	I.
		B. B. with soda gives globule of silver; malleable.	Hessite.	AgTe.	Lead-gray.	Gray.	Sectile.	2.5—3.	8.5	1.	IV.
	Soluble in nitric acid with the separation of gold.	Solution gives, with hydrochloric acid, a precip. of AgCl, and with sulphuric acid, of PbO,SO^3.	Müllerite (sylvanite containing lead).	$(Ag,Au,Pb)Te^3$.	Brass-yellow.			2.	8.	Easily.	V.
	On charcoal, with sulphur and iodide of potassium, gives a red sublimate (bismuth).	Fuses easily to a brittle silver-white globule.	TETRADYMITE.	$BiTe^3$, or $Bi(Te,S,Se)^3$	Steel-gray.		Basal.	1.5—2.	7.5	Easily.	III.
		Gives after a little blowing the selenium odor.	Joseite.	Bi, Te, S, Se.	Black-gray.		Basal.	1.5—2.	7.9	Easily.	III.
	After long heating gives a malleable metallic globule. Incompletely soluble in nitric acid.	Soluble in aqua-regia, with separation of chloride of silver.	Sylvanite (graphic tellurium).	$(Ag,Au)Te^3$.	Steel-gray.	Steel-gray.	Prismatic.	1.5—2.	8.	Easily.	IV.
		Same reactions (contains more silver).	Petzite.	$AuTe+3AgTe$.	Iron-black.	Iron-black.		2.5	9.	Easily.	IV.
	Heated with strong sulphuric acid gives a hyacinth-red or brownish-yellow solution; not a pure red like preceding.	Soluble in aqua-regia; in the solution SO_3 gives a precipitate (lead).	Nagyagite (foliated tellurium).	Pb, Au, Te, S.	Black-gray.	Gray.	Basal-fol.	1.—1.5	7.	Easily.	II.
	☞ Compare *Aikinite*, Div. 5, p. 68.										
DIVISION 4. *B. B. on charcoal, or in the open glass-tube, give dense antimony fumes.*	B. B. are nearly or completely volatile in a continued blast.	Tin-white. B. B. takes fire and continues to burn without further heating, and becomes covered with white needles of oxide of antimony.	ANTIMONY.	Sb.	Tin-white.	Tin-white.	Perfect.	3.5	6.2	1.	III.
		When pulverized and treated with caustic potassa is rapidly colored ochre-yellow, and for the most part dissolved.	**Stibnite** (antimony-glance).	SbS_3.	Lead to steel-gray.	Lead-gray.	Prismatic.	2	4.5	1.	IV.
		Gives in nitric acid a partial solution of a sky-blue color; this, with sulphuric acid, yields a white precipitate of sulphate of lead, and is rendered violet-blue on addition of an excess of NH_4O.	BOURNONITE.	$3(\text{Ɵu},Pb)S+SbS_3$.	Steel-gray.	Iron-black.		2.5—3.	5.8	1.	IV.
		Same reaction, but the aqua-regia solution is not precipitated by sulphuric acid.	Stylotypite.	$3(\text{Ɵu},Fe,Ag)S+SbS_3$.	Iron-black.	Iron-black.		3.	4.7	1.	IV.
		Oxidized by nitric acid to a white powder, imparting no color to the acid.	**Jamesonite.**	$2PbS+SbS_3$.	Lead-gray.		Basal.	2.—3.	5.6	1.	IV.
		Same as Jamesonite, not cleavable.	Zinkenite.	$PbS+SbS_3$.	Lead-gray.			3.—3.5	5.3	1.	IV.
		As above.	Boulangerite.	$3PbS+SbS_3$.	Lead-gray.			2.5—3.	5.9	1.	IV.
		As above (sometimes contains arsenic).	GEOCRONITE.	$5PbS+(Sb,As)S^3$.	Lead-gray.		Granular.	2.—3.	6.5	1.	IV.
		As above.	Plagionite.	Pb, S, Sb.	Lead-gray.			2.5.	5.4	1.	V.
		As above.	Meneghinite.	$4PbS,SbS_3$.	Lead-gray.			2.5	6.3	1.	V.
		Fused with sulphur and iodide of potassium gives a bismuth reaction.	Kobellite.	$3PbS+(Bi,Sb)S^3$.	Lead-gray.			Soft.	6.3	1.	Fibro
		☞ Compare *Galenite*, Div. 5, p. 67.									

(Page 67)

MINERALS WITH METALLIC LUSTRE.

A. Fusible from 1—5, or easily volatile.

DIVISION 4 (continued).

DIVISION 5 (in part).

A. Fusible from 1—5, or easily volatile.

DIVISION 4.—(*Continued.*) *B. B. on charcoal, or in the open glass-tube, give dense antimony fumes.*

General Characters.	Specific Characters.	Species.	Composition.	Color.	Streak.	Cleavage and Fracture.	Hardness.	Sp. Gr.	Fusibility.	Crystallization.
B. B. give with a mixture of borax and soda a malleable silver-bead, and the nitric solution yields with hydrochloric acid a precipitate of chloride of silver.	Gives no sulphur reaction.	Dyscrasite (antimonial silver).	Ag^3Sb.	Silver-white.	Silver-white.	Basal.	3.5—4.	9.6	1.5	IV.
	Gives sulphur reaction. The partial nitric solution yields with excess of ammonia a violet-blue color (copper).	FREIBERGITE (silver tetrahedrite).	Cu, Ag, SbS.	Steel-gray.	Gray.		3.5	4.8		I.
	Gives sulphur reaction, but no blue with ammonia.	STEPHANITE.	$5AgS + SbS^3$.	Iron-black.	Black.		2.5	6.26	1.	IV.
	As above.	Miargyrite.	$AgS + SbS_3$.	Iron-black.	Cherry-red.		2.5	5.2	1.	V.
	As above; the nitric solution gives a precipitate of sulphate of lead with SO_3.	Brogniardite.	$2(Pb,Ag)S + Sb,S_3$.	Black-gray.			3.	5.9	Easily.	I.
	Same.	Freieslebenite	$5(Pb,Ag)S + 2SbS_3$.	Steel-gray.	Gray.	Prismatic.	2.—2.5	6.—6.4	Easily.	V.
	☞ Compare *Pyrargyrite*, Div. 1. p. 72.									
Heated in a glass tube with soda gives a sublimate of mercury.	The nitric solution is rendered blue by excess of ammonia.	SPANIOLITE.	Cu, Hg, Sb, S.	Iron-black.	Red-brown.		3.5	5.1	1.5	I.
Give with soda on charcoal after long heating a globule of copper.	The nitric solution gives no precipitate with hydrochloric acid, but usually gives reactions for iron and zinc.	**Tetrahedrite.**	$4(ЄuS) + SbS_3$.	Lead-gray.	Dark-gray.		3.5	4.5—5.1	1.5	I.
	Very closely resembling the above in blowpipe reactions is the rare	Chalcostibite (antimonial-copper).	$ЄuS + SbS_3$.	Lead-gray.	Black.	Prismatic.	3.5	4.8	1.	IV.
Give after long heating on charcoal a magnetic globule.	Gives no sulphur reaction in open tube; difficultly fusible; but little acted on by hydrochloric acid; completely dissolved by aqua-regia.	Breithauptite.	Ni_2Sb.	Copper-red.	Red-brown.		5.5	7.5	3.	III.
	Easily dissolved in hydrochloric acid, with disengagement of sulphuretted hydrogen.	BERTHIERITE	$FeS + SbS_3$.	Steel-gray.			2.—3.	4.2	1.5	IV.?
	Easily fusible; hydrochloric acid has little effect; aqua-regia dissolves it with separation of sulphur.	Ullmannite.	$NiS_2 + NiSb$.	Steel-gray.			5.5	6.3	3.	I.

DIVISION 5. *B. B. with soda give a sulphur reaction, or placed in the open glass-tube give a sulphurous acid reaction, which reddens a strip of moistened blue litmus paper placed in the end, but do not give the reactions of the preceding division.*

General Characters.	Specific Characters.	Species.	Composition.	Color.	Streak.	Cleavage and Fracture.	Hardness.	Sp. Gr.	Fusibility.	Crystallization.
Malleable, can be cut with a knife like lead. In the nitric solution hydrochloric acid gives a heavy precipitate of chloride of silver.	The nitric solution is colored blue by excess of ammonia; moistened with HCl colors the flame blue.	Jalpaite (var. of Argentite).	(Ag, Єu,)S.	Gray-black.	Gray-black.	Malleable.	2.5	6.8	Easily.	I.
	Does not give the above reactions; with soda gives a globule of silver.	ARGENTITE (silver-glance).	AgS.	Gray-black.	Gray-black.	Malleable.	2.5	7.2	1.5	I.
	Differs only in crystalline form from argentite.	Acanthite.	AgS.	Gray-black.	Gray-black.	Malleable.	2.5	7.2	1.5	IV.
The roasted minerals give with borax a violet bead in O. F. (manganese).	The powder is leek-green.	Alabandite.	MnS.	Iron-black.	Green.	Cubic.	3.5	4.	3.	I.
	The powder is brownish-red.	Hauerite.	MnS^2.	Brown-black.	Brown-red.		4.	3.46	3.	I.
Streak red; mixed with soda in a closed tube gives metallic mercury.	Many varieties have a gray to black color, but the streak is red. ☞ The rare *Metacinnabarite* is amorphous HgS; has a black streak, H=3; G=7.72.	**Cinnabar.**	HgS.	Red.	Red.	Perfect.	2.5	8.9	Vol.	III.
B. B. with soda on coal gives a lead-globule and covers the coal with a yellow coat (oxide of lead).	Easily soluble in nitric acid, with separation of S. and $PbOSO_3$. The nitric solution gives no blue with ammonia.	**Galenite** (galena).	PbS.	Lead-gray.	Gray.	Cubic.	2.5	7.5	1.	I.
	☞ *Cuproplumbite* and *Huascolite* are respectively cupriferous and zinciferous varieties of galena.									

(Page 68)

MINERALS WITH METALLIC LUSTRE.

A. Fusible from 1—5, or easily volatile.

Division 5 (continued).

A.—Fusible from 1—5, or easily volatile.

DIVISION 5.—(Continued.)

B. B. with soda give a sulphur reaction, or placed in the open glass-tube give off sulphurous acid, which reddens a strip of moistened blue litmus paper placed in the end, but do not give the reactions of the preceding divisions.

General Characters.		Specific Characters.	Species.	Composition.	Color.	Streak.	Cleavage or Fracture.	Hardness.	Sp. Gr.	Fusibility.	Crystallization.
Moistened with HCl give to the flame the blue color of chloride of copper. Give with nitric acid a blue or green solution, which upon addition of ammonia in excess becomes violet or sky-blue.	With sulphur and iodide of potassium on coal give a red sublimate of the iodide of bismuth. The saturated nitric solution is rendered turbid by addition of water.	Gives with soda on coal a globule of copper.	Wittichenite (cupreous-bismuth).	3ꞒuS + BiS^3.	Steel-gray.	Black.		3.5	4.6—5.	Easily.	IV.
		In the nitric solution sulphuric acid gives a precipitate of $PbOSO_3$.	Aikinite.	3(Ꞓu,Pb)S + BiS^3.	Lead-gray.			2.—2.5	6.7	1.	IV.
		Gives with soda on coal a strongly magnetic globule containing nickel.	Grunauite.	Bi,Ni,Cu,Fe,S.	Steel-gray.	Dark-gray.	Octahedral.	4.5	5.1	Easily.	I.
		Same as Aikinite.	Chiviatite.	2(Ꞓu,Pb)S + 3BiS^3.	Lead-gray.				6.92	1.	Massi[ve]
		Same as Wittichenite.	Emplectite.	ꞒuS + BiS^3.	Tin-white.					Easily.	IV.
	Fuse to brittle steel-gray magnetic globules.	Brass-yellow color.	**Chalcopyrite** (copper pyrites).	ꞒuS + FeS + FeS^2.	Brass-yellow.	Green-black.	Uneven.	3.5	4.3	2.	II.
		Brass-yellow color; cleavage cubic.	Cubanite.	ꞒuS + FeS + 3FeS^2.	Bronze-yellow.	Red-bronze.	Cubic.	4.	4.1	Easily.	I.
		Brass-yellow color; the fresh fracture tarnishes to a golden-yellow in 24 hours.	Barnhardtite.	2ꞒuS + FeS + FeS^2.	Bronze-yellow.	Gray-black.		3.5	4.5	Easily.	Massiv[e]
		Color copper-red to yellow and intermediate shades; is called variegated copper; in the nitric solution sulphuric acid gives no precipitate.	**Bornite** (variegated copper).	(Ꞓu,Fe)S.	Copper-red, yellow, purple.	Black.		3.	5.	Easily.	I.
		Resembles bornite, but in the nitric solution sulphuric acid gives a precipitate of sulphate of lead.	Castillite.	Ꞓu,Pb,Fe,Ag,Zn,S.	Copper-red.	Black.	Foliated.	3.	5.2	Easily.	Massiv[e]
	Give none of the above reactions.	The nitric solution gives with HCl a heavy precipitate of AgCl.	Stromeyerite.	(Ꞓu,Ag)S.	Steel-gray.	Gray.		2.5—3.	6.3	Easily.	IV.
		B. B. in O. F. alone on coal yields a globule of copper. Soluble in nitric acid with separation of sulphur.	**Chalcocite** (copper glance).	ꞒuS.	Steel-gray.	Gray.	Conchoidal.	2.5—3.	5.7	Easily.	IV.
		Gives by itself no metallic malleable globule. Soluble in nitric acid, with separation of sulphur and binoxide of tin.	STANNITE (tin pyrites).	Ꞓu,Fe,Sn,Zn,S.	Steel-gray.	Black.		4.	4.4	Easily.	Massiv[e]
		☞ Compare *Tetrahedrite*, Div. 4, p. 67.									
The partial nitric solution is not blue. B. B. fuse to magnetic beads.		B. B. partially reduced to silver; the partial nitric solution gives a heavy precipitate of chloride of silver with HCl.	Sternbergite.	Ag,Fe,S.	Pinchbeck-brown.	Black.	Basal.	1.—1.5	4.2	Easily.	IV.
		The roasted mineral gives to the borax bead a sapphire-blue color. Soluble in nitric acid, forming a rose-red solution.	LINNAEITE.	2(Co,Ni)S + CoS^3.	Steel gray.	Black-gray.		5.5	4.9	Easily.	I.
		Gives like reactions, but also, when moistened with hydrochloric acid, imparts a blue color to the flame.	Carrollite.	2(Ꞓu,Co)S + CoS^2.	Tin-white.	Gray.		5.5	4.85	Easily.	I.
		The roasted mineral gives to the borax bead the violet color while hot, reddish-brown when cold, of nickel; gives no sulphur in the closed tube.	MILLERITE (capillary pyrites).	NiS.	Bronze-yellow	Bright.		3.—3.5	5.6	Easily.	III.
		As above, but gives sulphur in the closed tube.	Beyrichite.	3NiS + 2NiS^3.	Lead-gray.			3.—3.5	4.7	Easily.	III. ?
		Magnetic before fusion; color pinchbeck-brown. Reacts for nickel.	Pentlandite.	Ni,Fe,S.	Bronze-yellow.	Brown.		3.5—4.	4.6	Easily.	I.
		Give only the reaction for iron. Magnetic before fusion, gives but little sulphur in the closed tube.	**Pyrrhotite** (magnetic pyrites).	6FeS + FeS^2.	Bronze-yellow	Black-gray.	Basal.	4.	4.5	Easily.	III.
		Gives only the reactions of iron; not magnetic before fusion. Gives sulphur in the closed tube.	**Pyrite** (iron pyrites).	FeS^2.	Brass-yellow.	Brown-black.		6.—6.5	4.9	Easily.	I.
		Same as for pyrite; can be distinguished only by crystalline form.	**Marcasite** (white iron pyrites).	FeS_2.	Pale-yellow to white.	Black-gray.		6.—6.5	4.7	Easily.	III.

(Page 69)

MINERALS WITH METALLIC LUSTRE.

A. Fusible from 1—5, or easily volatile.

DIVISION 5 (concluded).

DIVISION 6.

A.—Fusible from 1—5, or easily volatile.

Division	General Characters.	Specific Characters.	Species.	Composition.	Color.	Streak.	Cleavage or Fracture.	Hardness.	Sp. Gr.	Fusibility.	Crystallization.
DIVISION 5.—(*Continued.*) *See preceding page.*	With sulphur and iodide of potassium give, on coal, a red sublimate of iodide of bismuth.	B. B. fuses in R. F. with effervescence, giving a globule of bismuth, and a bismuth coating on coal. Soluble in nitric acid.	BISMUTHINITE (bismuth glance).	BiS^3.	Lead-gray.	Gray.	Prismatic.	2.	6.4	1.	IV.
		As above, but gives a precipitate of sulphate of lead with sulphuric acid.	Chiviatite.	$2(\mathrm{Cu},Pb)S+3BiS^3$.	Lead-gray.	Gray.	Foliated.		6.92	1.	
		☞ Compare *Bismuth*, below.									
DIVISION 6. *Not belonging to the foregoing divisions.*	B. B. in a matrass yield metallic mercury and leave a spongy mass of silver.	Easily soluble in nitric acid.	Amalgam.	$AgHg^2$ and $AgHg^3$.	Silver-white.	Gray.		3.	13.7—14	1.	I.
		Yields less mercury in the closed tube.	Arquerite.	Ag^6Hg.	Silver-white.	Gray.	Malleable.		10.8		I.
	Fused with sulphur and iodide of potassium, coats the coal with a red sublimate of iodide of bismuth.	In the open glass-tube gives almost no fumes, and the metal becomes surrounded with fused oxide, which is dark-brown when hot, and yellow when cold.	BISMUTH.	Bi.	Reddish-white	White.	Basal.	2.5	9.7	1.	III.
	Colors the borax bead cobalt-blue.	Heated with phosphoric acid gives a violet solution (manganese).	Rabdionite.	Mn, Co, Fe, Cu, O.	Black.	Metallic greasy streak.		1.	2.8	3.	Stalact.
	Difficultly fusible. Heated in R. F. becomes magnetic.	Streak, cherry-red.	**Hematite** (specular iron).	$\ddot{\bar{F}}e$.	Steel-gray to black.	Red.	Scaly, fibrous, compact.	5.5—6.5	5.	Infus.	III.
	With soda on charcoal easily reduced to metallic copper.	☞ Compare *Cuprite* and *Melaconite*, Div. 3, p. 75, sometimes with metallic lustre.									
	Magnetic before heating.	Generally fusible above 5.	**Magnetite** (magnetic iron).	$\dot{F}e,\ddot{\bar{F}}e$.	Iron-black.	Black.	Octahedral.	5.5—6.5	4.9—5.2	5.	I.
		Gelatinize with hydrochloric acid. Sometimes magnetic from associated magnetite.	HORTONOLITE.	$(\dot{F}e,\dot{M}g,\dot{M}n)^2\dddot{S}i$.	Yellow-black.	Dirty-white.	Prismatic.	6.5	3.9	4.	IV.
			FAYALITE.	$\dot{F}e^2\dddot{S}i$.	Black.	Brown.	Prismatic.	6.5	4.1	3.	IV.
	The fine powder, boiled with aqua-regia, gradually assumes a yellowish color.	Boiled down with phosphoric acid gives a beautiful blue syrup (tungsten). The blue syrup is changed to violet by addition of nitric acid (manganese).	WOLFRAMITE	$(\dot{M}n,\dot{F}e)\dddot{W}$.	Black.	Black.	Prismatic.	5.5	7.3	3.	V.
	With borax in O. F. give an amethystine bead.	☞ Compare *Rhodonite*, Div. 5, p. 87, sometimes altered to a black metallic hydrous silicate; *Klipsteinite*, Div. 4, p. 85; and *Psilomelane*, Div. 1, p. 70, which in some varieties is fusible.									
	Gelatinize perfectly with hydrochloric acid.	Easily fusible, swells up but slightly. (See Div. 5, p. 78.)	ILVAITE.	$\dot{F}e,\ddot{\bar{F}}e,\dot{C}a,\dot{M}n,\dddot{S}i$.	Black.	Black.		5.5—6.	3.8—4.	2.5	IV.
		Easily fusible, swells up strongly. (See Div. 5, p. 78.)	ALLANITE.	$\ddot{\bar{A}}l,\dot{C}e,\dot{L}a,\dot{D}i,\dot{F}e,\dot{C}a,\dddot{S}i$.	Brown-black.	Gray.		5.5—6.	3.—4.2	2.5	V.
	With soda easily reduced to metallic lead.		Plattnerite.	$\ddot{P}b$.	Iron-black.	Brown.			9.3		
	When fused with soda, digested with water and filtered, a green solution is obtained, which neutralized with HCl gives a light-colored precipitate. If the latter is digested with strong HCl, and boiled with tin, then diluted with a like volume of water, it gives a clear sapphire-blue solution.		Samarskite.	$\dddot{\ddot{C}}b,\dot{F}e,\ddot{\bar{U}},\dot{Y}$.	Velvet-black.	Dark red-brown.		5.5—6.	5.6	4.5	IV.

(Page 70)

MINERALS WITH METALLIC LUSTRE.

B. Infusible or fusible above 5, and non-volatile.

DIVISION 1.

DIVISION 2.

B.—Infusible or fusible above 5, and non-volatile.

Division	General Characters.	Specific Characters.	Species.	Composition.	Color.	Streak.	Cleavage or Fracture.	Hardness.	Sp. Gr.	Crystallization.
DIVISION 1. *B. B. in O. F. a very small quantity gives to the borax-bead the amethystine red of manganese.*	With hydrochloric acid evolve chlorine. Contain little or no water.	Moistened with HCl colors the outer flame beautifully blue (chloride of copper).	Crednerite.	$\dot{Cu}^3\dddot{\overline{Mn}}^2$.	Black.	Black.	Basal.	4.5	5.	V.
		Color brownish-black.	BRAUNITE.	$2\dot{Mn}^2\ddot{Mn}+\dot{Mn}\dddot{Si}$.	Brown-black.	Black.		6.—6.5	4.7	II.
			Hausmannite.	$\dot{Mn}^2\ddot{Mn}$.	Brown-black.	Chestnut-brown.	Basal.	5.—5.5	4.7	II.
		Color iron-black to steel-gray.	**Pyrolusite.**	$\ddot{Mn}$.	Iron-black.	Black.		2.—5.	4.82	IV.
	Yields much water in the closed tube.	Prismatic cleavage very perfect.	MANGANITE.	$\dddot{\overline{Mn}}\dot{H}$.	Steel-gray.	Red-brown.	Prismatic.	4.	4.3	IV.
		In the hydrochloric solution sulphuric acid generally yields a white precipitate of sulphate of baryta.	PSILOMELANE	$\ddot{Mn},\dot{Ba},\dot{H}$.	Black.	Brown-black.		5.—6.	3.7—4.7	Amorph.
	☞ Compare *Franklinite*, Div. 2, below. *Hauerite* and *Alabandite*, Div. 5, p. 67.									
DIVISION 2. *B. B. on charcoal after long heating in R. F. become magnetic.*	Streak always cherry-red.	Decrepitates, and gives much water in the closed tube.	**Turgite** (hydro-hematite).	$\dddot{\overline{Fe}}^2\dot{H}$.	Reddish-black	Red.	Fibrous, compact.	5.—6.	4.14	
		Slowly soluble in hydrochloric acid.	**Hematite** (specular iron)	$\dddot{\overline{Fe}}$.	Reddish-black	Red.	Scaly, fibrous, compact.	6.—6.5	4.5—5.3	III.
	Magnetic without heating (sometimes but slightly). With salt of phosphorus in R. F. give a bottle-green glass, which fades on cooling.	With soda gives the manganese reaction, and on coal in R. F. gives a faint yellow sublimate (ZnO).	**Franklinite.**	$(\dot{Zn},\dot{Mn},\dot{Fe})\ (\dddot{\overline{Mn}},\dddot{\overline{Fe}})$.	Iron-black.	Reddish-brown.		5.5—6.5	5.1	I.
		Strongly magnetic, does not give above reactions. Difficultly fusible.	**Magnetite.**	$\dot{Fe}\dddot{\overline{Fe}}$.	Iron-black.	Black.	Octahedral.	5.5—6.5	4.9—5.2	I.
		In the solution after the oxidation of the protoxide of iron with chlorate of potash and its precipitation with an excess of ammonia, phosphate of soda gives a precipitate of the ammonio-phosphate of magnesia in the filtrate. Jacobsite gives a strong manganese reaction.	Jacobsite.	$(\dot{Mn},\dot{Mg})\ (\dddot{\overline{Mn}},\dddot{\overline{Fe}})$.	Black.	Black-brown.		6.	4.75	I.
			Magnesio-ferrite.	$\dot{Mg}\dddot{\overline{Fe}}$.	Black.	Black.		6.—6.5	4.5—4.6	I.
		☞ Compare *Menaccanite*, below.								
	The fine powder boiled with hydrochloric acid, filtered, and the filtrate boiled with tin-foil, gradually assumes a beautiful blue or violet color.	More easily decomposed by treating first with sulphuric acid and evaporating to dryness, and then treating with HCl and tin-foil.	**Menaccanite** (Titanic iron).	$(Ti,Fe)_2O^3$.	Black.	Black.		5.—6.	4.5—5.	III.
		☞ *Rutile*, *Anatase* and *Arkansite* sometimes become magnetic after long heating.								
	Streak ochre-yellow (sometimes has a sub-metallic lustre).	Much water in the closed tube.	**Limonite** (brown hematite).	$\dddot{\overline{Fe}}^2\dot{H}^3$.	Brown.	Yellow.	Fibrous, compact, earthy.	5.—5.5	3.6—4.	
	☞ Comp. *Siderite* and *Blende*, Div. 4, p. 92, sometimes with metallic lustre; also the minerals of the following section, especially *Chromite*.									

(Page 71)

MINERALS WITH METALLIC LUSTRE.

B. Infusible or fusible above 5, and non-volatile.

DIVISION 8.

B.—Infusible or fusible above 5, and non-volatile.

DIVISION 3.

Not included in the foregoing divisions.

General Characters.	Specific Characters.	Species.	Composition.	Color.	Streak.	Cleavage or Fracture.	Hardness.	Sp. Gr.	Crystallization.
Impart a beautiful emerald-green color to the beads of borax and salt of phosphorus when cold.	Sometimes strongly magnetic; only slightly attacked by hydrochloric acid.	**Chromite** (chromic iron)	$\dot{Fe}\ddot{Cr}$.	Iron-black.	Brown.	Uneven.	5.5	4.3	I.
☞ Compare *Cassiterite*, which with soda on coal is reduced to metallic tin.									
Very soft; soil the fingers.	B. B. in forceps colors the flame light-green, on charcoal with soda gives a sulphur reaction, and gives coating of molybdic acid.	**Molybdenite.**	MoS^2.	Blue-gray.	Greenish.	Foliated.	1.—1.5	4.6	V. ?
	Does not give the above, but deflagrates with nitre, affording carbonate of potassa.	**Graphite.**	C.	Iron-black.	Black.	Foliated.	1.—2.	2.	III.
Give to the salt of phosphorus-bead the violet color of titanic acid.	Crystallizes in cubes.	Perofskite.	$\dot{Ca}\ddot{Ti}$.	Iron-black to yellow.	Gray.		5.5	4.03	I.
	☞ Compare *Rutile* and *Brookite*, Div. 6, p. 95, sometimes with metallic lustre.								
Fused in a matrass with nitre evolves the peculiar odor of oxide of osmium.	Not perceptibly attacked by borax, salt of phosphorus, or nitro-hydrochloric acid.	IRIDOSMINE.	Ir, Os, Rd, Ru.	Tin-white.	Gray.		6.—7.	19.3--21.1	III.
Slightly attacked by acids.	B. B. immediately changes its color to yellow or white.	Yttrotantalite	$\dot{Ca}, \dot{Y}, \dot{U}, \dot{Fe}, \dddot{Ta}, \dddot{W}$.	Yellow to black.	Grayish.	Conchoidal.	5.5	5.7	IV.
	The powder fused with bi-sulphate of potash, then boiled with HCl, and filtered and the liquid evaporated with addition of tin-foil, it assumes a beautiful blue color, which rapidly fades, and gradually disappears upon addition of water.	Tantalite.	$\dot{Fe}, \dot{Mn}, \dddot{Ta}, \ddot{Sn}$.	Black.	Brown-black.	Brittle.	6.—6.5	7.—8.	IV.
	(same as above)	COLUMBITE.	$\dot{Fe}, \dot{Mn}, \dddot{Cb}, \dddot{Ta}, \ddot{Sn}$.	Black.	Red-black.	Brittle.	6.	5.4—6.5	IV.
	Gives like reactions.	Fergusonite.	$\dot{Y}, \dot{Fe}, \dot{U}, \dddot{Cb}$.	Black.	Pale-brown.	Conchoidal.	5.5—6.	5.8	II.
	☞ Compare *Polycrase*, Div. 4, p. 93; *Æschynite*, Div. 6, p. 95.								
Mostly soluble in nitric acid to a yellow fluid, from which ammonia throws down a sulphur-yellow precipitate.	With salt of phosphorus in R. F. a green bead, becoming yellow in O. F. Evaporated with phosphoric acid gives an emerald-green solution.	URANINITE (pitch-blende).	$\dot{U}\,\ddot{U}$.	Brownish-black.	Brown-black.	Conchoidal, uneven.	5.5	6.4—7.	I.

(Page 72)

MINERALS WITHOUT METALLIC LUSTRE.

A. Easily volatile or combustible.

B. Fusible from 1—5, and non-volatile.

I. *Yield a metal or a magnetic mass with soda.*

DIVISION 1.

Group	General Characters.	Specific Characters.	Species.	Composition.	Color.	Cleavage or Fracture.	Lustre.	Hardness.	Sp. Gr.	Fusibility.	Crystallization.
A.—B. B. easily volatile or combustible.	B. B. burns with a blue flame, emitting the odor of sulphurous acid.	Of a yellow color; when impure or mixed with earthy substances, gray or brown.	**Sulphur.**	S.	Sulphur-yellow.	Conchoidal.	Resinous.	1.5—2.5	2.	Easily.	IV.
	Fuse readily and volatilize, and B. B. on coal with soda in R. F. give off arsenical fumes.	Color aurora-red.	**Realgar.**	AsS.	Aurora-red.	Conchoidal.	Resinous.	1.5—2.	3.5	Easily.	V.
		Color lemon-yellow.	**Orpiment.**	AsS_3	Lemon-yellow	Foliated.	Pearly.	1.5—2.	3.48	Easily.	IV.
	Heated in a closed tube give a crystalline sublimate. B. B. with soda on coal give the strong garlic odor.	Occurs in thin plates with perfect cleavage.	Claudetite (arsenous acid).	$\ddot{A}s$.	White.	Prismatic.	Pearly.	2.5	3.8		IV.
		Color white.	Arsenolite (arsenous acid).	$\ddot{A}s$.	White.		Silky.	1.5	3.69	Vol.	I.
	Easily fusible and volatile, covering the coal with a white sublimate (oxide of antimony). Insoluble in water.	Dissolve mostly in HCl with the evolution of sulphuretted hydrogen. Heated with potash solution the powder becomes yellow.	KERMESITE.	$\ddot{S}b+2SbS_3$.	Cherry-red.	Basal.	Adamantine.	1.5	4.5	1.	V.
		Easily soluble in HCl, without evolution of gas. Unchanged by potash.	VALENTINITE	$\ddot{S}b$.	White.	Prismatic.	Adamantine.	2.5—3.	5.56	I.	IV.
		Same reactions as Valentinite; differs only in crystalline form.	SENARMONTITE.	$\ddot{S}b$.	White.	Octahedral.	Adamantine.	2.—2.5	5.22		I.
	Volatilize with dense white fumes; soluble in water. Treated with potash solution give an ammoniacal odor.	Volatile without fusion, its solution gives no precipitate with chloride of barium.	SAL AMMONIAC.	NH_4Cl.	White, yellow.		Vitreous.	1.5—2.	1.53	Vol.	I.
		Volatile with fusion, its solution gives a heavy precipitate with chloride of barium (sulphate of baryta).	Mascagnite.	$NH_4O\bar{S}+\dot{H}$.	White, gray, yellow.		Vitreous.	2.	1.7	Vol.	IV.
	With soda in the closed glass-tube give a sublimate of metallic mercury.	Streak red. Gives a reaction for sulphurous acid in the open glass-tube.	**Cinnabar.**	HgS.	Red.	Hexagonal.	Adamantine.	2.—2.5	9.	Vol.	III.
		Streak white. In the nitric solution nitrate of silver gives a heavy precipitate of the chloride of silver.	Calomel.	Hg_2Cl.	Gray-white.		Adamantine.	1.5	6.5	Vol.	II.
	Partly volatile; with soda on coal gives lead globules.	Deposits a lead-coating on charcoal.	Cotunnite.	PbCl.	Yellow-white.		Adamantine.	2.	5.2	Easily.	IV.
	☞ See also mineral coals in the appendix.										
B.—Fusible from 1—5, and not volatile or only partially volatile. I. *B. B. with soda on charcoal give a metallic globule or a magnetic mass.* DIVISION 1. *B. B. with soda on charcoal give a globule of silver.*	Streak red.	B. B. on coal gives an arsenical odor.	PROUSTITE (light-red silver ore).	$3AgS+AsS_3$.	Cochineal-red.	Conchoidal.	Adamantine.	2.5	5.5	1.	III.
		B. B. on coal gives a white sublimate of oxide of antimony.	PYRARGYRITE (dark-red silver ore).	$3AgS+SbS_3$.	Dark-red to black.	Conchoidal.	Adamantine.	2.5	5.8	1.	III.
		Same reactions as Proustite, but easily distinguished by its orange-yellow color and streak.	Xanthoconite.	Ag, As, S.	Pomegranate-yellow.		Adamantine.	2.	5.1		III.
		☞ Compare *Miargyrite*, Div. 4, page 67.									
	Malleable and sectile.	In a closed tube, with bisulphate of potassa, gives off hydrochloric acid vapors, fuses to a pale hyacinth-red globule, becomes yellow when cold.	CERARGYRITE.	AgCl.	Pearl-gray.		Resinous adamantine.	1.—1.5	5.5	I.	I.
		In closed tube, with bisulphate of potassa, gives off iodine vapors, fuses to a very dark, almost black globule.	Iodyrite.	AgI.	Lemon-yellow.	Basal.	Adamantine.	1.5	5.7	I.	III.
		In a closed tube, with bisulphate of potassa, gives off bromine vapors, fuses to an intense garnet-red globule, becoming yellow when cold.	Bromyrite.	AgBr.	Greenish-yellow.		Adamantine.	2.—3.	5.8—6.	I.	I.
			Embolite.	Ag(Cl, Br).	Green to dark-yellow.		Adamantine.	1.—1.5	5.3—5.8	I.	I.

* In minerals without metallic lustre there is frequently a wide range of color in a single species (for example, in Tourmaline and many other species, it varies from colorless to black); this property, therefore, can generally be used only as confirmatory connection with other characters in determining non-metallic mineral species. The *streak* in this group is generally paler than the color of mineral, and in a large majority of non-metallic minerals it is very nearly white.

(Page 73)

MINERALS WITHOUT METALLIC LUSTRE.

B. Fusible from 1—5, and non-volatile.

I. *Yield a metal or a magnetic mass with soda.*

DIVISION 2 (in part).

B.—Fusible from 1—5, and not volatile, or only partially volatile.

I. B. B. with soda on charcoal give a metallic globule or a magnetic mass.

DIVISION 2.

B. B. with soda on charcoal give a globule of lead.

General Characters.	Specific Characters.	Species.	Composition.	Color.	Cleavage or Fracture.	Lustre.	Hardness.	Sp. Gr.	Fusibility.	Crystallization.
B. B. on charcoal give coatings of lead and antimony.	Fused in a salt of phosphorus bead which has been saturated with oxide of copper, colors the flame blue (chloride of copper).	Nadorite.	Sb,Pb,O,Cl.	Brown-yellow.		Resinous.	3.	7.02		IV.
	Gives water in the closed tube.	BINDHEIMITE.	$\dot{P}b^3SbO^5b+4\ddot{H}$.	Brown-yellow.	Brittle.	Resinous.	4.	4.7		Amorph.
B. B. on charcoal give arsenical odors.	Fused in forceps in R.F. crystallizes on cooling. (Like Pyromorphite.)	MIMETITE.	$3\dot{P}b^3\dddot{A}s+PbCl$.	Yellow-brown.		Resinous.	3.5	7.1	I.	III.
	A variety of Mimetite containing phosphate of lime; gives the reaction for phosphoric acid.	Hedyphane.	$(\dot{P}b,\dot{C}a)^3(\dddot{A}s,\dddot{P})+PbCl$.	White.		Adamantine.	3.5—4.	5.45	I.	III.
The cold nitric solution gives with molybdate of ammonia a yellow precipitate (phosphomolybdate of ammonia).	Not easily reduced to lead on coal, but fuses to a globule, which, on cooling, becomes plainly crystalline; gives the chlorine reaction with salt of phosphorus and oxide of copper.	**Pyromorphite.**	$3\dot{P}b^3\dddot{P}+PbCl$.	White, brown, green.	Brittle.	Resinous.	3.5—4.	6.5—7.1	1.5	III.
Color red.	Imparts to the borax bead an emerald-green color, which in O.F. becomes light olive-green, then yellow, and finally colorless.	Dechenite (aræoxene).	$(\dot{P}b\dot{Z}n)VO^5$.	Red.		Greasy.	3.—4.	5.7	Easily.	Massive.
	Imparts to the borax bead an emerald-green color, which is constant in both flames. Streak orange.	CROCOITE (chromate of lead).	$\dot{P}b\dddot{C}r$.	Hyacinth-red.	Prismatic.	Vitreous.	2.5—3.	6.	1.5	V.
	As above. Streak brick-red.	Phœnicochroite.	$\dot{P}b^3\dddot{C}r^2$.	Hyacinth-red.	Perfect.	Resinous.	3.—3.5	5.7		IV.
	Gives with borax a yellow glass, which becomes colorless on cooling.	Minium.	Pb^3O^4.	Red.		Dull.	2.—3.		1.	
Color azure-blue.	With soda gives the reaction for sulphur. Heated with nitric acid sulphate of lead separates. Gives water in closed tube.	Linarite.	$\dot{P}b\dddot{S}+\dot{C}u\dot{H}$.	Azure-blue.	Prismatic.	Vitreous.	2.5	5.4	Easily.	V.
Dissolve in nitric acid with effervescence.	The solution gives with nitrate of silver a precipitate of AgCl.	Phosgenite.	$\dot{P}b\ddot{C}+PbCl$.	White.	3 cleavages.	Adamantine.	3.	6.2	Easily.	II.
	The partial solution gives with nitrate of baryta a precipitate of $BaOSO_3$.	Lanarkite.	$\dot{P}b\dddot{S}+\dot{P}b\ddot{C}$.	Greenish-white to yellow-gray.	Basal perfect.	Adamantine.	2.5	6.3—7.	Easily.	V.
	Not affected by the above reagents.	**Cerussite** (white lead).	$\dot{P}b\ddot{C}$.	White.	Conchoidal.	Vitreous to adamantine.	3.5	6.4	Easily.	IV.
	The same as lanarkite, but is orthorhombic in crystallization.	Leadhillite.	$\dot{P}b\dddot{S}+3\dot{P}b\ddot{C}$.	White, yellow-gray.	Prismatic.	Pearly to resinous.	2.5	6.3	1.5	IV.
	The same as lanarkite, but is hexagonal (rhombohedral).	Susannite.	$\dot{P}b\dddot{S}+3\dot{P}b\ddot{C}$.	White, yellow-gray.	Basal.	Resinous.	2.5	6.5	1.5	III.
Soluble in nitric acid without effervescence. The solutions give heavy precipitates with nitrate of silver.	Prismatic cleavage very perfect.	Mendipite.	$PbCl+2\dot{P}b$.	Colorless-white	Prismatic.	Pearly.	2.5	7.—7.1	Easily.	IV.
	Crystals tabular, cleavage imperfect.	Matlockite.	$PbCl+\dot{P}b$.	Green to yellow-white.	Basal, imperfect.	Pearly.	3.	7.2	Easily.	II.
Difficultly soluble in nitric acid.	B. B. with soda easily reduced with the formation of a sulphide.	**Anglesite.**	$\dot{P}b\dddot{S}$.	White.	Conchoidal.	Adamantine.	3.	6.1—6.3	1.5	IV.
Dissolves in hydrochloric acid with separation of PbCl to a greenish solution, which, diluted with water and agitated with tin-foil, assumes a blue color.	Heated on platinum-foil with a drop or two of strong sulphuric acid until copious fumes escape, and allowed to cool, then breathed upon, acquires an ultramarine-blue color.	**Wulfenite** (Molybdate of lead.)	$\dot{P}b\dddot{M}o$.	White-red, generally yellow.	Octahedral.	Resinous.	3.	6.9	1.5	II.
Decomposed by sulphuric acid, leaving a lemon-yellow residue. The acid is not colored.	With salt of phosphorus gives in O.F. a colorless glass, which in R.F. becomes blue on cooling.	Stolzite.	$\dot{P}b\dddot{W}$.	Brown, yellow to red.		Resinous.	3.	7.9	2.	II.

(Page 74)

MINERALS WITHOUT METALLIC LUSTRE.

B. Fusible from 1—5, and non-volatile.

I. *Yield a metal or a magnetic mass with soda.*

Division 2 (concluded).

Division 3 (in part).

B. Fusible from 1—5, and not volatile, or only partially volatile.

I. B. B. with soda on charcoal, give a metallic globule or a magnetic mass.

DIVISION 2.—(*Continued.*)

B. B. with soda on charcoal give a globule of lead.

General Characters.	Specific Characters.	Species.	Composition.	Color.	Cleavage or Fracture.	Lustre.	Hardness.	Sp. Gr.	Fusibility.	Crystallization.
B. B. with borax in R. F. give an emerald-green bead. Alcohol added to the concentrated hydrochloric solution gives an emerald-green color.	The color is not changed in O. F.; the others become yellow or colorless.	Vauquelinite.	$\dot{Cu}^3\dddot{Cr}^2 + 2\dot{Pb}^3\dddot{Cr}^2$.	Blackish to olive-green.		Adamantine resinous.	2.5—3.	5.6	Easily.	V.
	The nitric solution gives a precipitate or turbidity with nitrate of silver.	Vanadinite.	$\dot{Pb}^3VO^5 + \frac{1}{3}PbCl$.	Brown or yellowish.		Resinous.	2.75—3.	6.8	Easily.	III.
	Does not give the above reactions. B. B. on charcoal with soda gives a zinc coating.	Dechenite (variety Eusynchite).	$(\dot{Pb},\dot{Zn})VO^5$.	Yellowish-red or ochre-yellow.		Dull.	3.5	5.6	Easily.	Stalac.
	Much like vauquelinite. The nitric solution gives with molybdate of ammonia a yellow precipitate (phosphoric acid).	Laxmannite (Phosphochromite).	$\dot{Pb},\dot{Cu},\dddot{Cr},\overset{\cdot\cdot\cdot\cdot\cdot}{P}$.	Pistachio to olive-green.		Vitreous.	3.	5.77.	Easily.	V.
	Same as vanadinite: differs in crystalline form.	Descloizite.	$\dot{Pb}^2VO^5$.	Olive-brown to black.			3.5	5.8	Easily.	IV.
☞ Compare *Plumbogummite*, Div. 1, p. 89.										

DIVISION 3.

Moistened with hydrochloric acid give a beautiful blue color to the blowpipe flame, and with nitric acid give a solution which on addition of an excess of ammonia becomes violet-blue.

a. B. B. on charcoal evolve a strong arsenical odor; most of them alone on charcoal give a white brittle globule of arsenide of copper.

General Characters.	Specific Characters.	Species.	Composition.	Color.	Cleavage or Fracture.	Lustre.	Hardness.	Sp. Gr.	Fusibility.	Crystallization.
Fuses to a black magnetic slag.	Decrepitates and yields much water in the closed tube.	Chenevixite.	$(\bar{Fe},\dot{Cu}^3)^2\overset{\cdot\cdot\cdot\cdot\cdot}{As} + 3\dot{H}$.	Dark-green.			4.5	3.93 (?)	Easily.	Massive.
The nitric solution gives with sulphuric acid a precipitate of sulphate of lead.	In the closed tube gives off water and becomes black.	Bayldonite.	$(\dot{Pb},Cu)^4\overset{\cdot\cdot\cdot\cdot\cdot}{As} + 2\dot{H}$.	Grass to blackish-green.			4.5	5.35	Easily.	Massive.
B. B. fused in the forceps crystallize on cooling in radiated masses, covered with prismatic crystals.	In the matrass gives little water (4 per cent.).	OLIVENITE.	$\dot{Cu}^3(\overset{\cdot\cdot\cdot\cdot\cdot}{As},\overset{\cdot\cdot\cdot\cdot\cdot}{P}) + \dot{Cu}\dot{H}$.	Olive-, leek-, blackish-green.	Sometimes fibrous.	Adamantine to vitreous.	3.	4.1—4.4	2.	IV.
	In the matrass gives more water (7 per cent.).	Clinoclasite.	$\dot{Cu}^3\overset{\cdot\cdot\cdot\cdot\cdot}{As} + 3\dot{Cu}\dot{H}$.	Dark bluish-green.	Basal.	Pearly to vitreous.	2.5—3	4.19—4.36	2.	V.
B. B. in matrass decrepitate strongly and give much water.	Soluble in ammonia, with separation of carbonate of lime mechanically mixed with the mineral.	Tyrolite (Copper froth).	$\dot{Cu}^3\overset{\cdot\cdot\cdot\cdot\cdot}{As} + 2\dot{Cu}\dot{H} + 7\dot{H}$.	Apple-verdigris green.	Basal.		1.—2.	3.06	Easily.	IV.
	Soluble in ammonia without residue.	Chalcophyllite.	$\dot{Cu}^3\overset{\cdot\cdot\cdot\cdot\cdot}{As} + 5\dot{Cu}\dot{H} + 7\dot{H}$.	Emerald-grass green.	Basal.	Pearly.	2.	2.5	Easily.	III.
	The fused assay has an alkaline reaction.	Conichalcite.	$\dot{Cu},\dot{Ca},\overset{\cdot\cdot\cdot\cdot\cdot}{P},\overset{\cdot\cdot\cdot\cdot\cdot}{As},VO^5,\dot{H}$.	Pistachio to emerald-green.			4.5	4.12	Easily.	Massive.
Does not decrepitate in matrass; assumes a smalt-blue color when gently heated.	Loses 22 per cent. on ignition; soluble in ammonia with the separation of white flocks.	Liroconite.	$\dot{Cu},\ddot{\bar{Al}},\overset{\cdot\cdot\cdot\cdot\cdot}{As},\overset{\cdot\cdot\cdot\cdot\cdot}{P},\dot{H}$.	Sky-blue to green.		Vitreous.	2—2.5	2.9	Easily.	V.
Give none of the above reactions.	Loses 19 per cent. on ignition.	Euchroite.	$Cu^4\overset{\cdot\cdot\cdot\cdot\cdot}{As} + Cu\dot{H} + 6\dot{H}$.	Leek to emerald-green.	Prismatic.	Vitreous.	3.5—4	3.39	2.	IV.
	Loses only 5 per cent. on ignition.	Erinite.	$\dot{Cu}^3\overset{\cdot\cdot\cdot\cdot\cdot}{As} + 2\dot{Cu}\dot{H}$.	Grass to emerald-green.		Dull.	4.5	4.04		Amorph.
	Loses 13 per cent. on ignition.	Cornwallite.	$\dot{Cu}^3\overset{\cdot\cdot\cdot\cdot\cdot}{As} + 2\dot{Cu}\dot{H} + 3\dot{H}$.	Emerald to verdigris-green.	Amorphous.		4.5	4.16		Amorph.

(Page 75)

MINERALS WITHOUT METALLIC LUSTRE.

B. Fusible from 1—5, and non-volatile.

I. *Yield a metal or a magnetic mass with soda.*

DIVISION 3 (concluded).

B.—Fusible from 1—5, and not volatile, or only partially volatile.

I, *B. B. with soda on charcoal give a metallic globule or a magnetic mass.*

DIVISION 3.—(*Continued.*)

Moistened with hydrochloric acid give B. B. a beautiful blue color to the flame, and with nitric acid give a solution which on addition of an excess of ammonia becomes violet-blue.

b) B. B. emit no arsenical odor; most of them on charcoal yield a malleable copper-bead.

General Characters.	Specific Characters.	Species.	Composition.	Color.	Cleavage or Fracture.	Lustre.	Hardness.	Sp. Gr.	Fusibility.	Crystallization.
Color the flame blue without previous moistening with HCl. The nitric solution yields a precipitate of chloride of silver with nitrate of silver.	Gives much water in closed tube, and forms a gray sublimate.	**Atacamite.**	$3\dot{Cu}\dot{H} + Cu, Cl, \dot{H}$.	Leek-, black-, olive-, emerald-green.	Prismatic.	Vitreous.	3.5	4.25	Fusible.	IV.
	Nearly the same reactions.	Tallingite.	$4\dot{Cu}\dot{H} + Cu, Cl, \dot{H}$.	Blue to green.			3.	3.5 (?)	Fusible.	Massiv[e]
	Sulphuric acid gives a precipitate of sulphate of lead.	Percylite.	$Pb, Cu, Cl, O, \dot{H}$.	Sky-blue.			2.5			I.
	Yields no water in the closed tube.	Nantokite.	Cu_2Cl.	White.						
	☞ Compare *Atlasite*, below.									
B. B. with soda give a sulphuret which on moistening blackens silver.	Readily soluble in water; the others are not.	**Chalcanthite** (Blue vitriol).	$\dot{Cu}\dddot{S} + 5\dot{H}$.	Sky-blue.			2.5	2.21	Easily.	VI.
	Insoluble in water. The nitric solution gives a white precipitate with nitrate of baryta. In the open tube gives no odor of sulphurous acid.	Brochantite.	$\dot{Cu}\dddot{S} + 2\frac{1}{2}\dot{Cu}\dot{H}$.	Emerald to blackish-green.	Prismatic.		3.5—4	3.4—3.9	Easily.	IV.
	Heated in O. F. burns and emits the odor of sulphurous acid.	**Covellite.**	CuS.	Indigo-blue-black.	Basal.		1.5—2.	4.6		III.
	Resembles Brochantite, and has 16 per cent. of water. Brochantite has but 12.	Langite.	$\dot{Cu}\dddot{S} + 3\dot{Cu}\dot{H} + \dot{H}$.	Greenish-blue.			2.5—3	3.5		IV.
Easily and quietly soluble in acids.	The concentrated HCl solution gives a white precipitate of subchloride of copper on addition of water.	**Cuprite** (red copper ore).	$\dot{\bar{Cu}}$.	Cochineal-red.	Octahedral.	Earthy, adamantine.	3.5—4.	6.	Easily.	I.
	The hydrochloric solution gives no precipitate with water (sometimes effervesces with acids on account of impurities).	**Melaconite** (black copper ore).	$\dot{Cu}$.	Black to brownish-black.		Metallic to earthy.	3.	5.95	Difficultly.	IV.
Dissolve in nitric acid with effervescence giving off carbonic acid.	Gives much water in closed tube. Color green.	**Malachite.**	$\dot{Cu}\ddot{C} + \dot{Cu}\dot{H}$.	Grass to emerald-green.	Fibrous.	Silky to earthy	3.5—4.	3.8	2.	V.
	As above. Color blue.	**Azurite.**	$2\dot{Cu}\ddot{C} + \dot{Cu}\dot{H}$.	Blue.		Vitreous.	4.	3.7	2.	V.
	Gives with soda a zinc-coating on charcoal.	Aurichalcite.	$\dot{Cu}, \dot{Zn}, \ddot{C}, \dot{H}$.	Bluish-green.		Pearly.	2.		Difficultly.	Acicul[ar]
	The nitric solution gives with nitrate of silver a precipitate of chloride of silver.	Atlasite.	$\dot{Cu}, \ddot{C}, \dot{H}, Cl$.	Celandine to emerald-green		Vitreous-silky	3.—4.	3.85		
Easily and quietly soluble in nitric; the solutions give with molybdate of ammonia a yellow precipitate of phospho-molybdate of ammonia.	Loses 7 per cent. of water on ignition.	Libethenite.	$\dot{Cu}^3\overset{\cdot\cdot\cdot\cdot\cdot}{P} + \dot{Cu}\dot{H}$.	Dark olive-green.		Resinous.	4.	3.7	2.	IV.
	Loses 14 per cent. of water on ignition.	PSEUDOMALACHITE.	$\dot{Cu}^3\overset{\cdot\cdot\cdot\cdot\cdot}{P} + 2\dot{Cu}\dot{H} + \dot{H}$.	Dark-green.		Vitreous.	4.5—5.	4.2	2.	IV.
	Loses 10 per cent. of water on ignition.	Tagilite.	$\dot{Cu}_3\overset{\cdot\cdot\cdot\cdot\cdot}{P} + \dot{Cu}\dot{H} + 2\dot{H}$.	Verdigris to emerald-green		Vitreous.	3.—4.	4.07		V.
The nitric solution has a yellowish-green color, and gives, with an excess of ammonia, a bluish-green precipitate, and a blue solution.	The solution gives, when warmed with molybdate of ammonia, a yellow precipitate. Perfect basal cleavage.	Torbernite.	$\ddot{\bar{U}}_2\overset{\cdot\cdot\cdot\cdot\cdot}{P} + \dot{Cu}\dot{H} + 7\dot{H}$.	Grass-leek-apple to emerald-green.	Micaceous.	Pearly.	2.—2.5	3.5	2.5	II.
The powder mixed with soda and the mass fused, then boiled with water, the solution obtained acidified with HCl and then boiled down, the fluid becomes emerald-green, and when diluted with water, sky-blue.		Volborthite.	$\dot{Cu}, VO^3, \dot{H}$.	Olive-green to lemon-yellow.	Basal.	Pearly.	3.—3.5	3.5	Easily.	III.

(Page 76)

MINERALS WITHOUT METALLIC LUSTRE.

B. Fusible from 1—5, and non-volatile.

I. *Yield a metal or a magnetic mass with soda.*

DIVISION 4.

DIVISION 5 (in part).

B.—Fusible from 1—5, and not volatile, or only partially volatile.

I. *B. B. with soda on charcoal give a metallic globule or a magnetic mass.*

Division	General Characters.	Specific Characters.	Species.	Composition.	Color.	Cleavage or Fracture.	Lustre.	Hardness.	Sp. Gr.	Fusibility.	Crystallization.
DIVISION 4. *B. B. impart a beautiful sapphire-blue color to a borax bead.*	B. B. in matrass yields much water and becomes smalt-blue.	In HCl soluble to a rose-red solution.	ERYTHRITE (cobalt-bloom).	$\dot{Co}^3\dddot{As}+8\dot{H}$.	Crimson, peach-red.	Prismatic.	Pearly.	1.5–2.5	2.94	2.	V.
	Fuses with difficulty, colors the flame green.	Soluble in hydrochloric acid, with evolution of chlorine.	Heterogenite.	$O,\dot{Co},\dot{Cu},\ddot{Fe},\ddot{Bi},\ddot{Al},\dot{Ca}$.	Black—red-brown.			3.		Difficultly.	Amorph.
	The HCl and nitric solutions have a green color.	Ammonia gives a green precipitate, which is dissolved in an excess to a sapphire-blue solution.	Annabergite (always contains a little cobalt).	$Ni^3\dddot{As}+8H$.	Apple-green.		Earthy.	Soft.		Easily.	V.
DIVISION 5. *B. B. fused on charcoal in the R. F. give a black or gray magnetic mass, but do not give the reactions of the preceding divisions.* a) *During fusion evolve a strong arsenical odor.*	Fuse easily B. B. to magnetic beads. The color of the pulverized minerals are quickly changed to reddish-brown by a solution of caustic potash.	Amorphous.	Pitticite.	$\ddot{Fe},\dddot{As},\dddot{S},\dot{H}$.	Yellow to reddish-brown.			2.—3.	2.2—2.5		
		Crystallization isometric.	Pharmacosiderite.	$3\ddot{Fe}\dddot{As}+\ddot{Fe}\dot{H}^3+12\dot{H}$.	Green-red-brown, yellow.	Cubic.		2.5	3.	Easily.	I.
		Crystallization orthorhombic.	SCORODITE.	$\ddot{Fe}\dddot{As}+4\dot{H}$.	Leek-green to brown.			3.5—4.	3.2	Easily.	IV.
	Fibrous, with silky lustre.	Color brownish-yellow—9 p. c. water.	Arsenioside-rite.	$\dot{Ca},\ddot{Fe},\dddot{As},\dot{H}$.	Brownish-yellow.		Silky.	1.—2.	3.8	Easily.	
	Mostly soluble in water.	With excess of ammonia gives a blue solution. Sometimes contains arsenic.	Morenosite.	$\dot{Ni}\dddot{S}+7\dot{H}$.	Apple-green to bluish-green.		Vitreous.	2.	2.		
b) *Soluble in HCl without leaving a perceptible residue, and without gelatinizing.*	Gives much water (13 p. c.) in the closed tube, and colors the borax-bead blue.	Soluble in strong HCl with evolution of chlorine. Soluble in phosphoric acid to a violet fluid.	Rabdionite.	$\dot{Cu},\ddot{Mn},\ddot{Fe},\dot{Co},\dot{H}$.	Black.			Soft.	2.8	3.	
	Gives antimonial fumes on charcoal.	Gives water in the closed tube.	Stibioferrite.	$\ddot{Fe},SbO^5,\dot{H}$.	Yellow.		Resinous.	4.	3.52		IV.
	B. B. swell up and in the R. F. fuse perfectly to a magnetic slag. The solutions give with chloride of barium a heavy precipitate of sulphate of baryta, and with ammonia a greenish precipitate, which in the air changes to brownish-red; all except Pettkoite, give much water in the closed tube.	Gives little or no water in the closed tube.	Pettkoite.	$\dot{Fe},\ddot{Fe},\dddot{S}$.	Black.			2.5		Fuses.	
		Perfectly soluble in water.	MELANTERITE (copperas)	$\dot{Fe}\dddot{S}+7\dot{H}$.	Green.			2.	1.8		V.
		Soluble in water, leaving a yellow residue.	Botryogen.	$\dot{Fe},\ddot{Fe},\dddot{S},\dot{H}$.	Ochre-yellow to red.			2.5	2.04		V.
		Same reactions as Botryogen. Their powders are immediately turned brownish-red by solution of potassa.	Roemerite.	$\dot{R}\dddot{S}+\ddot{Fe}\dddot{S}^3+12\dot{H}$.	Yellowish-brown.			2.75	2.17		V.
			COQUIMBITE.	$\ddot{Fe}\dddot{S}^3+9\dot{H}$.	White to yellow.			2.5	2.		III.
			Jarosite.	$(\dot{K},\dot{Na})\dddot{S}+4\ddot{Fe}\dddot{S}+9\dot{H}$.	Ochre-yellow.			3.	3.2		III.
			Fibroferrite.	$\ddot{Fe}^2\dddot{S}^5+27\dot{H}$.	White to pale yellow.			1.5	1.84		Fib.
		Insoluble in water; powders yellow.	COPIAPITE.	$\ddot{Fe}^2\dddot{S}^5+18\dot{H}$.	Sulphur-yellow.		Pearly.	1.5	2.14		III.
			Raimondite.	$\ddot{Fe}^2\dddot{S}^3+7\dot{H}$.	Honey- to ochre-yellow.		Pearly.	3.	3.19		III.
			Carphosiderite.	$\ddot{Fe},\dddot{S},\dot{H}$.	Straw-yellow.		Resinous.	4.	2.5		Mass.
		Characterized by its color and octahedral crystallization.	Voltaite.	$\dot{Fe}\dddot{S}+\ddot{Fe}\dddot{S}^3+24\dot{H}$.	Black dark-green.		Resinous.				I.
	Soluble in heated HCl with effervescence.	Difficultly fusible; becomes by heating black and magnetic. ☞ Compare *Mesitite*, Div. 4, page 92.	Siderite (spathic-iron).	$\dot{Fe}\ddot{C}$.	Ash-gray to brownish-red.	Rhombohedral.	Pearly-vitreous.	4.	3.6—3.9	4.5	III.

(Page 77)

MINERALS WITHOUT METALLIC LUSTRE.

B. Fusible from 1—5, and non-volatile.

I. *Yield a metal or a magnetic mass with soda.*

DIVISION 5 (continued).

B. Fusible from 1—5, and not volatile, or only partially volatile.

I. *B. B. with soda on charcoal give a metallic globule or a magnetic mass.*

DIVISION 5.—(*Continued.*)

B. B. fused on charcoal in the R. F. give a black or gray magnetic mass but do not give the reactions of the preceding divisions.

	General Characters.	Specific Characters.	Species.	Composition.	Color.	Cleavage or Fracture.	Lustre.	Hardness.	Sp. Gr.	Fusibility.	Crystallization.
b) (*Continued.*) Soluble in HCl without leaving a perceptible residue and without gelatinizing.	The nitric solution gives with molybdate of ammonia a yellow precipitate. Moistened with sulphuric acid color the flame bluish-green (phosphoric acid).	Gives water in the closed tube.	Hureaulite.	$(\dot{M}n,\dot{F}e)^5\bar{\ddot{P}}^2+5\dot{H}$.	Orange to reddish-yellow.		Vitreous.	5.	3.2	Easily.	V.
		Gives the reaction for fluorine when fused in the closed tube with bisulphate of potassa.	TRIPLITE.	$\dot{R}^3\bar{\ddot{P}}+RFl.(\dot{R}=\dot{F}e,\dot{M}n)$	Brownish-black.	Cleavable in three directions.	Resinous.	5.	3.6	1.5	IV.
	With borax in O.F. dissolve to an amethystine glass (manganese).	Distinguished from triplite by its color.	Sarcopside.	$\dot{M}n,\dot{F}e,\bar{F}e,Fl,\bar{\ddot{P}}$.	Flesh-red to lavender-blue.		Silky.	4.	3.7	1.5	V. (?)
	Gives the above phosphoric acid reaction with molybdate of ammonia. The blowpipe flame is colored purple-red in streaks (lithia).	With borax gives the manganese reaction, but not so plainly as the minerals of the preceding section.	TRIPHYLITE.	$(\dot{F}e,\dot{M}n,\dot{L}i)^3\bar{\ddot{P}}$.	Greenish-gray, bluish, etc.	Perfect.	Resinous.	5.	3.54	1.5	IV.
	Gives the above phosphoric acid reaction with molybdate of ammonia. The solution with chloride of barium yields a heavy precipitate of sulphate of baryta.		Diadochite.	$\bar{F}e^3\bar{\ddot{P}}^2+2\bar{F}e\dddot{S}^2+32\dot{H}$.	Red, yellow, brown.	Brittle.	Resinous.	3.	2.03	Easily.	Amorphous
	Give the above phosphoric acid reaction with molybdate of ammonia. Moistened with sulphuric acid the flame is colored pale-green. Easily fusible. The borax-glass shows only the reactions for iron.	Loses 28 per cent. of water on ignition.	**Vivianite.**	$\dot{F}e^3\bar{\ddot{P}}+8\dot{H}$.	Different shades of blue.	Perfect.	Pearly-vitreous.	1.5—2.	2.6	1.5	V.
		Loses 10 per cent. on ignition.	DUFRENITE.	$\bar{F}e^2\bar{\ddot{P}}+3\dot{H}$.	Dark leek-green.	Radiated.	Silky.	3.5—4.	3.3	Easily.	IV.
		Loses 19 per cent. on ignition.	Borickite.	$(\bar{F}e,\dot{C}a^3)^5\bar{\ddot{P}}^2+15\dot{H}$.	Reddish-brown.		Waxy.	3.5	2.7	Easily.	Mass.
		Loses 33 per cent. on ignition.	Cacoxenite.	$\bar{F}e^2\bar{\ddot{P}}+12\dot{H}$ (with Fl).	Brownish yellow.	Fibrous, radiated.	Silky.	3—4.	3.38		
		☞ Compare *Beraunite.*	Beraunite.	$\bar{F}e,\bar{\ddot{P}},\dot{H}$.	Hyacinth-red, reddish-brown.	Foliated.	Metallic, pearly.	2.	2.87	Easily.	
	Streak cherry-red.	Generally fusible above 5.	**Hematite** (Specular-iron).	$\bar{F}e$.	Red to reddish-black.	Foliated, fibrous, compact.	Dull to brilliant metallic.	6.—6.5	4.5	5.	III.
c) Soluble in HCl, forming a jelly, or with the separation of silica.	In a matrass yields water, and with HCl forms a perfect jelly.	Fuses with slight puffing to a black glass.	Cronstedite.	$\dot{F}e,\dot{M}n,\dot{M}g,\bar{F}e,\ddot{S}i,\dot{H}$.	Raven-black.	Basal.	Vitreous.	3.5	3.35	Easily.	III.
	In the matrass yield water, and are decomposed by HCl without gelatinizing.	Radiated, sometimes foliated.	STILPNOMELANE (Chalcodite).	$\dot{F}e,\bar{F}e,\bar{A}l,\dot{M}g,\ddot{S}i,\dot{H}$.	Bronze-yellow to greenish-gray.	Radiated, compact.	Pearly to submetallic.	3.	2.76	Easily.	
		Micaceous.	Voigtite.	$\bar{A}l,\bar{F}e,\dot{F}e,\dot{M}g,\ddot{S}i,\dot{H}$.	Leek-green, yellow.	Micaceous.	Pearly.	2.5	2.91	Easily.	
		Massive.	Ekmannite.	$\bar{F}e,\dot{F}e,\dot{M}n,\dot{M}g,\ddot{S}i,\dot{H}$.	Leek-green to black.		Greasy.	2.5		Easily.	
		Massive.	Euralite.	$\bar{A}l,\bar{F}e,\dot{F}e,\dot{M}g,\ddot{S}i,\dot{H}$	Dark-green to black.			2.5	2.62	Easily.	
		Sometimes gelatinizes, sometimes does not.	Palagonite.	$\bar{A}l,\bar{F}e,\dot{M}g,\dot{C}a,\dot{N}a,\dot{K},\dot{H},\ddot{S}i$.	Yellow-red, black.		Vitreous, greasy.	4—5.	1.8—2.7	Easily.	

(Page 78)

MINERALS WITHOUT METALLIC LUSTRE.

B. Fusible from 1—5, and non-volatile.

I. *Yield a metal or a magnetic mass with soda.*

DIVISION 5 (continued).

B. Fusible from 1—5, and not volatile, or only partially volatile.

I. *B. B. with soda on charcoal give a metallic globule or a magnetic mass.*

DIVISION 5.—(*Continued.*)

B. B. fused on charcoal in the R. F. give a black or gray magnetic mass, but do not give the reactions of the preceding divisions.

c) (*Continued.*) Soluble in HCl, forming a jelly, or with the separation of silica.

General Characters.	Specific Characters.	Species.	Composition.	Color.	Cleavage or Fracture.	Lustre.	Hardness.	Sp. Gr.	Fusibility.	Crystallization.
Give little or no water in the closed tube; with HCl they gelatinize. Not cleavable.	Intumesces slightly; decrepitates slightly; fuses quietly to a black magnetic bead.	ILVAITE.	$(\frac{1}{3}\dot{R}^3+\frac{2}{3}\bar{F}e)^2\ddot{S}i^3$. $\dot{R}=\dot{F}e,\dot{C}a$.	Gray to iron-black.			5.5—6.	4.	2.5	IV.
	Swells much and fuses easily to a bulky brown or black glass. After separation of SiO_2 from the HCl solution, ammonia gives a precipitate which dissolve in oxalic acid, leaving a white residue, which ignited, treated with dilute HCl to separate carbonate of lime, and again ignited, gives a brick-red mass (Ce).	ALLANITE.	$\dot{C}a,\dot{C}e,\dot{F}e,\bar{A}l,\bar{F}e,\ddot{S}i$.	Pitch-brown to black.		Pitchy to resinous.	5.5—6.	3.—4.2	5.5	IV.
Crystalline and cleavable; gelatinize perfectly.	Magnetic.	FAYALITE.	$\dot{F}e^2\ddot{S}i$.	Dark-green brown to black.	Two cleavages at 90°.	Resinous.	6.5	4.	Easily.	IV.
	Decomposed by phosphoric acid the jelly immediately becomes violet when treated with nitric acid.	HORTONOLITE.	$(\dot{F}e,\dot{M}g,\dot{M}n)^2\ddot{S}i$.	Yellow to dark-yellow green.	Three cleavages.	Resinous.	6.5	3.91	4	IV.
	Same reaction.	Knebelite.	$(\dot{F}e,\dot{M}n)^2\ddot{S}i$.	Gray, red, brown to black.			6.5	4.12	Easily.	IV.
	Gives with soda a sublimate of oxide of zinc.	Roepperite.	$(\dot{F}e,\dot{M}n,\dot{Z}n,\dot{M}g)^2\ddot{S}i$.	Dark-green to black.	Rectangular.	Vitreous.	6.	4.	Diff.	IV.
Decomposed with separation of silica without gelatinizing. $F=2$.	Mixed with salt of phosphorus and oxide of copper tinges the flame green (chlorine).	Pyrosmalite.	$\dot{M}n,\dot{F}e,\ddot{S}i,Cl,\dot{H}$.	Brown to blackish-green.	Basal.	Pearly.	4.5	3.16	2.5	III.
	The HCl solution, boiled with tin, is colored violet (titanic acid).	Astrophyllite.	$\bar{A}l,\bar{F}e,\dot{M}n,\dot{M}g,\dot{F}e,\dot{N}a,\dot{K},\ddot{T}i,\ddot{S}i$.	Bronze-yellow.	Micaceous.	Pearly.	3	3.32	Easily.	IV.
Decomposed easily by HCl, leaving a residue of silica in the form of scaly flakes.	Occurs in granular scaly masses.	LEPIDOMELANE.	$(\frac{1}{4}\dot{R}^3+\frac{3}{4}\bar{R})^2\ddot{S}i^3$ $\dot{R},\bar{R}=\dot{K},\dot{M}g,\bar{A}l,\bar{F}e$.	Dark-green to black.	Micaceous.	Vitreous.	3.	3.	Easily.	III.?
In some varieties forms an imperfect jelly with HCl.	Not cleavable, easily fusible.	ALLOCHROITE (iron lime garnet).	$\dot{C}a^3\ddot{S}i+\bar{F}e^2\ddot{S}i^3$.	Green-yellow to black.		Greasy.	7.	3.7—4.	3.	I.
Fuse with difficulty; after long heating become magnetic. Decomposed by HCl without forming a jelly. Give water in matrass.	Amorphous.	Gillingite.	$\bar{F}e,\dot{M}n,\dot{F}e,\dot{M}g,\ddot{S}i,\dot{H}$.	Brownish-black.		Dull.	3.	3.04		Amorphous.
	Fibrous.	Xylotile.	$\bar{F}e,\dot{M}g,\dot{H},\ddot{S}i$.	Wood-brown.	Fibrous.	Silky.		2.4		
	☞ Compare *Limonite*, Div. 4, p. 92.									

d) Only slightly acted upon by hydrochloric acid.

General Characters.	Specific Characters.	Species.	Composition.	Color.	Cleavage or Fracture.	Lustre.	Hardness.	Sp. Gr.	Fusibility.	Crystallization.
Tinges the flame purple-red (lithia).	Very perfectly cleavable in one direction (micaceous).	**Lepidolite.**	$\bar{A}l,\bar{F}e,\dot{K},\dot{L}i,\ddot{S}i,Fl$.	Rose-red, gray-white.	Micaceous.	Vitreous.	2.5—3.	2.8—3.	2.—2.5	IV.
Imparts a violet color to the borax bead.	Some specimens contain enough iron to become magnetic.	**Rhodonite.**	$\dot{M}n\ddot{S}i$.	Rose-red, brownish-red.	Perfect.	Vitreous.	5.5—6.5	3.61	2.5	VI.
Decomposed by aqua-regia with separation of a yellow powder (tungstic acid).	Boiled with phosphoric acid give a blue syrup; with soda and nitre on platinum foil give the bluish-green manganese reaction.	WOLFRAM.	$(\dot{F}e,\dot{M}n)\dddot{W}$.	Black.	Prismatic.	Sub-metallic.	5.—5.5	7.1—7.5.	2.5—3	V.
	Same reactions.	Megabasite.	$(\dot{M}n,\dot{F}e)\dddot{W}$.	Brown.	Prismatic.	Sub-metallic.	3.5—4.	6.4—6.9	Easily.	V.
	Same reactions, contains no iron.	Hübnerite.	$\dot{M}n\dddot{W}$.	Brown-red.	Prismatic.	Adamantine.	4.5	7.1	Easily.	V.
Fuses quietly at 3. Gelatinizes after fusion.	Not easily cleavable.	**Almandine-Garnet.**	$(\frac{1}{2}\dot{F}e^3+\frac{1}{2}\bar{A}l)^2\ddot{S}i^3$.	Red or brownish-red.		Vitreous.	7.—7.5.	3.7—4.	3.	I.

(Page 79)

MINERALS WITHOUT METALLIC LUSTRE.

B. Fusible from 1—5, and non-volatile.

I. *Yield a metal or a magnetic mass with soda.*

DIVISION 5 (concluded).

DIVISION 6.

B. Fusible from 1—5, and not volatile or only partially volatile.

I. B. B. with soda on charcoal give a metallic globule or a magnetic mass.

Division 5.—(*Continued.*) *B. B. fused on charcoal in the R. F. give a black or gray magnetic mass, but do not give the reactions of the preceding divisions.*

d. (*Continued.*) Only slightly acted upon by hydrochloric acid.

General Characters.	Specific Characters.	Species.	Composition.	Color.	Cleavage or Fracture.	Lustre.	Hardness.	Sp. Gr.	Fusibility.	Crystallization.
Fuse quietly to a black shining glass.	Fused with soda, and then dissolved in HCl and treated with ammonia to separate iron, the filtrate gives with oxalate of ammonia a heavy precipitate (lime).	Babingtonite.	$3\dot{R}^3\ddot{Si}^2 + \overline{Fe}\ddot{Si}^3$. $\dot{R} = \dot{Ca}, \dot{Fe}, \dot{Mn}$.	Dark green-black.		Splendent.	5—6.	3.36	2.5	VI.
	Gives no lime when treated as above.	Acmite.	$(\dot{Fe}, \dot{Na})^3\ddot{Si}^2 + 2\overline{Fe}\ddot{Si}^3$.	Red-brown to blackish-green.	Cleavable at angle of 93°.	Vitreous.	6.	3.4	2.	V.
	☞ Compare *Augite*, Div. 6, p. 88.									
Easily fusible (1.7—2) with strong intumescence and escape of gas bubbles to a black glass.	Gives water in the closed tube.	Crocidolite.	$\dot{Fe}, \dot{Mg}, \dot{Na}, \ddot{Si}, \dot{H}$.	Green to lavender-blue.	Fibrous.	Silky.	4.	3.2	Easily.	
	Yields no water in a matrass.	ARFVEDSONITE.	$\overline{Fe}, \dot{Fe}, \dot{Mn}, \dot{Na}, \ddot{Si}$.	Black.	Perfect at an angle 123°.	Vitreous.	6	3.4	2.	V.
Fuses at 3 without swelling. Gives water in matrass.	Occurs in loosely granular masses, or filling cavities in rocks.	**Glauconite** (Green earth).	$\overline{Fe}, \overline{Al}, \dot{Fe}, \dot{Mg}, \dot{K}, \ddot{Si}, \dot{H}$.	Deep-olive to sea-green.	Scaly.	Dull.	Soft.	1.—2.	2.2—2.4	
☞ Compare *Amphibole* Div. 6, p. 88, *Tourmaline*, Div. 6, p. 87. Compare *Lepidomelane*, Subdivision *c*, p. 78.										

Division 6. *Not belonging to the foregoing divisions.*

General Characters.	Specific Characters.	Species.	Composition.	Color.	Cleavage or Fracture.	Lustre.	Hardness.	Sp. Gr.	Fusibility.	Crystallization.
Easily soluble in HCl, yielding a colorless solution, which becomes blue on agitation with tin-foil.	B. B. on charcoal fuses, fumes, and is absorbed. In R. F. with salt of phosphorus gives a bead which when cold is beautifully green.	Molybdite.	$\dddot{Mo}$.	Sulphur-orange, yellow.		Silky, earthy.	1.—2.	4.5	1.	IV.
Fused with sulphur and iodide of potassium on charcoal give a fine red sublimate on the coal (bismuth). ☞ Compare *Walpurgite*, p. 82.	Gelatinizes perfectly with HCl.	Eulytite.	$\dddot{Bi}^2\ddot{Si}^3$.	Dark hair-brown to yellow.		Resinous.	4.5	6.1	Easily.	I.
	Does not gelatinize; dissolves with effervescence.	Bismutite.	$\dddot{Bi}, \ddot{C}, \dot{H}$.	White to yellow.		Dull.	4.—4.5	6.8—7.6	Easily.	Amorph.
	With salt of phosphorus gives a green bead in R. F.	Pucherite.	$\dddot{Bi}, VO^4$.	Reddish-brown.	Basal.	Vitreous adamantine.	4.	5.91	Easily.	IV.
☞ Compare *Samarskite*, Div. 6, p. 69; *Allanite* and *Lepidomelane*, Div. 5, p. 78.										

(Page 80)

MINERALS WITHOUT METALLIC LUSTRE.

B. Fusible from 1—5, and non-volatile.

II. *Yield no metal or magnetic mass with soda.*

DIVISION 1 (in part).

B.—Fusible from 1—5, and non-volatile or only partially volatile.

II. *B. B. with soda on charcoal give no metallic globule or magnetic mass.*

DIVISION 1.

B. B. after fusion and continued heating on charcoal or in the forceps have an alkaline reaction, and change the color of moistened turmeric paper to red-brown.

a) Easily and completely soluble in water.

General Characters.	Specific Characters.	Species.	Composition.	Color.	Cleavage or Fracture.	Lustre.	Hardness.	Sp. Gr.	Fusibility.	Crystallization.
B. B. on charcoal deflagrate strongly.	Fused on platinum wire colors the flame violet. In the solution bichloride of platinum produces a yellow crystalline precipitate.	Nitre.	$\dot{K}\dddot{N}$.	White.		Vitreous.	2.	1.93	Easily.	IV.
	Fused on platinum wire colors the flame strongly yellow. Bichloride of platinum produces no precipitate.	SODA NITRE.	$\dot{N}a\dddot{N}$.	White.		Vitreous.	1.5—2	2.2	Easily.	III.
In a matrass yield much water; the aqueous solutions react alkaline, and effervesce on addition of an acid.	Rapidly effloresces on exposure to the air and changes to thermonatrite.	Natron.	$\dot{N}a\ddot{C}+10\dot{H}$.	Gray-white.		Earthy.	1.5	1.4	Easily.	V.
	Effloresces.	Thermonatrite.	$\dot{N}a\ddot{C}+\dot{H}$.	Gray-white.			1.5	1.5—1.6	Easily.	IV.
	Does not alter on exposure.	TRONA.	$\dot{N}a^2\ddot{C}^3+4\dot{H}$.	Gray-white.			2.5—3.	2.11	Easily.	V.
The aqueous solution does not react alkaline; does not effervesce with acids. Chloride of barium gives an abundant white precipitate of sulphate of baryta, which is insoluble in acids.	The solution gives a white precipitate with soda. Ignited and treated with cobalt solution yields a flesh-red mass (50 per cent. water).	EPSOMITE (epsom salt).	$\dot{M}g\dddot{S}+7\dot{H}$.	Colorless-white.		Vitreous.	2.25	1.7	Easily.	IV.
	With soda yields a white precipitate. Ignited and treated with cobalt solution yields a blue mass.	KALINITE (potash alum).	$\dot{K}\dddot{S}+\overline{A}l\dddot{S}^3+24\dot{H}$.	White.		Vitreous.	2.25	1.75	Easily.	I.
	In the concentrated solution bichloride of platinum yields a yellow precipitate.	Aphthitalite.	$\dot{K}\dddot{S}$.	White.		Vitreous.	3.	1.73	Easily.	IV.
	Not affected by the above reagents; yields water in the closed tube.	MIRABILITE (glauber salt).	$\dot{N}a\dddot{S}+10\dot{H}$.	White.		Vitreous.	1.5—2.	1.48	Easily.	V.
	Not affected by the above reagents; yields no water in the closed tube.	Thenardite.	$\dot{N}a\dddot{S}$.	White.		Vitreous.	2.—3.	2.55	Easily.	IV.
	Like epsomite—14 per cent. water.	Loeweite.	$(\dot{M}g,\dot{N}a)\dddot{S}+Aq$.	Yellow-white, red.		Vitreous.	2.5	2.37	Easily.	II.
	Like epsomite—13 per cent. water.	Kieserite.	$\dot{M}g\dddot{S}+\dot{H}$.	White.		Dull.	2.5	2.51	Easily.	IV.
	Like epsomite—21.5 per cent. water.	Bloedite.	$(\dot{M}g,\dot{N}a)\dddot{S}+2\dot{H}$.	White, orange-red.					Easily.	V.
	Like epsomite but does not effloresce in air.	Simonyite.	$(\dot{M}g,\dot{N}a)\dddot{S}+2\dot{H}$.	Colorless to blue-green, yellow.			2.5	2.24	Easily.	V.
	Like epsomite—loses 26.8 water when heated to 133° C.	Picromerite.	$(\dot{K},\dot{M}g)\dddot{S}+3\dot{H}$.	White.		Silky.	2.5		Easily.	V.
Yield no precipitates in the aqueous solutions with chloride of barium or alkalies; with nitrate of silver yield a heavy precipitate of chloride of silver; the reaction is not alkaline.	Yields a heavy precipitate with bichloride of platinum.	**Sylvite.**	KCl.	Colorless to white.	Cubic.	Vitreous.	2.	1.9—2.	Easily.	I.
	Yields no precipitate with bichloride of platinum.	**Halite** (common salt).	NaCl.	Colorless, white, red, purple.	Cubic.	Vitreous.	2.5	2.15	Easily.	I.
Moistened with strong sulphuric acid gives a green flame (boric acid).	Reaction alkaline; does not effervesce with acids; bubbles, swells up, and fuses to a clear bead B. B.	**Borax.**	$\dot{N}a\dddot{B}^2+10\dot{H}$.	Gray-white.		Vitreous.	2.5	1.72	Easily.	V.

(Page 81)

MINERALS WITHOUT METALLIC LUSTRE.

B. Fusible from 1—5, and non-volatile.

II. *Yield no metal or magnetic mass with soda.*

Division 1 (concluded).

B.—Fusible from 1—5, and not volatile, or only partially volatile.

II. *B. B. with soda on charcoal give no metallic globule or magnetic mass.*

DIVISION 1.

B. B. after fusion and continued heating on charcoal or in the forceps, have an alkaline reaction and change the color of moistened turmeric paper to red-brown.

b) Insoluble or difficultly soluble in water.

General Characters.	Specific Characters.	Species.	Composition.	Color.	Cleavage or Fracture.	Lustre.	Hardness.	Sp. Gr.	Fusibility.	Crystallization.
Fusibility = 1. Alone colors the flame yellow; moistened with strong sulphuric acid colors the flame green (boric acid).	Gives much water in closed tube; partially soluble in hot water; the solution is alkaline. (Gives boric acid reaction with sulphuric acid and alcohol.)	ULEXITE.	$\dot{N}a, \dot{C}a, \dddot{B}, \dot{H}$.	White.	Fibrous.	Silky.	1.	1.65	1.	
Soluble in dilute hydrochloric acid with effervescence.	Gives much water in the closed tube.	Gay-lussite.	$\dot{N}a\ddot{C} + \dot{C}a\ddot{C} + 5\dot{H}$.	White.		Vitreous, pearly.	2.—3.	1.99	Easily.	V.
	The dilute solution gives a heavy precipitate with sulphuric acid; fused in the forceps, colors the flame green.	**Witherite.**	$\dot{B}a\ddot{C}$.	White-gray.		Vitreous.	3.5	4.3	2.	IV.
	The HCl solution gives a precipitate with ammonia (phosphate of lime). The nitric solution, warmed with molybdate of ammonia, gives a yellow precipitate.	Staffelite.	$\dot{C}a^3\overset{\cdot\cdot\cdot\cdot\cdot}{P}, \dot{C}a\ddot{C}$.	Leek-green to green-yellow.			4.	3.13		Stalact.
Quietly soluble in much hydrochloric acid; the solution gives with chloride of barium an abundant precipitate ($BaO SO_3$). The solution neutralized by ammonia gives with oxalate of ammonia a precipitate of oxalate of lime.	In closed tube yields much water.	**Gypsum.**	$\dot{C}a\dddot{S} + 2\dot{H}$.	Colorless, gray-white.	In 3 directions.	Silky, vitreous.	2.	2.3	2.5—3.	V.
	Yields little water in the closed tube. In its solution bichloride of platinum gives a yellow precipitate. Partially soluble in water.	POLYHALITE.	$\dot{K}\dddot{S} + \dot{M}g\dddot{S} + 2\dot{C}a\dddot{S} + 2\dot{H}$.	Yellow to brick-red.		Vitreous.	2.5	2.77	1.5	IV. (?)
	Yields no water, and is not precipitated by bichloride of platinum. Partially soluble in water.	GLAUBERITE.	$\dot{N}a\dddot{S} + \dot{C}a\dddot{S}$.	Yellow to gray.		Vitreous.	2.5	2.7	1.5	V.
	Yields no water; does not precipitate by bichloride of platinum; insoluble in water.	**Anhydrite.**	$\dot{C}a\dddot{S}$.	Colorless, white-blue, red.	Perfect in 3 directions.	Vitreous.	3.5	2.9	2.5—3.	IV.
	☞ Compare *Celestite*, below, which in fine powder is slightly acted on by acids.									
Very little acted upon by HCl. B. B. with soda give a sulphur reaction.	Fused in the forceps colors the flame yellowish-green.	**Barite.**	$\dot{B}a\dddot{S}$.	All colors, white-yellow, blue.	Basal, perfect.	Vitreous.	2.5—3.5	4.5	3.	IV.
	Fused in the forceps colors the flame red.	**Celestite.**	$\dot{S}r\dddot{S}$.	Colorless, white, blue.	Basal, perfect.	Vitreous.	3.—3.5	3.9	3.	IV.
Heated on charcoal evolves an arsenical odor.	Yields water in a matrass.	Pharmacolite.	$\dot{C}a^2\overset{\cdot\cdot\cdot\cdot\cdot}{As} + 6\dot{H}$.	White-gray.		Vitreous.	2.—2.5	2.7	Easily.	V.
When fused with bisulphate of potassa in a matrass, yield vapors of hydrofluoric acid, which corrode the glass.	Easily fusible in the flame of a candle. (F = 1.)	**Cryolite.**	$3NaFl + Al^2Fl^3$.	White to black.	Basal perfect.	Vitreous.	2.5	3.	1.	IV. ?
	In the closed tube decrepitates and generally phosphoresces.	**Fluorite** (fluor spar).	$CaFl$.	All colors.	Octahedral.	Vitreous.	4.	3.18	3.	I.
	Same as cryolite (occurs in granular masses).	Chiolite.	$3NaFl + 2Al^2Fl^3$.	Snow-white.			4.	2.72	I.	II.
	The same, but in closed tube yields water, which has a strongly acid reaction.	PACHNOLITE (*Thomsenolite*)	$3(Ca, Na)Fl + Al^2Fl^3 + 2\dot{H}$	Colorless-white.		Vitreous.	2.5—4.	2.75	Easily.	V.
	Yields no water in the closed tube.	Arksutite.	$2(Ca, Na)Fl + Al^2Fl^3$.	White.		Vitreous.	2.5	3.1	Easily.	Mass.
	Yields no water in the closed tube.	Chodneffite.	$2NaFl + Al^2Fl^3$.	White.			4.	3.	Easily.	II.
	Yields water in the closed tube.	Gearksutite.	$2CaFl + Al^2Fl^3 + 4\dot{H}$.	White.		Earthy.	2.			
Effervesces with concentrated hydrochloric acid; the solution when evaporated gelatinizes.	B. B. immediately becomes white and opaque; fuses at 2.5 with intumescence to a white blistered glass, which placed on turmeric paper gives an alkaline reaction.	CANCRINITE (near nephelite).	$\dddot{\bar{A}l}, \dot{C}a, \dot{N}a, \ddot{C}, \dddot{S}i$.	White, pink, gray-yellow.	Hexagonal.	Vitreous.	5.—6.	2.5	2.5	III.

(Page 82)

MINERALS WITHOUT METALLIC LUSTRE.

B. Fusible from 1—5, and non-volatile.

II. *Yield no metal or magnetic mass with soda.*

Division 2 (in part).

B.—Fusible from 1—5, and non-volatile or only partially volatile.

II. *B. B. with soda on charcoal give no metallic globule or magnetic mass.*

DIVISION 2. *Soluble in hydrochloric acid, some also in water. The solution is not gelatinized by evaporation.*

General Characters.	Specific Characters.	Species.	Composition.	Color.	Cleavage or Fracture.	Lustre.	Hardness.	Sp. Gr.	Fusibility.	Crystallization.
Give arsenical fumes on charcoal.	Fuses easily; with strong sulphuric acid it gives off hydrofluoric acid, which corrodes glass.	Durangite.	$\ddot{\bar{Al}}, \ddot{\bar{Fe}}, \dot{Mn}, \dot{Na}, \dot{Li}, \dddot{\bar{As}}, Fl$.	Orange-red.	Prismatic.	Vitreous.	5.	4.	2.	V.
	Gives an amethystine bead with salt of phosphorus (oxide of manganese).	Chondrarsenite.	$\dot{Mn}^5 \dddot{\bar{As}} + 2\frac{1}{2}\dot{H}$.	Yellow-red.			3.		Easily.	Gran.
	Gives a green bead with salt of phosphorus (oxide of uranium; with S + KI gives a red sublimate on charcoal (iodide of bismuth).	Walpurgite.	$\ddot{\bar{Bi}}, \ddot{\bar{U}}, \dddot{\bar{As}}, \dot{H}$.	Wax-yellow.	Scaly.	Adamantine.		5.8		V.
	Gives a green bead with salt of phosphorus, but no reaction for bismuth.	Trögerite.	$\ddot{\bar{U}}^5 \dddot{\bar{As}}^2 + 20\dot{H}$.	Lemon-yellow	Tabular.			3.3		V.
	Gives on charcoal a coating of oxide of zinc.	Adamite.	$\dot{Zn}^3 \dddot{\bar{As}} + \dot{Zn}\dot{H}$.	Violet to honey-yellow.	Distinct.	Vitreous.	3.5	4.34	Easily.	IV.
Soluble in water. Colors the borax bead violet when hot (oxide of manganese)	Gives much water (40 p. c.) in the closed tube.	Fauserite.	$\dot{Mg}\dddot{S} + 2\dot{Mn}\dddot{S} + 15\dot{H}$.	Red to yellow-white.	Distinct.	Vitreous.	2.—2.5	1.89	Easily.	IV.
Soluble in water. Give a sulphur reaction with soda on charcoal. Fuse when first heated, and swell up to an infusible mass.	Moistened with a potash or soda solution gives an odor of ammonia.	Tschermigite (ammonia alum).	$NH_4O\dddot{S} + \ddot{\bar{Al}}\dddot{S}^3 + 24\dot{H}$.	Colorless to white.		Vitreous.	1.—2.	1.50		I.
	After fusion moistened with nitrate of cobalt and again ignited becomes blue (alumina).	Alunogen.	$\ddot{\bar{Al}}\dddot{S}^3 + 18\dot{H}$.	Yellow, red-white.		Silky.	1.5—2.	1.7		V.
	After fusion moistened with nitrate of cobalt and again ignited becomes green (oxide of zinc).	Goslarite (zinc vitriol).	$\dot{Zn}\dddot{S} + 7\dot{H}$.	White.	Prismatic.	Vitreous.	2.—2.5	1.95	Easily.	IV.
Treated with caustic potash or soda gives the odor of ammonia.	Gives much water in a matrass.	STRUVITE.	$(NH_40, \dot{Mg})^2 \dddot{\bar{P}} + 12\dot{H}$.	Yellow to brown-white.	Basal.	Vitreous.	2.	1.7	Easily.	IV.
B. B. fuse easily with intumescence, and color the flame green (boric acid). Give the boric acid reaction with sulphuric acid and alcohol.	Imparts a violet color to the hot borax bead (oxide of manganese).	Sussexite.	$(\dot{Mn}, \dot{Mg})^2 \dddot{B} + \dot{H}$.	Gray-white.	Fibrous.	Silky.	3.	3.42	2.	
	Soluble in water.	Sassolite (boric acid).	$\dot{H}^3 \dddot{B}$.	Yellow to white.	Scaly.	Pearly.	1.	1.48	1.	VI.
	Insoluble in water, gives 26 p. c. water on ignition.	Hydroboracite	$\dot{Ca}^3 \dddot{B}^4 + \dot{Mg}^3 \dddot{B}^4 + 18\dot{H}$.	White.	Foliated.		2.	1.9—2.	Easily.	Fibrous.
	Gives little or no water.	BORACITE.	$\dot{Mg}_3 \dddot{B}^4 + \frac{1}{2}\dot{Mg}Cl$.	White, gray-green.		Vitreous.	4.5—7.	2.97	2.	I.
	Like Hydroboracite, but contains only 7 p. c. water.	Szaibelyite.	$3\dot{Mg}^5 \dddot{B}^2 + 4\dot{H}$.	White-yellow.			3.—4.	3.	Easily.	
	Like Hydroboracite. Its nitric solution gives a yellow precipitate with molybdate of ammonia.	Lüneburgite.	$2(\dot{Mg}, \dot{H})\dddot{\bar{P}} + \dot{Mg}\dddot{B} + 7\dot{H}$.							
	☞ Compare *Borax*, Div. I., p. 80.									
Give with borax a violet bead (manganese.)	☞ Compare *Alabandite* and *Hauerite*, which give off sulphuretted hydrogen when treated with HCl. (See Div. 5, p. 67.)									
Moistened with strong sulphuric acid color the flame pale bluish-green. The nitric solutions give with molybdate of ammonia a yellow precipitate (phospho-molybdate of ammonia).	Fuses at 3.—3.5 with bubbling; soluble in dilute hydrochloric acid.	Wagnerite.	$2\dot{Mg}^3 \dddot{\bar{P}} + (Mg, Na)Fl$.	Yellow.		Vitreous.	5.5	3.07	3.5	V.
	In the closed tube phosphoresces with a faint white light.	Kjerulfine.	$2\dot{Mg}^3 \dddot{\bar{P}} + CaFl$.	Pale-red.		Greasy.	4.—5.	3.15	3.	V.
	Fuses quietly at 5; insoluble in dilute hydrochloric acid.	**Apatite.**	$\dot{Ca}^3 \dddot{\bar{P}} + \frac{1}{3}Ca(ClFl)$.	Sea-green, blue, yellow, red, white.		Vitreous.	5.	2.9—3.2	4.5—5.	III.
	Reacts like apatite, but also gives much water in the closed tube (26 per cent.).	Brushite.	$(\frac{2}{3}\dot{Ca} + \frac{1}{3}\dot{H})^3 \dddot{\bar{P}} + 4\dot{H}$.	Yellow-white.	Perfect.	Pearly-vitreous.	2.—2.5	2.21	Easily.	V.
	Same as above. Water=18 per cent.	Isoclasite.	$\dot{Ca}^3 \dddot{\bar{P}} + \dot{Ca}\dot{H} + 4\dot{H}$.	Snow-white.	Perfect.	Pearly-vitreous.	1.5	2.92		V.

(Page 83)

MINERALS WITHOUT METALLIC LUSTRE.

B. Fusible from 1—5, and non-volatile.

II. *Yield no metal or magnetic mass with soda.*

Division 2 (concluded).

Division 3 (in part).

B.—Fusible from 1–5, and not volatile or only partially volatile.

II. *B.B. with soda on charcoal give no metallic globule or magnetic mass.*

DIVISION 2.—(*Continued.*) *Soluble in hydrochloric acid without gelatinization.*

General Characters.	Specific Characters.	Species.	Composition.	Color.	Cleavage or Fracture.	Lustre.	Hardness.	Sp. Gr.	Fusibility.	Crystallization.
Fuse at 2, coloring the flame purple-red (lithia). Phosphoresce with a light-blue light.	Soluble with difficulty in strong acids. Fused with bisulphate of potassa evolves hydrofluoric acid. The nitric solution gives a yellow precipitate with molybdate of ammonia.	Amblygonite.	($\frac{1}{4}$(L̇iṄa)^3+$\frac{3}{4}$Äl)^{4}P̈ with part of the O replaced by Fl.	Green, gray-white.	Cleavable at 105°.	Vitreous.	6.	3.11	2.	VI.
	A like mineral, with 4 per cent. of water. Gives a pure lithia flame.	HEBRONITE.		Gray-white.	Cleavable at 105°.	Vitreous.	6.	3.04	2.	VI.
With salt of phosphorus in O. F. give a yellow glass which in R. F. becomes green (Ü).	Fuses with ease in the matrass. The solution in HCl has a yellow color, and gives with ammonia a yellowish precipitate.	Autunite.	Ü^{2}P̈+ĊaḢ+7Ḣ.	Lemon to sulphur-yellow.	Basal.	Pearly.	2.—2.5	3.1	2.5	IV.
	☞ Compare *Torbernite.* Div. 3, p. 75.			White.						

DIVISION 3. *Soluble in hydrochloric acid, forming a stiff jelly upon evaporation.*

a) B. B. in the closed tube give water.

General Characters.	Specific Characters.	Species.	Composition.	Color.	Cleavage or Fracture.	Lustre.	Hardness.	Sp. Gr.	Fusibility.	Crystallization.
In matrass gives little water. B.B. fuses to a clear glass, tinging the flame green.	The dilute acid solution colors turmeric paper red (boric acid).	**Datolite.**	(Ċa^2,Ḣ^3,B̈)S̈i.	Colorless, white-green, yellow-red.		Vitreous.	5.5	3.		V.
The dilute HCl solution gives with sulphuric acid a precipitate of the sulphate of baryta.	Prismatic cleavage perfect.	Edingtonite.	Äl, Ḃa, S̈i, Ḣ.	White-pink.	Prismatic.	Vitreous.	4.5	2.7	Easily.	II.
Fuses quietly at 2, without swelling or intumescence, to a clear transparent glass.	Carbonate of ammonia produces little or no precipitate in the HCl solution, after the alumina has been separated by ammonia.	NATROLITE.	Ṅa, Äl, S̈i^3, Ḣ^2.	White to red.		Vitreous.	5.5	2.25	2.	IV.
Fuses with intumescence. In the HCl solution chloride of barium produces a precipitate. ($BaOSO_3$.)		Ittnerite.	Äl, Ċa, Ṅa, Ḣ, S̈, S̈i.	Ash-gray.		Vitreous.	5.5	2.4	Easily.	I.
Sometimes curls up in worm-like forms on fusion.	Fuses to a voluminous frothy shining slag, which in R.F. further fuses to a vesicular slightly transparent globule; becomes electric on heating.	SCOLECITE.	Ċa, Äl, S̈i^3, Ḣ^3.	White.	Prismatic.	Vitreous.	5.5	2.2	2.2	V.
	Fuses, emitting air-bubbles to a white translucent enamel.	LAUMONTITE.	Ċa, Äl, S̈i^4, Ḣ^4.	White-gray, red.	Prismatic.	Pearly.	3.5	2.3	Easily.	V.
	Fuses with difficulty on the edges, worming like scolecite.	Chalcomorphite.	S̈i, Äl, Ċa, Ḣ, C̈.	White.		Glassy.	5.	2.54		III.
	Resembles scolecite, but is not pyroelectric.	Mesolite.	(ĊaṄa)Äl^3, S̈i, 3Ḣ.	White.	Fibrous.	Silky.	5.	2.3	Easily.	?
	Resembles scolecite, but is not pyroelectric.	Thomsonite.	(ĊaṄa), Äl, 2S̈i, 2½Ḣ.	White.	Prismatic.	Vitreous.	5.	2.35	2.	IV.
Fuse at 3 with slight intumescence.	Often decrepitates. Found in rectangular-terminated crystals. Often in twins consisting of 3 or 4 crystals united around a common axis.	Phillipsite.	(Ċa, K̇), Äl, 4S̈i, 5Ḣ.	White (red).		Vitreous.	4.—4.5	2.2	3.	IV.
	Usually has the appearance of the square octahedron.	Gismondite.	Äl, Ċa, K̇, S̈i, Ḣ.	Bluish-white, white.		Splendent.	4.5	2.26	Easily.	IV.
☞ Compare *okenite, apophyllite, analcite,* belonging to the next section.										

(Page 84)

MINERALS WITHOUT METALLIC LUSTRE.

B. Fusible from 1—5, and non-volatile.

II. *Yield no metal or magnetic mass with soda.*

DIVISION 3 (concluded).

B. Fusible from 1—5, and non-volatile or only partially volatile.

II. *B. B. with soda on charcoal give no metallic globule or magnetic mass.*

Division 3.—(*Continued.*) *Soluble in hydrochloric acid, forming a stiff jelly upon evaporation.*

b) B. B. in the closed tube give no water, or but traces.

General Characters.	Specific Characters.	Species.	Composition.	Color.	Cleavage or Fracture.	Lustre.	Hardness.	Sp. Gr.	Fusibility.	Crystallization.
☞ Compare *datolite* of previous section.										
Give with borax in O. F. an amethystine glass (oxide of manganese). ☞ Compare *Willemite*, p. 91.	Heated with hydrochloric acid evolves sulphuretted hydrogen; not cleavable.	Helvite.	$(\frac{1}{2}(\dot{Mn},\dot{Fe})+\frac{1}{2}\dot{Be})^2\ddot{Si}+\frac{1}{3}MnS$.	Wax or honey-yellow.		Resinous.	6.—6.5	3.2	3.	I.
	B. B. with soda on charcoal a slight coating of zinc. Heated with HCl evolves HS.	Danalite.	$(\frac{1}{2}(\dot{Zn},\dot{Fe},\dot{Mn})+\frac{1}{2}\dot{Be})^2\ddot{Si}+\frac{1}{3}ZnS$.	Flesh-red, gray.		Vitreous.	5.5—6.	3.43	Easily.	I.
	Gives off no sulphuretted hydrogen. Perfect cleavage in one direction.	TEPHROITE.	$\dot{Mn}^2\ddot{Si}$.	Reddish-brown, ash-gray.		Vitreous.	6.	4.	3.5	IV.
With soda on charcoal give a sulphur reaction.	Color sky-blue. Fuses with difficulty at 4.5 to a white glass.	Hauynite.	$(\frac{1}{4}\dot{Na}^3+\frac{3}{4}\dddot{\bar{Al}})^2\ddot{Si}^3+\dot{Ca}\dddot{S}$.	Green to blue.	Dodecahedral.	Vitreous.	5.5—6.	2.5	4.5	I.
	Color sky-blue. Gives off sulphuretted hydrogen when treated with HCl.	Lapis-Lazuli.	$\dot{Ca},\dot{Na},\dddot{\bar{Al}},\dddot{\bar{Fe}},S,\ddot{Si}$.	Azure-blue.		Vitreous.	5.—5.5	2.4	3.	I.
	Fuses quietly at 4.5. Mostly crystallized in rhombic dodecahedrons.	Nosite.	$(\frac{1}{4}\dot{Na}^3+\frac{3}{4}\dddot{\bar{Al}})^2\ddot{Si}^3+\frac{1}{2}\dot{Na}\dddot{S}$.	Gray to black.		Vitreous.	5.5	2.3	4.5	I.
	Fuses at 3 with intumescence. Massive granular.	Scolopsite.	$\dddot{\bar{Al}},\dot{Ca},\dot{Na},\dddot{S},Cl,\ddot{Si},\dot{H}$.	Grayish-white.	Splintery.	Resinous.	5.	2.53	3.	Massi
Fused with a bead of salt of phosphorus which has been saturated with oxide of copper, tinge the flame blue (chloride of copper). In the nitric solution nitrate of silver gives a precipitate of the chloride of silver.	Fuses to an opaque pistachio-green bead. In the dilute HCl solution turmeric paper assumes an orange color (reaction for zirconia).	Eudialyte.	$(\frac{2}{3}(\dot{Ca},\dot{Na},\dot{Fe})^2+\frac{1}{3}\ddot{Zr})^2\ddot{Si}$.	Rose to brown-red.	Basal.	Vitreous.	5.5	2.9	2.5	III.
	Fuses to a clear colorless glass.	SODALITE.	$(\frac{1}{4}\dot{Na}^3+\frac{3}{4}\dddot{\bar{Al}})^2\ddot{Si}^3+\frac{1}{2}NaCl$.	Gray, green, blue, yellow-white.		Vitreous.	5.5—6.	2.3	3.5—4.	I.
In the hydrochloric acid solution, after separation of the silica, ammonia gives a precipitate.	Fuses with intumescence to a vesicular glass which cannot be perfectly rounded by fusion.	Meionite.	$(\frac{1}{3}(\dot{Ca},\dot{Na})^3+\frac{2}{3}\dddot{\bar{Al}})^2\ddot{Si}^3$.	Colorless to white.		Vitreous.	5.5	2.7	3.	II.
	Fuses quietly. After the separation of the alumina by an excess of ammonia, gives a copious precipitate with oxalate of ammonia. Occurs in square and octagonal prisms.	Melilite (Humboldtilite).	$(\frac{2}{3}(\dot{Ca},\dot{Mg},\dot{Na})^3+\frac{1}{3}(\dddot{\bar{Al}},\dddot{\bar{Fe}}))^2\ddot{Si}^3$.	White, yellow, brown.	Basal.	Vitreous.	5.	2.95	3.	II.
	Does not give the above reaction with oxalate of ammonia. Found massive and in hexagonal prisms. Fuses without intumescence.	NEPHELITE (Elaeolite).	$\dot{Na},\dot{K},\dddot{\bar{Al}},\dddot{\bar{Fe}},\ddot{Si}$.	Colorless and green-red.	Hexagonal.	Vitreous to greasy.	5.5—6.	2.6	3.5	III.
	☞ Compare *Cancrinite*, Div. 1, p. 81.									
	Behaves like melilite, but is less fusible. F=4.	Barsowite (var. Anorthite).	$\dot{Ca},\dot{Mg},\dddot{\bar{Al}},\dddot{\bar{Fe}},\ddot{Si}$.	White.	Granular.	Vitreous.	5.5—6.	2.75	4.	VI.
In the hydrochloric solution, after separation of the silica, ammonia gives little or no precipitate, but carbonate of ammonia causes a copious separation of carbonate of lime.	Fuses quietly to a colorless translucent glass.	WOLLASTONITE.	$\dot{Ca}\ddot{Si}$.	White-gray.	Basal.	Vitreous.	4.5—5.	2.9	4.5	V.
	☞ Compare *Pectolite*, Div. 4, p. 85.									
	☞ Also compare the difficultly fusible minerals *Gehlenite*, Div. 5, p. 94; *Tachylite*, Div. 4, p. 86; and *Willemite*, Div. 2, p. 91.									

(Page 85)

MINERALS WITHOUT METALLIC LUSTRE.

B. Fusible from 1—5, and non-volatile.

II. *Yield no metal or magnetic mass with soda.*

DIVISION 4 (in part).

B.—Fusible from 1—5, and non-volatile, or only partially volatile.

II. *B. B. with soda on charcoal give no metallic globule or magnetic mass.*

DIVISION 4.

Soluble in hydrochloric acid, leaving a residue of silica without forming a perfect jelly.

a) B. B. in the closed tube give water.

General Characters.	Specific Characters.	Species.	Composition.	Color.	Cleavage or Fracture.	Lustre.	Hardness.	Sp. Gr.	Fusibility.	Crystallization.
With borax gives the amethystine color of manganese.	Treated with HCl evolves chlorine, and silica separates as a slimy powder. Gives 9 per cent. of water on ignition.	Klipsteinite.	$\dddot{\bar{Mn}}, \dot{Mn}, \dddot{Si}, \dot{H}$.	Dark liver-brown to black.		Dull to sub-metallic.	5—5.5.	3.5		Amorph.
Easily decomposed by HCl, the silica separating in gelatinous lumps. After the separation of the silica, the solution gives with ammonia no or only a slight precipitate.	Fuses with slight intumescence to a white enamel-like glass. Yields but little water. After fusion gelatinizes perfectly with hydrochloric acid.	PECTOLITE.	$(\frac{4}{6}\dot{C}a+\frac{1}{6}\dot{N}a+\frac{1}{6}\dot{H})\dddot{Si}$.	White to gray.	Fibrous.	Silky.	5.	2.7	2.	V.
	Fuses at 1.5; colors the flame violet (potash); yields much water; after fusion is but slightly attacked by acids.	APOPHYLLITE.	$(\frac{1}{2}(\dot{C}a,\dot{K})+\frac{1}{2}\dot{H})^2\dddot{Si}+\dot{H}\dddot{Si}$	Colorless, white, rose-red, yellow.	Basal.	Vitreous pearly.	5.	2.3	1.5	II.
	Fuses at 2.5—3, with frothing to a milk-white glass; yields much water; after fusion but slightly attacked by acids.	Okenite.	$(\frac{1}{2}\dot{H}+\frac{1}{2}\dot{C}a)\dddot{Si}+\frac{1}{2}\dot{H}$.	White.	Fibrous.	Pearly.	4.5—5.	2.3	Easily.	IV. ?
	☞ Compare *Xonaltite* and *Sepiolite*, Div. 5, p. 93.									
Decomposed by HCl like the preceding. After the separation of the silica the solution gives with ammonia a copious precipitate.	B. B. at first becomes opaque, but fuses quietly to a clear glass. Occurs usually in trapezohedrons and cubes.	ANALCITE.	$\dddot{\bar{A}}l, \dot{N}a, \dddot{Si}^4, \dot{H}^2$.	Colorless to white, gray, green, yellow, red.	Not cleavable.	Vitreous.	5.—5.5	2.28	2.5	I.
The dilute HCl solution gives with sulphuric acid a white precipitate ($\dot{B}a\dddot{S}$).	Fuses at 3 with intumescence. (Contains 13 p. c. of water.) ☞ Compare *Harmotome*, p. 87.	Brewsterite.	$\dddot{\bar{A}}l,(\frac{2}{3}\dot{S}r+\frac{1}{3}\dot{B}a),\dddot{Si}^6,\dot{H}^5$.	Yellowish-white to gray.	Prismatic.	Pearly vitreous.	5.	2.45	3.	V.
B. B. swell up more or less and fuse with contortions to enamel-like masses. In the solution from which the silica has been separated ammonia produces a precipitate.	Yields but little water (4.3 per cent.). The others give from 15 to 20 per cent.	Prehnite.	$\dot{C}a^2,(\dddot{\bar{A}}l,\dddot{\bar{F}}e),\dddot{Si}^3,\dot{H}^5$.	Apple to oil green, white.	Basal.	Vitreous.	6.—6.5	2.9	2.	IV.
	Distinguished by its rhombohedral crystallization and imperfect cleavage.	CHABAZITE.	$(\frac{2}{3}\dot{C}a+\frac{1}{3}(\dot{N}a,\dot{K})),\dddot{\bar{A}}l,\dddot{Si}^4,\dot{H}^6$.	White, flesh-red.		Vitreous.	4.—5.	2.1	Easily.	III.
	Perfectly cleavable in one direction. Orthorhombic. B. B. intumesces strongly.	STILBITE.	$\dot{C}a,\dddot{\bar{A}}l,\dddot{Si}^6,\dot{H}^6$.	White, yellow-red.	Prismatic.	Pearly vitreous.	3.5—4.	2.16	2.—2.5	IV.
	Perfectly cleavable in one direction. Monoclinic. Lustre very pearly on one face. B. B. intumesces strongly.	HEULANDITE.	$\dot{C}a,\dddot{\bar{A}}l,\dddot{Si}^6,\dot{H}^5$.	White-red.	Clinodiagonal.	Pearly vitreous.	3.5—4.	2.2	2.—2.5	V.
	One perfect cleavage. Intumescence less.	Hypostilbite.	$(\dot{N}a,\dot{C}a),\dddot{\bar{A}}l,4\frac{1}{2}\dddot{Si},\dot{H}^6$.	White.	Fibrous.	Vitreous.	3.5—4.	2.2	Easily.	
	Fuses with scarcely any intumescence.	Mordenite.	$(\dot{N}a,\dot{C}a),\dddot{\bar{A}}l,\dddot{Si}^9,\dot{H}^6$.	White.	Concretionary.	Silky.	5.	2.08	Easily.	
These minerals, the hardness of which is not above 3, are softer than the other minerals of this division.	Fuses at 3.5—4 with intumescence; not cleavable. (Water = 9 p. c.)	Chonicrite.	$\dddot{\bar{A}}l,\dot{M}g,\dot{C}a,\dddot{Si},\dot{H}$.	White-yellow.		Silky.	2.5—3.	2.9	3.5—4.	
	Fuses quietly at 4.; cleavable in one direction. (Water = 11 p. c.)	Pyrosclerite.	$(\frac{2}{3}(\dot{M}g,\dot{F}e)^3+\frac{1}{3}(\dddot{\bar{A}}l,\dddot{\bar{C}}r))^2\dddot{Si}^3+3\dot{H}$.	Apple to emerald-green.	Micaceous.	Pearly.	3.	2.74	4.	V. ?
	Exfoliates in worm-like forms.	Vermiculite.	$\dot{M}g,\dot{F}e,\dddot{\bar{A}}l,\dddot{Si},\dot{H}$.	Brown-yellow.	Micaceous.	Pearly.	1.5	2.75		VI. ?
	Exfoliates prodigiously.	JEFFERISITE.	$\dot{M}g,\dddot{\bar{F}}e,\dddot{\bar{A}}l,\dddot{Si},\dot{H}$.	Brown-yellow.	Micaceous.	Pearly.	1.5	2.3		IV. ?
	Swells up; fuses with difficulty. (Water = 13 p. c.)	Jollyte.	$(\frac{1}{3}(\dot{F}e,\dot{M}g)^3+\frac{2}{3}\dddot{\bar{A}}l)^2\dddot{Si}^3+4\dot{H}$.	Brown.			3.	2.61	Difficult.	Amorph.
	Swells up and fuses to a white enamel. (Water = 21 p. c.)	Kerrite.	$\dot{M}g,\dddot{\bar{F}}e,\dddot{\bar{A}}l,\dddot{Si},\dot{H}$.	Greenish-yellow.	Micaceous.	Pearly.	1.5	2.3		
	Swells up and fuses to a brown glass. (Water = 11 p. c.)	Maconite.	$\dot{K},\dot{M}g,\dddot{\bar{F}}e,\dddot{\bar{A}}l,\dddot{Si},\dot{H}$.	Dark-brown.	Micaceous.	Pearly.	2.	2.8		
	Fuses with difficulty to a white enamel. Water = 4 p. c.)	Willcoxite.	$\dot{K},\dot{N}a,\dot{M}g,\dot{F}e,\dddot{\bar{A}}l,\dddot{Si},\dot{H}$.	Gray.	Micaceous.	Pearly.	1.5			
	Exfoliates slightly; fuses with difficulty to a brown-yellow blebby mass. (Water = 13 p. c.)	Dudleyite.	$\dot{N}a,\dot{M}g,\dddot{\bar{F}}e,\dddot{\bar{A}}l,\dddot{Si},\dot{H}$.	Bronze.	Micaceous.	Pearly.				

(Page 86)

MINERALS WITHOUT METALLIC LUSTRE.

B. Fusible from 1—5, and non-volatile.

II. *Yield no metal or magnetic mass with soda.*

Division 4 (concluded).

B.—Fusible from 1—5, and non-volatile, or only partially volatile.

II. *B. B. with soda on charcoal give no metallic globule or magnetic mass.*

DIVISION 4.—(*Continued.*)

Soluble in hydrochloric acid, leaving a residue of silica without forming a perfect jelly.

General Characters.	Specific Characters.	Species.	Composition.	Color.	Cleavage or Fracture.	Lustre.	Hardness.	Sp. Gr.	Fusibility.	Crystallization.
a) (*Continued*) B. B. in the closed tube give water.										
H = 4.—4.5. Cleavable.	Fuses quietly at 3. to a milk-white globule. The dilute HCl solution colors turmeric paper orange-yellow (zirconia).	Catapleiite.	$\ddot{Z}r, \dot{N}a, \dot{C}a, \dddot{S}i, \dot{H}$.	Yellow-brown.	Prismatic.	Vitreous.	6.	2.8	3.	III.
	Fuses at first with intumescence, then quietly at 2.5—3. to a yellow-brown glass. With salt of phosphorus in the reducing flame gives a violet color (titanic acid).	Mosandrite.	$\ddot{C}e, \dot{C}a, \dot{N}a, \ddot{T}i, \dddot{S}i, \dot{H}$.	Reddish-brown.	Prismatic.	Resinous.	4.	2.95	3.	IV. ?
Difficultly fusible (F=5.)	Absorbs water with avidity. ($\dot{H}$ = 10 p. c.)	SEPIOLITE.	$\dot{M}g^2\dddot{S}i^3 + 2\dot{H}$.	Gray-white.		Dull.	2.—2.5		5.	
	Does not absorb water. (Water = 20 p. c.)	DEWEYLITE.	$\dot{M}g, \dddot{S}i, \dot{H}$.	White, yellow, red.		Greasy.	3.	2.2	5.	
Fuses at 2.5 to an opaque black shining glass. Difficultly decomposed by hydrochloric acid.	Yields but little water. The hydrochloric solution gives with ammonia a heavy greenish-gray precipitate.	Sordavalite.	$\ddot{\bar{A}}l, \dot{F}e, \dot{M}g, \dddot{S}i, \dot{H}$.	Gray-black.		Resinous.	2.5	2.58	2.5	
b) B. B. in the closed tube give no water, or but traces.										
	☞ Compare *Pectolite*, *Chonicrite* and *Prehnite* of the preceding subdivision.									
☞ Compare *Lapis-lazuli*, Div. 3, p. 84.	Generally gelatinizes. Color, sky-blue.									
Micaceous; also scaly massive.	Fuses easily in the candle flame, and B. B., with intumescence to a gray enamel giving a lithia-flame.	Cryophyllite.	$\ddot{\bar{A}}l, \dot{F}e, \dot{K}, \dot{L}i, \dddot{S}i, \dot{H}$.	Black, green to brown-red.	Micaceous.	Pearly.	2.5	2.91	1.5—2.	IV.
Fuses easily to a black slag.	The silica separates as gelatinous lumps.	Tachylite.	$\dot{F}e, \dot{M}g, \dot{C}a, \dot{N}a, \ddot{\bar{A}}l, \dddot{S}i, \dot{H}$.	Gray, pitch-black.		Vitreous.	6.5	2.6	2.5	
The HCl solution evaporated with addition of tin-foil assumes a violet color (titanic acid).	Fuses quietly. Difficultly decomposed; the silica separates as a slimy powder.	Schorlomite.	$\ddot{\bar{F}}e, \dot{C}a, \ddot{T}i, \dddot{S}i$.	Black.		Vitreous.	7.—7.5	3.8	3.	
	Fuses with much effervescence. Easily decomposed, the silica separating in gelatinous lumps.	Tscheffkinite.	$\dot{C}e, \dot{F}e, \ddot{T}i, \dddot{S}i$.	Black.		Vitreous.	5.—5.5	4.5	Easily.	
Fuse with intumescence at 2.5 to a white vesicular glass, which cannot easily be further fused.	Cleavable in two directions.	**Wernerite** (Scapolite).	$\ddot{\bar{A}}l, \ddot{\bar{F}}e, \dot{C}a, \dot{N}a, \dot{K}, \dddot{S}i$.	White, gray, blue, green, red.	Prismatic.	Vitreous to greasy.	5.—6.	2.6—2.8	2.5	II.
	☞ Compare *Meionite*, Div. 3, p. 84.									
The silica separates in flocks; the acid solution when boiled with tin becomes beautifully blue (Columbium reaction).	The solution colors turmeric paper orange-yellow (zirconia reaction). Easily fusible at 3 to a light-green, much-blistered glass.	Wöhlerite.	$\dot{C}a, \dot{N}a, \ddot{Z}r, \ddot{C}b, \dddot{S}i$.	Yellow-brown.	Prismatic.	Vitreous.	5.5	3.41	3.	IV.
Cleaves in two directions with an angle of 94°.	Fusibility = 3.5. Often striated, and shows beautiful play of colors.	LABRADORITE	$(\dot{C}a, \dot{N}a)\dddot{S}i + \ddot{\bar{A}}l\dddot{S}i^2$.	White, gray-brown, green.	Angle 94°.	Vitreous.	6.	2.7	3.5	VI.
	Fusibility = 4.5. Gelatinizes with acids.	Anorthite.	$\dot{C}a\dddot{S}i + \ddot{\bar{A}}l\dddot{S}i$.	Colorless, white, gray.	Two equal cleavages.	Vitreous.	6.—7.	2.7	4.5	VI.
Gives the chlorine reaction with oxide of copper.	Difficultly fusible.	Microsommite	$\dot{C}a, \dot{K}, NaCl, \ddot{\bar{A}}l, \dddot{S}i$.	Colorless.		Vitreous.	6.	2.6	5.	III.
☞ Compare *Grossularite*, *Sphene* and *Danburite*, Div. 6, p. 87; also *Tephroite*, Div. 3, p. 84.										

(Page 87)

MINERALS WITHOUT METALLIC LUSTRE.

B. Fusible from 1—5, and non-volatile.

II. *Yield no metal or magnetic mass with soda.*

DIVISION 5.

DIVISION 6 (in part).

B.—B. B. fusible from 1—5, and non-volatile or only partially volatile.

II. *B. B. with soda on charcoal give no metallic globule or magnetic mass.*

Division	General Characters.	Specific Characters.	Species.	Composition.	Color.	Cleavage or Fracture.	Lustre.	Hardness.	Sp. Gr.	Fusibility.	Crystallization.
DIVISION 5. *Slightly attacked by hydrochloric acid. B. B. give a deep amethystine color to the borax bead (oxide of manganese).*	Gives water in the matrass. Found in fibrous radiated masses.		Carpholite.	$(\bar{A}l, \bar{F}e, \bar{M}n)^2 \dddot{S}i^3 + 3\dot{H}$.	Straw-yellow.	Stellate, fibrous.	Silky.	5.—5.5	2.9	3.5	IV.
	Fuses quietly at 3. Cleavage indistinct, sometimes dodecahedral.		SPESSARTITE (manganese garnet).	$(\frac{1}{2}(\dot{M}n, \dot{F}e) + \frac{1}{2}\bar{A}l)^2 \dddot{S}i^3$.	Brownish-red.		Vitreous.	7.	4.2	3.	I.
	Fuses with intumescence at 2.—2.5. Plainly cleavable in one direction.		Piedmontite.	$(\frac{1}{3}\dot{C}a^3 + \frac{2}{3}(\bar{M}n, \bar{F}e, \bar{A}l))^2 \dddot{S}i^3$.	Cherry-red to reddish-brown	Prismatic.	Vitreous.	6.5	3.4	3.	V.
	Fuses quietly at 3. Plainly cleavable at an angle of 92°.		RHODONITE (manganese spar).	$\dot{M}n\dddot{S}i$.	Rose-red, brown.	Prismatic.	Vitreous.	6.	3.6	2.5	VI.
	☞ Compare *Axinite* in next section.										
DIVISION 6. *Not belonging to the foregoing divisions.*	Fused alone colors the flame green (boric acid).	Fuses at 3 to a globule which while hot is clear, but becomes cloudy on cooling. Yields no water in the closed tube.	Danburite.	$\dot{C}a^2\dddot{S}i + \dddot{B}^2\dddot{S}i^3$.	Pale-yellow.		Vitreous.	7.	2.9	3.	VI.
		Yields water in the closed tube.	Howlite.	$\dot{C}a, \dddot{B}, \dddot{S}i, \dot{H}$.	White.		Sub-vitreous.	3.5	2.55	Easily.	Amorph
	The powder is soluble in hydrochloric acid, leaving a yellow residue of tungstic acid.	When the acid solution is boiled with metallic zinc, it becomes colored intensely blue, but soon bleaches on dilution.	Scheelite.	$\dot{C}a\dddot{W}$.	White, brown, green-red.		Vitreous.	4.5—5.	6.	5	II.
	Micaceous. Give to the blowpipe flame the purple-red color of lithia.	Fuses at 2. Gives in the closed tube little or no water.	Lepidolite.	$\bar{A}l, \bar{F}e, \dot{M}n, \dot{K}, \dot{L}i, \dddot{S}i, Fl$.	White-gray pink.	Micaceous.	Pearly.	2.5	3.	2.5	IV.
		B. B. vermicular exfoliations. Gives in the closed tube much water.	Cookeite.	$\bar{A}l, \dot{L}i, \dot{K}, \dddot{S}i, \dot{H}, Fl$.	White.	Micaceous.	Pearly.	2.5	2.7	Difficultly.	
	Micaceous, but do not give the lithia flame.	Swells up B. B. and gives much water in the closed tube (11 per cent.)	Thermophyllite (serpentine).	$\dot{M}g, \dddot{S}i, \dot{H}$.	Brown to white.	Foliated.	Pearly.	2.5	2.6	5.	
		Fuses quietly. Easily decomposed by sulphuric acid.	Euphyllite.	$\bar{A}l, \dot{K}, \dot{N}a, \dddot{S}i, \dot{H}$.	White.	Foliated.	Pearly.	3.5	2.8	4.—4.5	
		Fuses quietly. Difficultly decomposed by sulphuric acid.	MARGARITE.	$\bar{A}l, \dot{C}a, \dot{N}a, \dddot{S}i, \dot{H}$.	White, red, gray.	Micaceous.	Pearly.	4.	2.99	4.—4.5	
		☞ Compare *Muscovite* and *Biotite*, Div. 6, page 94.									
	Not micaceous. Give to the blowpipe flame the purple-red color of lithia.	Fuses quietly to a white enamel. ☞ Compare *Amblygonite*, p. 83.	PETALITE.	$\bar{A}l, \dot{L}i, \dot{N}a, \dddot{S}i$.	White, gray-pink.	Basal.	Greasy.	6.5	2.45	3.5	V.
		Intumesces, throwing out fine branches, which fuse to a clear glass.	SPODUMENE.	$(\frac{1}{3}(\dot{L}i, \dot{N}a)^3 + \frac{4}{3}\bar{A}l)\dddot{S}i^3$.	White-gray, green-pink.	Prismatic.	Pearly.	6.5	3.18	3.5	V.
	Phosphoresces when heated, or when struck with a hammer.	Fuses quietly at 3 to a transparent colorless glass. With salt of phosphorus in the open tube gives the fluorine reaction.	Leucophanite.	$\dot{C}a, \dot{N}a, \dot{B}e, \dddot{S}i, Fl$.	Green-white.	Basal.	Vitreous.	3.5—4.	2.97	3.	IV.
	Gives water in a matrass; the partial HCl solution gives a precipitate with sulphuric acid (baryta).	Usually occurs in twin crystals.	HARMOTOME.	$\dot{B}a, \bar{A}l, \dddot{S}i^4, \dot{H}^6$.	White-red.		Vitreous.	4.5	2.45	3.5	IV.
	Fused with a mixture of fluor-spar and bisulphate of potassa momentarily colors the blowpipe flame green.	Fuses easily, with much effervescence, coloring the flame pale-green to a dark-green glass. The fine powder of the fused mineral gelatinizes with acids.	AXINITE.	$\bar{A}l, \bar{M}n, \bar{F}e, \dot{C}a, \dddot{S}i, \dddot{B}$.	Clove-brown to pearl-gray.		Vitreous.	6.5—7.5	3.27	2.	VI.
		Different varieties vary much in blowpipe characters; all become electric by heating. Some gelatinize after fusion.	Tourmaline.	$\bar{A}l, \bar{F}e, \dot{M}n, \dot{M}g, \dddot{S}i, \dddot{B}, Fl$.	Black, brown, green, blue, pink, white.		Vitreous.	6.5—7.5	2.9—3.3	3.—5.	III.
	Partially decomposed by hydrochloric acid; the solutions when boiled with tin become violet (titanic acid).	Fuses with slight intumescence to a blackish glass.	Titanite. (Sphene).	$(\dot{C}a + \ddot{T}i)\dddot{S}i$.	Brown, green, yellow, black.	Prismatic.	Vitreous.	5.—5.5	3.5	3.	V.
		Differs in crystalline form.	Guarinite.	$(\dot{C}a + \ddot{T}i)\dddot{S}i$.	Honey-yellow.	Prismatic.	Vitreous.	6.	3.48	3.	II.
		Fuses with brisk intumescence to a blackish mass.	Keilhauite (Yttrotitanite.)	$\dot{C}a, \dot{Y}, \bar{F}e, \bar{A}l, \ddot{T}i, \dddot{S}i$.	Brown-black.		Resinous.	6.5	3.7	3.	IV.

(Page 88)

MINERALS WITHOUT METALLIC LUSTRE.

B. Fusible from 1—5, and non-volatile.

II. *Yield no metal or magnetic mass with soda.*

DIVISION 6 (concluded).

B.—B. B. Fusible from 1—5, and non-volatile, or only partially volatile.

II. *B. B. with soda on charcoal give no metallic globule or magnetic mass.*

DIVISION 6.—(Continued.)

Not belonging to the foregoing divisions.

General Characters.	Specific Characters.	Species.	Composition.	Color.	Cleavage or Fracture.	Lustre.	Hardness.	Sp. Gr.	Fusibility.	Crystallization.
Hardness 6. Fuse quietly.	Fuses at 5. Has two perfect cleavages at 90°.	**Orthoclase.**	$\dot{K}, \ddot{\bar{A}}l, \dddot{Si}^6$.	Colorless, white, flesh-red, gray-green.	Right-angle.	Vitreous.	6.	2.5—2.6	5.	V.
	Fuses at 4. Shows striations on one cleavage surface.	**Albite.**	$\dot{N}a, \ddot{\bar{A}}l, \dddot{Si}^6$.	Colorless, white-gray, dull-green.	93°30′.	Vitreous.	6.	2.6	4.	VI.
	Fuses at 3.5. Striations as above.	**Oligoclase.**	$\dot{N}a, \dot{C}a, \ddot{\bar{A}}l, \dddot{Si}$.	White, flesh-red.	93°.	Vitreous.	6.	2.6—2.7	3.5	VI.
	Fuses at 3.5. Striations as above. Gives water in the closed tube. Phosphorescent.	Tschermakite.	$\dot{N}a, \dot{M}g, \ddot{\bar{A}}l, \dddot{Si}, \dot{H}$	Gray-white.	94°.	Vitreous.	6.	2.64	3.5	VI.
	Fused with soda, the silica separated from the hydrochloric solution, gives with sulphuric acid a precipitate (baryta).	Hyalophane.	$\dot{K}, \dot{B}a, \ddot{\bar{A}}l, \dddot{Si}$.	White, flesh-red.	2 cleavages.	Vitreous.	6.	2.9	5.	V.
	☞ Compare *Labradorite*, Div. 4, p. 86.									
Hardness=6.5. Fuse with swelling and intumescence to a slaggy mass. They gelatinize with acids after fusion.	Fuses to a white or yellow slag.	ZOISITE.	$(\frac{1}{3}\dot{C}a^3 + \frac{2}{3}(\ddot{\bar{A}}l, \ddot{\bar{F}}e))^2\dddot{Si}^3$.	White-ash gray.	Prismatic.	Vitreous.	6.—6.5	3.—3.3	3.—3.5	IV.
	Fuses to a black or dark-brown slag.	**Epidote** (Pistacite).	$(\frac{1}{3}\dot{C}a^3 + \frac{2}{3}(\ddot{\bar{A}}l, \ddot{\bar{F}}e))^2\dddot{Si}^3$.	Gray, pistachio-green, brown-yellow.	2 cleavages.	Vitreous.	6.—7.	3.2—3.5	3.—3.5	V.
Hardness, 6.5—7.5. Gelatinize with acids after fusion.	Fuses quietly at 3 (grossular) to 4.5 (pyrope).	**Garnet** (in part).	$(\frac{1}{2}\dot{R}^3 + \frac{1}{2}\ddot{\bar{R}})^2\dddot{Si}$.	White, red-brown, black.	Dodecahedral.	Vitreous.	6.5—7.5	3.2—4.3	3.—4.5	I.
	Fuses with intumescence at 3.	**Vesuvianite** (Idocrase).	$(\frac{2}{3}\dot{C}a^3 + \frac{1}{3}(\ddot{\bar{A}}l, \ddot{\bar{F}}e))^2\dddot{Si}^3$.	Brown-green, yellow, blue.		Vitreous.	6.5	3.3—3.4	3.	II.
	Resembles grossular (but does not gelatinize after fusion).	Monzonite.	$\ddot{\bar{A}}l, \dot{F}e, \dot{C}a, \dot{N}a, \dddot{Si}$.	Gray-green.		Vitreous.	6.	3.	3.	Mass.
Hardness 6. Cleavable at an angle of 93°.	Includes many varieties, from the colorless *diopside* and white *malacolite* to black *augite*; light-colored varieties fuse to a white glass, while the dark give a black glass. The *species* is recognized by the cleavage and habit of crystal, the *variety* only by experience.	**Pyroxene.**	$\dot{R}\dddot{Si}$, sometimes $(\dot{R}^3, \ddot{\bar{R}})(\dddot{Si}, \ddot{\bar{A}}l\frac{2}{3})^3$. $\dot{R} = \dot{C}a, \dot{M}g, \dot{F}e, \dot{Z}n, \dot{M}n$, $\ddot{\bar{R}} = \ddot{\bar{A}}l, \ddot{\bar{F}}e$.	Colorless, white, gray, brown, green, and black.	87° & 93°.	Vitreous.	5.5—6.	3.2—3.5	2.5—5.	V.
Hardness 5.5. Cleavable at an angle of 124°.	Fuses to a white glass.	Tremolite.	$(\dot{C}a, \dot{M}g)\dddot{Si}$.	White.	Bladed.	Pearly, vitreous.	5.5	2.9—3.1	3.5	V.
	Finely fibrous with fibres easily separable.	Asbestus.		White.	Fibrous.	Silky.				
	Fuses to a black or green glass.	Actinolite.	$(\dot{C}a, \dot{M}g, \dot{F}e)\dddot{Si}$.	Green, brown.	124°30′ and 55°30.	Vitreous.	5.5	3.—3.2	4.	V.
	As above under *pyroxene*. The species includes *tremolite*, *asbestus*, *actinolite*, and many darker colored varieties. Can be recognized by the cleavage, but the varieties can only be learned by experience.	**Amphibole** (Hornblende).	Like pyroxene.	Like pyroxene	124°30 and 55°30′.	Vitreous.	5.5	2.9—3.4	2.5—5.	V.
Fuses at 4. Exfoliates, and yields water in a matrass.	Occurs in thin short fibrous layers.	Gümbelite.	$\ddot{\bar{A}}l, \dot{K}, \dddot{Si}, \dot{H}$.	Green-white.	Fibrous.	Pearly.			4.	
Fuses at 2. Gives water in a matrass.	Fuses with intumescence to a white glass.	Wilsonite (alt'd Scapolite).	$\ddot{\bar{A}}l, \dot{K}, \dot{M}g, \dddot{Si}, \dot{H}$.	White to red.	Cleaves at right angles.	Dull.	3.	2.7	2.	II.
Fuse with swelling up, at 3.5—4. to a vesicular white glass or enamel. They are amorphous, volcanic products, and are not homogeneous.	Characterized by an intense vitreous lustre.	OBSIDIAN.	$\dddot{Si}, \ddot{\bar{A}}l, \ddot{\bar{F}}e, \dot{C}a, \dot{M}g, \dot{K}, \dot{N}a$.	White, gray, green, yellow, black.	Break with sharp edges. Conchoidal.		6.	2.2—2.8	3.5—4.	
	Characterized by a strong fatty lustre.	PITCHSTONE.								
	Characterized by a mother-of-pearl lustre; sometimes yields water.	PEARLSTONE.								
	Characterized by a vesicular froth-like structure.	PUMICE.								

(Page 89)

MINERALS WITHOUT METALLIC LUSTRE.

C. Infusible or fusible above 5.

DIVISION 1 (in part).

C.—Infusible or fusible above 5.

Division 1.

First ignited B. B. then moistened with cobalt solution and again ignited assume a beautiful blue color. (It is necessary to pulverize hard anhydrous minerals before treatment.)

a) B. B. in the closed tube give water.

General Characters.	Specific Characters.	Species.	Composition.	Color.	Cleavage or Fracture.	Lustre.	Hardness.	Sp. Gr.	Crystallization.
With soda on coal give a sulphur reaction.	Insoluble in hydrochloric acid. (13 p. c. water.)	Alunite.	$\dot{K}\dddot{S}+3\bar{A}l\dddot{S}+6\dot{H}$.	White-gray.	Basal.	Vitreous.	3.5—4.	2.6	III.
	Easily soluble in hydrochloric acid. (47 p. c. water.)	ALUMINITE.	$\bar{A}l\dddot{S}+9\dot{H}$.	White.		Dull.	1.—2.	1.66	
	B. B. becomes black, burns and falls to pieces.	Pissophanite.	$\bar{A}l, \bar{F}e, \dddot{S}, \dot{H}$.	Light to olive-green.		Vitreous.	1.5	1.96	
	Like aluminite. (37 p. c. water.)	Felsobanyite.	$\bar{A}l^2\dddot{S}+10\dot{H}$.	White-yellow.	Perfect.	Pearly.	1.5	2.33	IV.
	☞ Compare *Kalinite*, *Tschermigite*, and *Alunogen*, which are soluble in water.								
With soda on coal gives a globule of lead.	B. B. puffs up and half melts without becoming fluid. The solution gives with molybdate of ammonia a yellow precipitate.	Plumbogummite.	$\bar{A}l, \dot{P}b, \overset{.....}{P}, \dot{H}$.	White, reddish-yellow, gray-green.		Resinous.	4.—5.	4.8	
With soda on coal gives a zinc coating.	Soluble in hydrochloric acid, forming a perfect jelly.	**Calamine** (electric calamine.)	$\dot{Z}n^2\dddot{S}i+\dot{H}$.	Colorless, white-yellow, green, blue.	Prismatic.	Vitreous.	4.5—5.	3.5	IV.
Give the phosphoric acid reaction when fused with magnesium in the closed tube (see **134**). Mostly soluble in caustic potassa, also if to this solution an excess of nitric acid is added, and some molybdate of ammonia, a yellow precipitate is thrown down.	Contains 27 p. c. of water.	WAVELLITE.	$\bar{A}l^3\overset{.....}{P}^2+12\dot{H}$ with Fl.	White yellow, gray; brown, blue, green.	Radiated.	Pearly.	3.5—4.	2.3	IV.
	Contains 40 p. c. of water.	Evansite.	$\bar{A}l^2\overset{.....}{P}+\bar{A}l\dot{H}^3+15\dot{H}$.	White.		Vitreous.	3.5—4.	1.94	
	Contains 24 p. c. of water.	Peganite.	$\bar{A}l^2\overset{.....}{P}+6\dot{H}$.	Deep-green, gray, white.		Vitreous.	3.—3.5	2.5	IV.
	Contains 29 p. c. of water.	Fischerite.	$\bar{A}l^2\overset{.....}{P}+8\dot{H}$.	Grass to olive-green.		Vitreous.	5.	2.46	IV.
	Contains 4 p. c. of water.	Berlinite.	$\bar{A}l\overset{.....}{P}+\frac{1}{2}\dot{H}$.	White-gray-red.		Vitreous.	6.	2.64	Massive.
	Contains 27 p. c. of water.	Zepharovichite	$\bar{A}l\overset{.....}{P}+6\dot{H}$.	Green, yellow, gray-white.		Vitreous.	5.	2.37	Compact
	Contains 6 p. c. of water.	Trolleite.	$\bar{A}l\overset{.....}{P}+\frac{1}{3}\bar{A}l\dot{H}^3$.	Pale-green.		Vitreous.	5.5	3.10	Compact
	Contains 24 p. c. of water.	Sphaerite.	$\bar{A}l^5\overset{.....}{P}^2+16\dot{H}$.	Gray-red.		Vitreous.	4.	2.53	
	Contains 23 p. c. of water.	Redondite.	$\bar{F}e, \bar{A}l, \overset{.....}{P}, \dot{H}$.	Gray-yellow.		Dull.	3.5	2.	Massive.
	Contains 12 p. c. of water.	Amphithalite.	$\bar{A}l, \dot{C}a, \overset{.....}{P}, \dot{H}$.	Milk-white.			6.		Massive.
	Contains 12 p. c. of water.	Tavistockite.	$(\frac{1}{3}\dot{C}a^3+\frac{1}{3}\bar{A}l)^2\overset{.....}{P}+3\dot{H}$.	White.		Pearly.			Acicular.
	Contains 21 p. c. of water.	Coeruleolactite.	$\bar{A}l^3\overset{.....}{P}^2+10\dot{H}$.	Milk-white to blue.	Uneven.	Vitreous.	5.	2.5	
Soluble in hydrochloric acid, with the separation of gelatinous silica.	Gelatinizes perfectly. H = 3. (Water 42 p. c.)	ALLOPHANE.	$\bar{A}l\dddot{S}i+6\dot{H}$.	White, blue, yellow, green.	Brittle.	Resinous, vitreous.	3.	1.87	Amorph.
	Has a lamellar structure. H = 4. (Water 30 p. c.)	Samoite.	$\bar{A}l^2\dddot{S}i^3+10\dot{H}$.	White, gray, yellow.		Resinous.	4.5	1.8	Stalac.
	Very soft. H = 1—2. (Water = 16 p. c.)	Halloysite.	$\bar{A}l\dddot{S}i^2+3\dot{H}$.	White, gray, green, yellow, red.		Waxy.	1.—2.	2.	
	Very soft. H = 1—2. (Water = 33½ p. c.)	Collyrite.	$\bar{A}l^2\dddot{S}i+9\dot{H}$.	White.		Glimmering.	1.—2.	2.1	Amorph.
Fused in a closed tube with bisulphate of potassa gives the fluorine reaction.	Gives water in the closed tube, which reacts for fluorine.	Ralstonite.	$\bar{A}l, Ca, Mg, Fl, \dot{H}$.	Colorless-white.		Vitreous.	4.5	2.5	I.
Easily soluble in caustic potassa.	Hardness = 2.5—3. Water 34½ p. c.	GIBBSITE.	$\bar{A}l\dot{H}^3$.	White, yellow, red.		Dull.	2.5—3.	2.3	III.
Very easily cleavable in one direction.	Water = 15 p. c. H = 6.5.	DIASPORE.	$\bar{A}l\dot{H}$.	White, gray, brown, blue, green.		Vitreous, pearly.	6.5—7.	3.4	IV.
	Water = 13 p. c. H = 1.—2.5.	**Kaolinite.**	$\bar{A}l\dddot{S}i^2+2\dot{H}$.	White, gray, brown.		Pearly.	1.—2.	2.5	IV.
	Water = 15 p. c. H = 1. Occurs in scales.	Pholerite.	$\bar{A}l^2\dddot{S}i^3+4\dot{H}$.	White, gray, red.		Pearly.	1.—2.	2.5	IV.

(Page 90)

MINERALS WITHOUT METALLIC LUSTRE.

C. Infusible or fusible above 5.

Division 1 (concluded).

C.—Infusible or fusible above 5.

DIVISION 1.—(*Continued.*) *First ignited B. B., then moistened with cobalt solution and again ignited, assume a beautiful blue color. (It is necessary to pulverize the hard anhydrous minerals before treatment.)*

Group	General Characters.	Specific Characters.	Species.	Composition.	Color.	Cleavage or Fracture.	Lustre.	Hardness.	Sp. Gr.	Crystallization.
a) (*Continued.*) B. B. in the closed tube give water.	Usually amorphous, clay-like or chalky. ☞ Compare *Kaolinite* and *Pholerite*, above; *Kaolinite* forms the basis of most clays.	Tough; can be cut into chips; imperfectly decomposed by sulphuric acid.	Cimolite.	$\ddot{\bar{A}}l^2\ddot{S}i^9+3\dot{H}$.	White, gray, red.		Dull.	Soft.	2.2	Amorph
		Unctuous. Forms a pasty mass with water.	Clay.	$\ddot{\bar{A}}l,\ddot{S}i,\dot{H}$.	All colors.		Dull.	Soft.		Amorph
		Water = 35 p. c. Falls to pieces in water.	Schrötterite.	$\ddot{\bar{A}}l^8\ddot{S}i^3+30\dot{H}$.	White-green.		Resinous.	3.5	2.	
		Water = 25 p. c. Falls to pieces in water.	Miloschite.	$(\ddot{\bar{A}}l,\ddot{\bar{C}}r)\ddot{S}i+3\dot{H}$.	Blue-green.			1.5	2.13	
	☞ Compare *Lazulite, Svanbergite, Pyrophyllite, Seybertite, Myelin*, and *Agalmatolite* of the following section, which give a little water in the matrass.									
b) B. B. in the closed tube gives no water, or but traces.	With soda on coal give a sulphur reaction.	The partial nitric solution gives a reaction for phosphoric acid with molybdate of ammonia.	Svanbergite.	$\ddot{\bar{A}}l,\dot{C}a,\dot{N}a,\dddot{\bar{P}},\dddot{S},\dot{H}$.	Yellow, or yellowish-brown.		Vitreous.	5.	3.3	III.
		Gives no phosphoric acid.	Alumian.	$\ddot{\bar{A}}l\dddot{S}^2$.	White.		Vitreous.	2.—3.	2.74	?
	Colors the flame green when moistened with sulphuric acid and ignited.	B. B. swells, loses its blue color, and falls into small pieces. Not acted upon by acids.	LAZULITE.	$\ddot{\bar{A}}l\dddot{\bar{P}}+(\dot{M}g,\dot{F}e)\dot{H}$.	Azure-blue.		Vitreous.	5.—6.	3.1	V.
	With soda on coal gives a zinc coating.	Gelatinizes perfectly with hydrochloric acid.	**Willemite.**	$\dot{Z}n^2\ddot{S}i$.	Colorless, brown, yellow, red, green.		Vitreo-resinous.	5.5	3.9—4.2	III.
	Very soft. H = 1.—3.	The micaceous variety swells up B. B. into fan-like forms. Compact or slaty varieties do not exfoliate.	**Pyrophyllite.**	$\ddot{\bar{A}}l,\ddot{S}i^3+\dot{H}$.	White, gray, green.	Micaceous to scaly.	Pearly.	1.—2.	2.9	IV.
		Unaltered B. B.; unacted upon by acids.	Agalmatolite.	$\ddot{\bar{A}}l,\dot{K},\ddot{S}i,\dot{H}$.	White, gray, green.	Massive.	Dull.	2.—2.5	2.8	Massive
		Somewhat decomposed by acids.	Myelin.	$\ddot{\bar{A}}l,\ddot{S}i$.	Yellow-red, white.		Dull.	2.	2.5	
		Like pyrophyllite.	Westanite.	$\ddot{\bar{A}}l,\ddot{S}i,\dot{H}$.	Brick-red.			2.5		Radiate
	Very distinctly foliated.	The foliæ are very elastic. Not acted upon by sulphuric acid.	**Muscovite.**	$\ddot{\bar{A}}l,\ddot{\bar{F}}e,\dot{K},\dot{N}a,\ddot{S}i,\dot{H}$.	Gray, white, brown, green.	Micaceous.	Pearly.	2.5	2.8—3.	IV.
		Not so cleavable; foliæ not elastic; decomposed by sulphuric acid.	SEYBERTITE.	$\ddot{\bar{A}}l,\ddot{\bar{F}}e,\dot{M}g,\dot{C}a,\ddot{S}i,\dot{H}$.	Yellow-red, brown.	Foliated.	Pearly.	4.5	3.1	IV.
	Not affected by acids.	Fused in the open tube with salt of phosphorus gives the fluorine reaction.	TOPAZ.	$\ddot{\bar{A}}l,\ddot{S}i,Fl$.	Colorless, white, blue, green, yellow.	Basal.	Vitreous.	8.	3.5	IV.
		Fused with a mixture of bisulphate of potassa and fluor spar gives a green flame (boric acid). Pyroelectric.	RUBELLITE (var. tourmaline).	$\ddot{\bar{A}}l,\dot{L}i,\dot{N}a,\dot{K},\dot{M}n,\ddot{\bar{B}},\ddot{S}i,Fl$.	Violet, rose-red.		Vitreous.	7.5	3.	III.
		Decomposed in a bead of salt of phosphorus leaving a skeleton of silica. Cleavable in two directions at 91½°.	**Andalusite.**	$\ddot{\bar{A}}l\ddot{S}i$.	White, gray, yellow-red.	Prismatic.	Vitreous.	7.5	3.2	IV.
		Decomposed like the preceding. In bladed crystals. Cleavage very perfect at 106°.	**Cyanite.**	$\ddot{\bar{A}}l\ddot{S}i$.	Blue, white, gray, green, black.	Prismatic.	Vitreous, pearly.	5.—7.	3.6	VI.
		Commonly fibrous. Decomposed like the preceding.	FIBROLITE.	$\ddot{\bar{A}}l\ddot{S}i$.	White, brown, green, red.	Prismatic.	Vitreous.	6.—7.	3.2	V.
		Slowly but perfectly soluble in salt of phosphorus; very hard; H = 9.	**Corundum.**	$\ddot{\bar{A}}l$.	White, gray, blue, all colors.	Rhombohedral.	Vitreous.	9.	4.	III.
		Slowly but perfectly soluble in salt of phosphorus. H = 8.5.	CHRYSOBERYL.	$\dot{B}e^3\ddot{\bar{A}}l$.	Asparagus to emerald-green.		Vitreous.	8.5	3.7	IV.
		☞ Compare *Spinel* and *Beryl*, p. 96.								

☞ *Leucite*, the hardness of which is not above 6, and *Cassiterite*, which gives globules of tin with soda, sometimes give blue with nitrate of cobalt. Quartz gives a lighter blue, with an inclination toward red.

(Page 91)

MINERALS WITHOUT METALLIC LUSTRE.

C. Infusible or fusible above 5.

DIVISION 2.

DIVISION 3.

C.—Infusible or fusible above 5.

Division	General Characters.	Specific Characters.	Species.	Composition.	Color.	Cleavage or Fracture.	Lustre.	Hardness.	Sp. Gr.	Crystallization.
DIVISION 2. *Moistened with cobalt solution and ignited B. B. assume a green color.*	Dissolve in hydrochloric acid with effervescence.	Gives much water in the closed tube.	HYDROZINCITE.	$\dot{Zn}\ddot{C}+2\dot{Zn}\dot{\bar{H}}$.	White, gray, yellow.		Dull.	2.—2.5	3.7	
		Gives little or no water in the closed tube.	**Smithsonite.**	$\dot{Zn}\ddot{C}$.	White, gray, green, blue, yellow, red.		Vitreous.	5.	4.4	III.
	With hydrochloric acid form a perfect jelly.	Gives much water in the closed tube. Pyroelectric.	**Calamine.**	$\dot{Zn}^2\dddot{Si}+\dot{\bar{H}}$.	White, gray, green, blue, yellow, red.	Prismatic.	Vitreous.	5.	3.5	IV.
		Gives no water in the closed tube.	**Willemite.**	$\dot{Zn}^2\dddot{Si}$. (often with $\dot{Mn}$).	White, gray, brown, green, yellow, red.		Vitreo-resinous.	5.5	4.	III.
	☞ Compare *Goslarite*, *Sphalerite*, and *Cassiterite*.									
DIVISION 3. *After ignition B. B. have an alkaline reaction and change the color of moistened turmeric paper to red-brown.*	Give much water in the closed tube.	Dissolves easily and quietly in hydrochloric acid.	**Brucite.**	$\dot{Mg}\dot{\bar{H}}$.	White, gray, green.	Basal.	Pearly.	2.5	2.35	III.
		As above, gives a strong manganese reaction with borax.	Pyrochroite.	$(\dot{Mn},\dot{Mg})\dot{\bar{H}}$.	White to bronze.	Basal.	Pearly.	2.5		
		Effervesces in hot HCl; the concentrated solution gives no precipitate with sulphuric acid.	HYDROMAGNESITE.	$3(\dot{Mg}\ddot{C}+\dot{\bar{H}})+\dot{Mg}\dot{\bar{H}}$.	White.		Silky-dull.	3.5	2.1	V.
		Effervesce in hot HCl; the concentrated solutions give a precipitate with sulphuric acid.	Hydrodolomite.	$(\dot{Ca}.\dot{Mg})\ddot{C}+\frac{1}{3}\dot{\bar{H}}$.	Yellow, gray, green, white.		Vitreous.		2.5	
			Predazzite.	$2\dot{Ca}\ddot{C}+\dot{Mg}\dot{\bar{H}}$.	White to gray-white.		Vitreous.	3.5	2.63	
			Pencatite.	$\dot{Ca}\ddot{C}+\dot{Mg}\dot{\bar{H}}$.	Blue-gray.		Vitreous.	3.	2.5	
	Effervesce and are soluble in cold dilute acid; the dilute solution gives no precipitate with sulphuric acid; but the strong solution does.	Usually shows a distinct rhombohedral cleavage.	**Calcite.**	$\dot{Ca}\ddot{C}$.	Colorless, white, and of all tints.	Rhombohedral.	Vitreous.	3.	2.6—2.8	III.
		Is not cleavable. B. B. falls to pieces.	**Aragonite.**	$\dot{Ca}\ddot{C}$.	Colorless, white, yellow, red, blue.		Vitreous.	3.5—4.	2.9—3.	IV.
		☞ Compare *Strontianite*, below.								
	Effervesce and are soluble in hot but not in cold dilute hydrochloric acid.	The concentrated solution gives with sulphuric acid a precipitate of sulphate of lime.	**Dolomite.**	$\dot{Mg}\ddot{C}+\dot{Ca}\ddot{C}$.	White, gray, brown, etc.	Rhombohedral.	Vitreous to pearly.	3.5—4.	2.8—2.9	III.
		The concentrated solution gives no precipitate with sulphuric acid.	**Magnesite.**	$\dot{Mg}\ddot{C}$.	White, yellow, gray, brown, green.	Rhombohedral.	Vitreous.	3.5—4.5	3.—3.1	III.
		☞ Compare *Siderite* and *Diallogite*, Div. 4, p. 92. Compare also the two following minerals.								
	Effervesce and dissolve in cold dilute hydrochloric acid; the very dilute solution gives a precipitate with sulphuric acid.	Imparts to the flame a bright-red color.	**Strontianite.**	$\dot{Sr}\ddot{C}$.	White, gray, yellow, green.	Prismatic.	Vitreous.	3.5—4.	3.7	IV.
		Imparts to the flame a yellowish-green color.	Barytocalcite.	$\dot{Ba}\ddot{C}+\dot{Ca}\ddot{C}$.	White, gray, yellow, green.	Prismatic.	Vitreous.	4.	3.6	V.
	☞ Compare *Yttrocerite*, also *Talc* and *Muscovite*, which sometimes have an alkaline reaction after fusion.									

(Page 92)

MINERALS WITHOUT METALLIC LUSTRE.

C. Infusible or fusible above 5.

DIVISION 4 (in part).

C.—Infusible or fusible above 5.

DIVISION 4.

Nearly or perfectly soluble in hydrochloric or nitric acid, without gelatinizing or leaving a considerable residue of silica.

General Characters.	Specific Characters.	Species.	Composition.	Color.	Cleavage or Fracture.	Lustre.	Hardness.	Sp. Gr.	Crystallization.
Colors the flame carmine-red (lithia).	With salt of phosphorus gives reactions for copper and cobalt.	Lithiophorite.	$\ddot{\overline{\mathrm{Mn}}}, \ddot{\overline{\mathrm{Al}}}, \dot{\mathrm{Fe}}, \dot{\mathrm{Co}}, \dot{\mathrm{Cu}}, \dot{\mathrm{Ba}}, \dot{\mathrm{Li}}, \dot{\mathrm{H}}$.	Bluish-black.		Dull.	3.	3.2—3.6	
With soda on coal easily reduced to metallic antimony, and give the antimony coating.	Yields little or no water in the closed tube.	Cervantite.	$\mathrm{SbO^3, SbO^5}$.	Yellowish.		Pearly.	4.5	4.08	IV.
	Yields 5 per cent. of water.	Stibiconite.	$\mathrm{SbO^4} + \dot{\mathrm{H}}$.	Yellow-red to white.		Pearly.	4.—5.5	5.28	Mass.
	Yields 15 per cent. of water.	Volgerite.	$\mathrm{SbO^5} + 5\dot{\mathrm{H}}$.	White.	Pulverulent	Dull.		6.6	Mass.
Soluble in heated hydrochloric acid with effervescence (carbonic acid).	B. B. becomes magnetic, with borax gives the nickel reaction.	ZARATITE (Emerald-nickel).	$\dot{\mathrm{Ni}}\ddot{\mathrm{C}} + 2\dot{\mathrm{Ni}}\dot{\mathrm{H}} + 4\dot{\mathrm{H}}$.	Emerald-green.		Vitreous.	3.—3.25	2.6	
	B. B. does not become magnetic. In O. F. colors the bead intensely violet (manganese).	DIALLOGITE (Rhodochrosite)	$\dot{\mathrm{Mn}}\ddot{\mathrm{C}}$.	Rose-red, gray, brown.	Rhombohedral.	Vitreous. pearly.	3.5—4.5	3.5	III.
	B. B. becomes magnetic. In the solution, after separation of the iron with ammonia, gives a heavy crystalline precipitate with phosphate of soda.	MESITITE.	$2\dot{\mathrm{Mg}}\ddot{\mathrm{C}} + \dot{\mathrm{Fe}}\ddot{\mathrm{C}}$.	Yellowish-white, gray, brown.	Rhombohedral.	Vitreous, pearly.	4.—4.5	3.35	III.
	B. B. becomes magnetic; with borax gives only the reactions for iron.	**Siderite.**	$\dot{\mathrm{Fe}}\ddot{\mathrm{C}}$. (with $\dot{\mathrm{Mn}}, \dot{\mathrm{Ca}}, \dot{\mathrm{Mg}}$.)	Ash-gray to brown-red.	Rhombohedral.	Vitreous.	3.5—4.5	3.7—3.9	III.
	Like Siderite, but after separation of the iron by ammonia gives a heavy precipitate with oxalate of ammonia.	ANKERITE.	$\dot{\mathrm{Ca}}\ddot{\mathrm{C}} + (\dot{\mathrm{Mg}}, \dot{\mathrm{Fe}}, \dot{\mathrm{Mn}})\ddot{\mathrm{C}}$.	White, gray, red.	Rhombohedral.	Vitreous.	3.5—4.	2.95—3.1	III.
	Yields much water in matrass; does not become magnetic. Effervesces at first and then dissolves quietly.	Hydrotalcite.	$\ddot{\overline{\mathrm{Al}}}, \dot{\mathrm{Mg}}, \dot{\mathrm{H}}$.	White.	Basal.	Pearly.	2.	2.04	III.
	Slowly soluble in HCl; the not too acid solution gives with oxalic acid a white precipitate which on ignition becomes brick-red (oxide of cerium).	Parisite.	$(\dot{\mathrm{Ce}}, \dot{\mathrm{La}}, \dot{\mathrm{Di}})\ddot{\mathrm{C}} + \frac{1}{2}(\mathrm{Ca, Ce})\mathrm{Fl}$.	Brown-yellow.	Basal.	Resinous.	4.5	4.35	III.
	☞ Compare *Smithsonite*, Div. 2, p. 91.								
Heated in R. F. become black and magnetic; quietly but difficultly soluble in HCl.	Streak yellow, usually crystalline. Water =10 per cent.	**Göthite.**	$\ddot{\overline{\mathrm{Fe}}}\dot{\mathrm{H}}$.	Dark-red, brown, black.	Prismatic.	Sub-metallic.	5.—5.5	4.3	IV.
	Streak yellow, not crystalline. Water = $14\frac{1}{2}$ per cent.	**Limonite.**	$\ddot{\overline{\mathrm{Fe}}}{}^2\dot{\mathrm{H}}^3$.	Brown-yellow, black.		Dull to sub-metallic.	5.	3.6—4.	
	Streak red. Water = 5.3 per cent.	**Turgite** (Hydro-hematite).	$\ddot{\overline{\mathrm{Fe}}}{}^2\dot{\mathrm{H}}$.	Brown-black.		Dull to sub-metallic.	5.5	4.1—4.6	
	☞ Compare *Hematite*, Div. 2, page 70.								
In the open tube give sulphurous acid. B. B. with soda give a sulphur reaction.	B. B. with soda deposits the brownish-red coating of oxide of cadmium.	Greenockite.	CdS.	Orange to honey-yellow.	Prismatic.	Adamantine.	3.—3.5	4.9	III.
	B. B. with soda on charcoal gives a coating of oxide of zinc.	**Sphalerite (Blende).**	(Zn,Fe)S.	White, yellow, green, brown, black.	Dodecahedral.	Resinous.	3.5—4.	3.9—4.2	I.
With borax give an amethystine bead (manganese).	On charcoal with soda gives a coating of oxide of zinc.	**Zincite.**	$\dot{\mathrm{Zn}}$, colored by manganese.	Orange-yellow to deep-red.	Basal.	Adamantine.	4.—4.5	5.68	III.
	Gives much water in the closed tube.	WAD (Bog manganese).	$\ddot{\overline{\mathrm{Mn}}}, \dot{\mathrm{H}}$.	Gray, dull-black.		Dull.			
With borax give a deep blue bead (cobalt).	With soda on platinum wire gives a manganese reaction.	WAD (var. Asbolite).	$\ddot{\overline{\mathrm{Mn}}}, \dot{\mathrm{Co}}, \dot{\mathrm{H}}$.	Black.		Dull.	2.—2.5	3.1—3.3	
With salt of phosphorus in O. F. give a yellow bead, which in R. F. becomes deep green (uranium).	The nitric solution gives a heavy precipitate with nitrate of baryta.	Zippeite.	$\ddot{\overline{\mathrm{U}}}, \dddot{\mathrm{S}}, \dot{\mathrm{H}}$.	Yellow.		Silky.	3.		
	Gives no precipitate with nitrate of baryta.	URANINITE (Pitch blende).	$\ddot{\overline{\mathrm{U}}}\dot{\mathrm{U}}$.	Gray, brown, black.		Resinous.	5.5	6.4—8.	I.
Colors the flame green, and when moistened with hydrochloric acid colors the flame blue (copper).	The nitric solution gives a yellow precipitate with molybdate of ammonia (phosphoric acid). In the closed tube much water.	Turquois.	$\ddot{\overline{\mathrm{Al}}}, \dot{\mathrm{Cu}}, \overline{\mathrm{P}}, \dot{\mathrm{H}}$.	Sky-blue to green.		Dull.	6.	2.6—2.8	

(Page 93)

MINERALS WITHOUT METALLIC LUSTRE.

C. Infusible or fusible above 5.

DIVISION 4 (concluded).

DIVISION 5 (in part).

C. Infusible or fusible above 5.

Division	General Characters.	Specific Characters.	Species.	Composition.	Color.	Cleavage or Fracture.	Lustre.	Hardness.	Sp. Gr.	Crystallization.
DIVISION 4.—(Continued.) *Nearly or perfectly soluble in hydrochloric acid or nitric acid without gelatinizing or leaving a residue of silica.*	Moistened with sulphuric acid color the flame pale-green. Give the phosphoric acid reaction when fused with magnesium in the closed tube. The nitric solutions give a precipitate with molybdate of ammonia (phosphoric acid).	The nearly neutral solution gives a precipitate with oxalate of ammonia (oxalate of lime).	**Apatite.**	$\dot{C}a^3\dddot{P} + \frac{1}{3}Ca(Cl,Fl)$.	Colorless, white, blue, yellow, green.		Vitreous.	5.	3.2	III.
		Fused with soda, the mass treated with water, and filtered, the residue dissolved in little HCl, the solution gives with oxalic acid a precipitate which ignited becomes brick red (oxide of cerium).	Monazite.	$\dot{C}e, \dot{L}a, \dot{D}i, \ddot{T}h, \dddot{P}$.	Yellow, clove-red, brown.	Basal.	Resinous.	5.—5.5	5.2	V.
		After fusion becomes magnetic. Difficultly soluble in HCl.	Childrenite.	$\bar{\ddot{A}}l, \dot{F}e, \dot{M}n, \dddot{P}, \dot{H}$.	Yellow-brown to brownish-black.		Vitreous.	4.5—5.	3.18	IV.
	Fused with bisulphate of potassa, the mass dissolved in dilute hydrochloric acid and boiled with tin, gives a deep blue solution.	The dilute acid solution colors turmeric paper orange-yellow (zirconia).	Polycrase (Polymignite).	$\bar{\ddot{F}}e, \ddot{C}e, \dot{Y}, \ddot{Z}r, \ddot{T}i, \ddot{C}b$.	Black.		Sub-metallic.	5.5—6.5	4.8—5.1	IV.
	With bisulphate of potassa, or strong sulphuric acid, give the reaction for hydrofluoric acid.	Gives reaction for the oxide of cerium. (See Monazite, above.)	Fluocerite.	$CeFl + Ce^2Fl^3$.	Yellow, tile-red.		Weak.	4.—5.	4.7	III.
		Evolves carbonic acid when treated with acids.	Bastnäsite. (Hamartite).	$CeFl + 2(\dot{C}e, \dot{L}a)\ddot{C}$.	Wax-yellow.	Distinct.	Greasy.	4.	4.93	IV.?
		Like fluocerite; but has an imperfect cleavage in two directions.	Yttrocerite.	(Ca,Ce,Y)Fl.	White, gray, blue.		Weak, vitreous.	4.5	3.45	
DIVISION 5. *Gelatinize with hydrochloric acid or are decomposed with the separation of silica.* a) B. B. in the closed tube give water.	Fused with soda on charcoal, effervesce and yield a globule of copper.	With hydrochloric acid forms a perfect jelly. (Water = 11 per cent.)	Dioptase.	$\dot{C}u\ddot{S}i + \dot{H}$.	Emerald-green.	Rhombohedral.	Vitreous.	5.	3.3	III.
		Decomposed without gelatinization. (Water = 20 per cent.)	**Chrysocolla.**	$\dot{C}u\ddot{S}i + 2\dot{H}$.	Blue to green.		Vitreous.	2.—4.	2.2	
		As above. (Water = 16 per cent.)	Cyanochalcite.	$\dot{C}u, \dddot{P}, \ddot{S}i, \dot{H}$.	Azure-blue.		Dull.	4.5	2.79	
	Color yellow; after separation of the silica, the solution gives with ammonia a sulphur-yellow precipitate ($\bar{\ddot{U}}$).	Water = $12\frac{1}{2}$ per cent. In acicular crystals.	Uranotil.	$\bar{\ddot{U}}, \dot{C}a, \ddot{S}i, \dot{H}$.	Lemon-yellow.		Vitreous.		3.96	IV.
	Color white; massive; very hard.	After separation of the silica ammonia gives no precipitate, but oxalate of ammonia throws down oxalate of lime.	Xonaltite.	$4\dot{C}a\ddot{S}i + \dot{H}$.	White-gray.				2.71	
	Gelatinize with hydrochloric acid.	The not too acid solution gives a precipitate with oxalic acid which becomes brick-red on ignition.	CERITE.	$(\dot{C}e, \dot{L}a, \dot{D}i)^2\ddot{S}i + \dot{H}$.	Cherry-red, clove-brown.		Resinous.	5.5	4.9	
		Does not gelatinize after ignition.	Thorite.	$\ddot{T}h\ddot{S}i + 1\frac{1}{2}\dot{H}$.	Orange, brown-black.		Resinous.	4.5—5.	5.—5.4	I.
	Gives to the borax bead in both O. F. and R. F. an emerald-green color (chromium).	Yields much water in closed tube. B. B. blackens.	Wolchonskoite.	$\bar{\ddot{C}}r, \bar{\ddot{A}}l, \bar{\ddot{F}}e, \dot{M}g, \ddot{S}i, \dot{H}$.	Blue, grass-green.		Dull.	2.—2.5.	2.3	Amorphous
	With borax in O.F. gives a violet bead, becoming red-brown on cooling (nickel.)	In closed tube blackens and gives much water.	Genthite.	$\dot{N}i, \dot{M}g, \ddot{S}i, \dot{H}$.	Apple to emerald-green.		Resinous.	3.—4.	2.4	Amorphous
	After long heating in R.F. become magnetic.	In the solution, after precipitation of the oxide of iron by ammonia, phosphate of soda gives a precipitate (magnesia).	Xylotile.	$\bar{\ddot{F}}e, \dot{M}g, \dot{F}e, \ddot{S}i, \dot{H}$.	Wood-brown to green.	Asbestiform	Glimmering.		2.4	Fib.
		Gives only reactions for iron.	Chloropal.	$(\dot{F}e, {}^3\bar{\ddot{F}}e)\ddot{S}i^3 + 4\frac{1}{2}\dot{H}$.	Pistachio-green to yellow.		Earthy.	2.5—4.5	2.	Mass.
		☞ Compare *Gillingite*, Div. 5, p. 78.								
	Moistened with cobalt solution B.B. become pink.	Gelatinizes with hydrochloric acid. Very light; absorbs water. B. B. shrivels up.	SEPIOLITE (Meerschaum).	$\dot{M}g^2\ddot{S}i^3 + 2\dot{H}$.	White, yellow, red.		Dull.	2.—2.5	1.5	Mass.
		Greasy feel; does not adhere to the tongue.	CEROLITE.	$\dot{M}g, \ddot{S}i, \dot{H}$.	Green, yellow, white.	Conchoidal.	Resinous.	2.—2.5	2.3	Mass.

(Page 94)

MINERALS WITHOUT METALLIC LUSTRE.

C. Infusible or fusible above 5.

DIVISION 5 (concluded).

DIVISION 6 (in part).

C.—Infusible or fusible above 5.

Division 5.—(Continued.) *Gelatinize with hydrochloric acid or are decomposed with the separation of silica.*

Group	General Characters.	Specific Characters.	Species.	Composition.	Color.	Cleavage or Fracture.	Lustre.	Hardness.	Sp. Gr.	Crystallization.
a)—(*Continued.*) B. B. in the closed tube give water.	Decomposed by hydrochloric acid without gelatinizing. Loses on ignition 12-13 per cent. water.	Serpentine; varies in color from white to black; structure massive or compact, fibrous and foliated. Ordinarily it is green, compact, and has a dull greasy lustre. *Retinalite* is a variety with a resinous lustre; *porcellophite* is soft, white, dull and earthy; *bowenite* is hard, compact and apple-green; *bastite* is foliated with a bronzy lustre; *marmolite* is thin-foliated and pearly; *picrolite* is columnar or coarsely fibrous; *chrysolite* is fine fibrous.	**Serpentine.**	$2\dot{Mg}\ddot{Si}+\dot{Mg}\dot{H}^2$, with a small amount of $\dot{Fe}$, and frequently colored green by iron, nickel or chromium.	White, gray, various shades of oil-green, apple-green, yellow, red and black.	Tough.	Sub-resinous, greasy, pearly, resinous, silky, and earthy.	2.5—5.5	2.5—2.65	Only found in pseudomorphs.
	Decomposed like the preceding, but give only a little water in closed tube.	Micaceous, with flexible but not elastic laminæ.	Penninite.	$8(\dot{Mg}^3,\bar{\dddot{Al}}),9\ddot{Si},12\dot{H}$.	Green, gray, red.	Foliated.	Pearly.	2.5	2.7	III.
		☞ Compare *pro-chlorite*, *ripidolite* and *delessite*. p. 95.								
		Crystalline foliated.	Monradite (Pyroxene).	$\dot{Mg},\dot{Fe},\ddot{Si},\dot{H}$.	Yellow.		Vitreous.	6.	3.27	Granular
		Very soft, with a soapy-feel.	Neolite.	$\dot{Mg},\bar{\dddot{Al}},\ddot{Si},\dot{H}$.	Green.		Silky.	1.—2.	2.77	Fibrous.
		Pearly lustre; perfect cleavage in one direction.	SEYBERTITE.	$\dot{Mg},\dot{Ca},\bar{\dddot{Al}},\bar{\dddot{Fe}},\ddot{Si},\dot{H}$.	Yellow, copper-red, reddish-brown.	Foliated.	Pearly, sub-metallic.	4.—5.	3.—3.1	IV.
b) B. B. in the closed tube give no water or but traces.	Decomposed by hydrochloric acid with the formation of a jelly.	B. B. swells up and often glows with a bright light; strongly heated becomes grayish-green.	Gadolinite.	$\dot{Y},\dot{Ce},\dot{Fe},\dot{Be},\ddot{Si}$.	Blackish-green to black.		Vitreous.	6.5—7.	4.—4.5	IV.
		With salt of phosphorus gives the fluorine reaction.	**Chondrodite.**	$\dot{Mg}^8,\ddot{Si}^3,Fl$.	White, red, yellow, brown, green.		Vitreous resinous.	6.5	3.2	IV.
		Fusible in very thin splinters; does not swell.	Gehlenite.	$(\frac{1}{2}(\dot{Ca},\dot{Mg})^3+\frac{1}{2}(\bar{\dddot{Al}},\bar{\dddot{Fe}}))\ddot{Si}$.	Gray-white.		Resinous.	5.5—6.	3.	II.
		Infusible.	**Chrysolite** (olivine).	$(\dot{Mg},\dot{Fe})^2\ddot{Si}$.	Olive-green.	Prismatic.	Vitreous.	7.	3.3—3.5	IV.
		After precipitation of the iron by ammonia, gives a precipitate with oxalate of ammonia (lime). Fusibility=5.	Monticellite.	$(\frac{1}{2}\dot{Ca}+\frac{1}{2}\dot{Mg})^2\ddot{Si}$.	White-gray.	Prismatic.	Vitreous.	5.—5.5	3.—3.2	IV.
		☞ Compare *Roepperite*. p. 78.								
	Decomposed by hydrochloric acid with separation of gelatinous silica.	Perfect cleavage in one direction.	Forsterite.	$\dot{Mg}^2\ddot{Si}$.	White-gray.	Prismatic.	Vitreous.	6.—7.	3.2—3.3	IV.
		☞ Compare *Monradite*, *Neolite*, and *Seybertite* above.								
	Decomposed without forming a jelly.	Generally crystallizes in trapezohedrons.	LEUCITE.	$\dot{K}\ddot{Si}+\bar{\dddot{Al}}\ddot{Si}^3$.	White-gray.		Vitreous.	5.5	2.4	I.

Division 6. *Not belonging to the foregoing divisions.*

Group	General Characters.	Specific Characters.	Species.	Composition.	Color.	Cleavage or Fracture.	Lustre.	Hardness.	Sp. Gr.	Crystallization.
a) Hardness under 7.	Micaceous; foliæ elastic. Give little or no water in the closed tube. Soft. H=1.-2.5.	Decomposed by strong sulphuric acid (optic axial angle not exceeding 5°).	**Biotite.**	$(\frac{1}{2}(\dot{Mg},\dot{K})^3+\frac{1}{2}(\bar{\dddot{Al}},\bar{\dddot{Fe}}))^2\ddot{Si}^3$.	Green-black.	Foliated.	Splendent.	2.5	3.	III.
		Not decomposed by strong sulphuric acid (optic axial angle 44°-78°).	**Muscovite.**	$\bar{\dddot{Al}},\bar{\dddot{Fe}},\dot{K},\ddot{Si},\dot{H}$.	White, gray, brown, green, yellow, red.	Foliated.	Pearly.	2.5	3.	IV.
		Like muscovite (optic axial angle 109°-128°).	MARGARITE.	$(\dot{Ca},\dot{Na})\ddot{Si}+\bar{\dddot{Al}}'\ddot{Si}+\dot{H}$.	White, gray, yellow, pink.	Foliated.	Pearly.	3.5—4.5	2.99	IV.
		Decomposed by sulphuric acid (optic axial angle 3°-20°, rarely less than 5°).	**Phlogopite.**	$(\frac{2}{3}(\dot{Mg},\dot{K})^3+\frac{1}{3}\bar{\dddot{Al}})^2\ddot{Si}^3$.	Yellow, red, white.	Foliated.	Pearly.	2.5	2.8	IV.
		Decomposed by sulphuric acid (optic characters like muscovite).	MARGARODITE.	Muscovite + $\dot{H}$.	White-gray.	Foliated.	Pearly.	2.5	2.8	IV.
		Like muscovite; when decomposed by soda the hydrochloric solution gives a precipitate with sulphuric acid (baryta).	Oellacherite.	$\dot{Ba},\dot{K},\dot{Mg},\bar{\dddot{Al}},\ddot{Si},\dot{H}$.	White, gray.	Foliated.	Pearly.		2.9	
	Gives little water in closed tube (not always foliated); has a greasy feel. Soft.	When foliated the foliæ are not elastic.	Talc.	$\dot{Mg}^6\ddot{Si}^5+2\dot{H}$.	White, apple to dark-green.	Foliated, compact.	Pearly.	1.	2.7	IV.

(Page 95)

MINERALS WITHOUT METALLIC LUSTRE.

C. Infusible or fusible above 5.

DIVISION 6 (continued).

C.—Infusible or fusible above 5.

DIVISION 6.—(*Continued.*) *Not belonging to the foregoing divisions.*

a)—(*Continued.*) Hardness under 7.

General Characters.	Specific Characters.	Species.	Composition.	Color.	Cleavage or Fracture.	Lustre.	Hardness.	Sp. Gr.	Crystallization.
Micaceous, the foliæ usually not elastic. Give much water in the closed tube. Decomposed by sulphuric acid.	B. B. whitens and fuses on edges to a gray-yellow enamel.	RIPIDOLITE.	$\dot{Mg}^6, \ddot{\bar{Al}}, \ddot{Si}^3, \dot{H}^4$.	Shades of green to red.	Foliated.	Splendent, pearly.	2.5	2.7	V.
	Becomes black and magnetic.	PROCHLORITE	$(\frac{4}{5}(\dot{Mg},\dot{Fe})^3 + \frac{3}{5}\ddot{\bar{Al}})\ddot{Si} + 1\frac{1}{2}\dot{H}$.	Green-black.	Foliated.	Pearly.	1.—2.	2.7—2.9	III.
	Occurs with short fibrous structure; can be decomposed by hydrochloric acid.	Delessite.	$\dot{Mg}, \ddot{\bar{Al}}, \ddot{\bar{Fe}}, \ddot{Si}, \dot{H}$.	Dark olive-green.			1.—2.5	2.89	
	Like ripidolite.	Leuchtenbergite.	$(\frac{2}{3}\dot{Mg}^3 + \frac{1}{3}\ddot{\bar{Al}})\ddot{Si} + 1\frac{1}{2}\dot{H}$.	White.	Basal.	Pearly.	2.5	2.65	III.
	Like ripidolite. Often gives reactions for chromium.	PENNINITE.	$8(\dot{Mg}^3, \ddot{\bar{Al}}), 9\ddot{Si}, 12\dot{H}$.	Green, gray, red.	Basal.	Pearly.	2.5	2.7	III.
	Easily distinguished by its hardness.	CHLORITOID.	$(\frac{1}{4}(\dot{Fe},\dot{Mg})^3 + \frac{3}{4}\ddot{\bar{Al}})^4\ddot{Si}^3 + 3\dot{H}$.	Gray, green, black.	Basal.	Vitreous.	5.—6.	3.5—3.6	V. ?
With salt of phosphorus give an emerald-green bead.	☞ See *wolchonskoite*, Div. 5, p. 93, and *chromite*, Div. 3, p. 71.								
With soda on coal reduced to metallic tin.	Its high specific gravity is very noticeable.	**Cassiterite.**	$\ddot{Sn}$.	Brown-black.		Adamantine and dull.	6.—7.	6.4—7.1	II.
Fused with carbonate of soda or with bisulphate of potash, dissolved in hydrochloric acid and boiled with tin, the solution becomes violet (titanic acid). ☞ Compare *Scheelite*, p. 87.	Moistened with sulphuric acid colors the flame green (boric acid).	Warwickite.	$\dot{Mg}, \dot{Fe}, \ddot{Ti}, \ddot{B}$.	Brown-black.	Prismatic.	Sub-metallic.	3.—4.	3.4	V. ?
	Prismatic cleavage.	**Rutile.**	$\ddot{Ti}$.	Red, brown, yellow, black.	Prismatic.	Adamantine.	6.5	4.2	II.
	Octahedral cleavage.	OCTAHEDRITE	$\ddot{Ti}$.	Blue, brown, red, black.	Octahedral.	Adamantine.	5.5	3.8—3.9	II.
	No cleavage.	BROOKITE.	$\ddot{Ti}$.	Yellow, red, brown, black.		Adamantine.	5.5—6.	3.9—4.2	V.
	☞ Compare *perofskite*, Div. 3, p. 71.								
Fused with carbonate of soda, dissolved in hydrochloric acid, and boiled with tin, the solution becomes violet (titanic acid).	The residue from the solution in water dissolved in HCl colors turmeric paper orange-yellow (zirconia). B. B. swells up.	Æschynite.	$\ddot{Zr}, \ddot{\bar{Fe}}, \dot{Ce}, \dot{Y}, \dddot{Cb}, \ddot{Ti}$.	Black.		Resinous.	5.—6.	5.1	IV.
	B. B. unchanged.	Euxenite.	$\dot{Y}, \dot{U}, \dot{Ce}, \ddot{Ti}, \dddot{Cb}, \dddot{Ta}$.	Brown-black.		Brilliant.	6.5	4.9	IV.
	Found in octahedrons.	Pyrochlore.	$\dot{Ca}, \dot{Ce}, \dddot{Cb}$.	Brown-red.		Vitreous.	5.5	4.3	
Gives water in the matrass. With soda fuses with effervescence to a clear glass.	Mostly soluble in caustic potassa; hydrated silica is precipitated by addition of sufficient chloride of ammonium.	OPAL.	$\ddot{Si}\dot{H}$.	Colorless, milk-white, yellow, brown, red.		Vitreous.	6.—6.5	2.—2.3	Amorp[hous]
Moistened with sulphuric acid colors the flame light-green. ☞ Compare *Lazulite*, p. 90.	Difficultly soluble in phosphorus salt to a colorless glass.	Xenotime.	$(\dot{Y}, \dot{Ce})^3\dddot{\dot{P}}$.	Yellow, brown, red.	Prismatic.	Resinous.	4.—5.	4.5	II.
With phosphorus salt gives in O. F. a colorless bead, which in R. F., or better with tin on charcoal, becomes blue (when cold).	Decomposed by nitric acid, leaving a yellow residue of tungstic acid, which is soluble in alkalies.	**Scheelite.**	$\dot{Ca}\dddot{W}$.	White, brown, yellow, red.		Vitreous.	4.5—5.	6.	II.
	Soluble in alkalies; not affected by nitric acid; occurs in soft earthy masses.	Tungstite.	$\dddot{W}$.	Yellow.		Dull.			
Amorphous. Gives much water in closed tube.	Soluble in sulphuric acid.	Beauxite.	$(\ddot{\bar{Al}}, \ddot{\bar{Fe}})\dot{H}^2$.	White, brown, red.		Dull.		2.55	
	☞ Compare *Kaolinite*. Div. 1, p. 89.								
Cleavable.	Cleavable in two directions at 93°; the cleavage surfaces show pearly lustre.	ENSTATITE.	$\dot{Mg}\ddot{Si}$.	White, gray, green, brown.	Prismatic.	Metalloidal.	5.5	3.2	IV.
	Cleavable in two directions, 124½°; fainter lustre than enstatite	ANTHOPHYLLITE.	$\dot{Fe}\ddot{Si} + 3\dot{Mg}\ddot{Si}$.	Brown, gray, green.	Prismatic.	Silky.	5.5	3.2	IV.
	Much like enstatite; on charcoal yields a magnetic mass.	HYPERSTHENE.	$(\dot{Mg}, \dot{Fe})\ddot{Si}$.	Brown, green, black.	93°.	Metalloidal.	5.—6.	3.39	IV.
☞ Compare *Childrenite*, Div. 4, p. 93; and *Orthoclase* and *Hyalophane*, Div. 6, p. 88. Also *Staurolite*, p. 96.									

(Page 96)

MINERALS WITHOUT METALLIC LUSTRE.

C. Infusible or fusible above 5.

DIVISION 6 (concluded).

MINERAL COAL.

C.—Infusible or Fusible above 5.

DIVISION 6.—(Continued.)

Not belonging to the foregoing divisions.

Hardness 7 or more than 7.

☞ Compare *Cassiterite*, *Rutile*, and *opal* which are very near 7 in hardness.

General Characters.	Specific Characters.	Species.	Composition.	Color.	Cleavage or Fracture.	Lustre.	Hardness.	Sp. Gr.	Crysta- tion
Pulverized and fused with borax, colors the bead emerald-green (Chromium).	B. B. becomes blackish green, but cools to original color.	Ouvarovite (chrome garnet).	$(\frac{1}{3}\dot{Ca}^3+\frac{1}{3}\ddot{\bar{Cr}})^3\ddot{Si}^3$	Emerald Green.		Vitreous.	7.5	3.5	I.
B. B., infusible and unaltered. With soda fuses, with effervescence to a clear glass (when pure).	Rock crystal, rose quartz amethyst, chalcedony, agate, jasper, flint, etc., are varieties of quartz. *Tridymite* is a hexagonal form of silica with a specific gravity of 2.2—2.3.	**Quartz.**	$\ddot{Si}$.	Colorless, white, smoky, yellow, red, and all colors.	Conchoidal.	Vitreous.	7.	2.6	III.
H = 7. Do not fuse to a clear glass with soda.	Difficultly fusible. F. = 5—5.5.	IOLITE.	$2(\dot{Mg},\dot{Fe})\ddot{Si}+\ddot{\bar{Al}}^2\ddot{Si}^3$	Blue.		Vitreous.	7.	2.6	IV.
	Infusible.	**Staurolite.**	$\ddot{\bar{Al}},\ddot{\bar{Fe}},\dot{Fe},\dot{Mg},\ddot{Si}$.	Brown, red, black.		Vitreous-resinous.	7.	3.6	IV.
H = **7.5.**	B. B. becomes colorless. Fused with soda, and the fusion dissolved in hydrochloric acid, the dilute acid solution colors turmeric paper orange-yellow (zirconia).	ZIRCON.	$\ddot{Zr}\ddot{Si}$.	Colorless, red-gray, brown.		Adamantine	7.5	4.4—4.6	II.
	B. B. becomes milk white. Hexagonal prisms, with basal cleavage.	**Beryl.**	$(\frac{1}{2}\dot{Be}^3+\frac{1}{2}\ddot{\bar{Al}})\ddot{Si}^3$	Colorless, pink, blue-yellow and green.		Vitreous.	7.5—8.	2.6—2.7	III.
	B. B. becomes milk white. Monoclinic prisms, with right-angled cleavage.	Euclase.	$(\frac{1}{6}\dot{H}^3+\frac{2}{6}\dot{Be}^3+\frac{3}{6}\ddot{\bar{Al}})\ddot{Si}$.	Mountain-green-blue, white.	Prismatic.	Vitreous.	7.5	3.1	V.
	B. B. unchanged. Hexagonal prisms and pyramids, no basal cleavage.	Phenacite.	$\dot{Be}^2\ddot{Si}$.	Colorless, yellow-red.	Conchoidal.	Vitreous.	7.5—8.	3.	III.
H = 8. Gives with salt of phosphorus in open tube the fluorine reaction.	B. B. the yellow varieties become rose-red, crystallizes in prisms with perfect basal cleavage.	TOPAZ.	$\ddot{\bar{Al}},\ddot{Si},Fl$.	Colorless, white, yellow, blue, pink.	Basal.	Vitreous.	8.	3.5	IV.
H = 7.5—8. Occurs generally in octahedrons.	With soda and borax on charcoal gives a coating of oxide of zinc.	GAHNITE (zinc spinel).	$(\dot{Zn},\dot{Mg}),(\ddot{\bar{Al}}\ddot{\bar{Fe}})$.	Green, black.	Conchoidal.	Vitreous.	7.5.—8.	4.4—4.9	I.
	Soluble when pulverized in a bead of salt of phosphorus.	**Spinel.**	$(\dot{Mg},\dot{Fe}),(\ddot{\bar{Al}},\ddot{\bar{Fe}})$.	Red, blue, green, yellow, brown and black.	Conchoidal.	Vitreous.	8.	3.5—4.1	I.
H = 10.	Characterized by its hardness.	Diamond.	C.	Colorless to black.	Octahedral.	Adamantine	10.	3.5—3.6	I.

MINERAL COAL.

☞ The native hydrocarbons are, for the most part, mixtures more analogons to rocks than true mineral species, and no attempt is made to classify them here, other than to state a few facts in regard to some varieties of mineral-coal, as given by Von Kobell

General Characters.	Specific Characters.	Variety.	Composition.	Color.	Streak.	Lustre.	Hardness.	Sp. Gr.
Does not take fire in a lamp flame.	In closed tube yields a little water, and very little tarry product. B. B. burns with a feeble flame without fusing, leaving little ash; boiled with potash solution gives to it no color.	**Anthracite.**	C = 80—94 p. c.	Black.	Black.	Brilliant.	2.—2.5	1.3—1.7
Take fire in a lamp flame, and burn with a deep yellow flame, giving an empyreumatic odor. B. B. in glass tube give drops of tar or oil. Air dried *Brown coal* (Lignite) contains frequently from 15 to 20 p. c., or more of water, which it loses when dried at 110° C.	Imparts but little color to potash solution. The powder boiled with ether imparts to it scarcely any color.	**Bituminous coal.**	50—85 p. c. residue on ignition.	Black.	Black.	Resinous.		1.2—1.3
	Imparts little color to potash solution. The powder boiled with ether imparts to it a wine or brown-red color; very fusible; flows in the flame of a candle like wax.	**Asphaltum.**	C,H,O.	Brown-black.	Brown.	Resinous.		1.—1.8
	Imparts to potash solution a brown color.	**Brown coal.**	Very variable.	Brown-black.	Brown.	Dull-resinous.		

INDEX TO MINERALS

IN

CHAPTER IV.

www.ingramcontent.com/pod-product-compliance
Lightning Source LLC
LaVergne TN
LVHW021409110826
845150LV00007B/1844